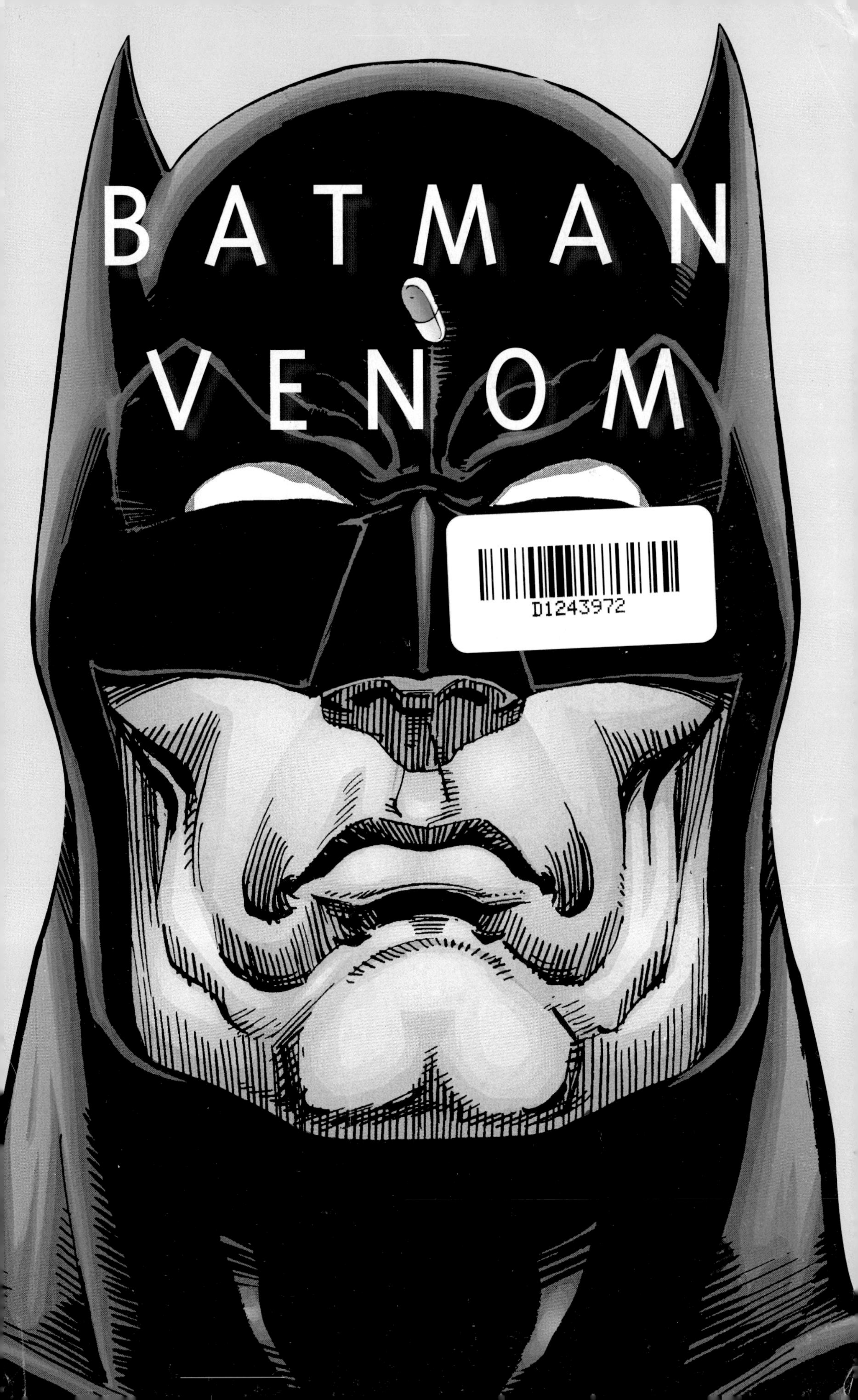
BATMAN
VENOM

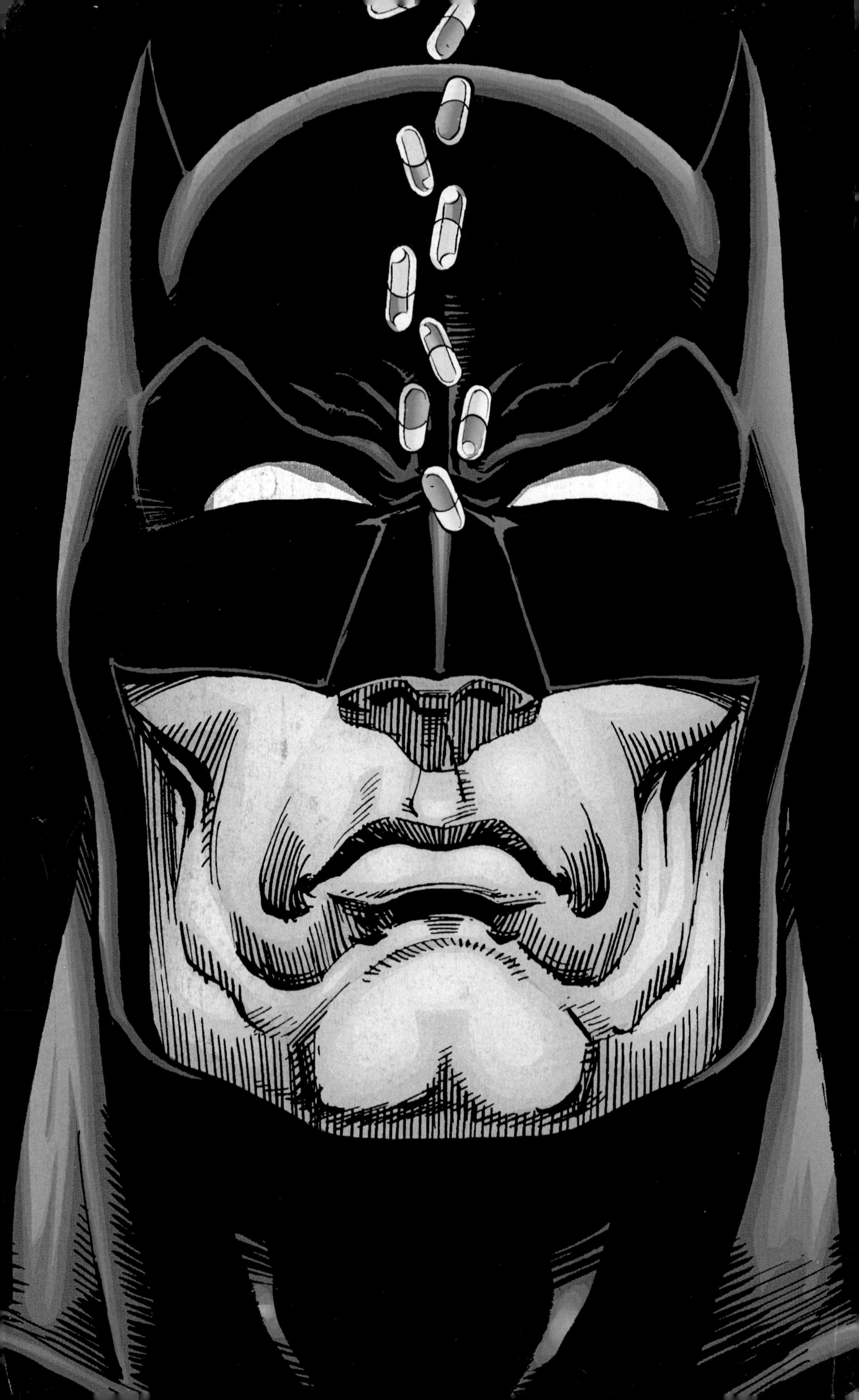

BATMAN VENOM

DENNIS O'NEIL Story

TREVOR VON EEDEN Layouts

RUSSELL BRAUN Pencils

JOSÉ LUIS GARCÍA-LÓPEZ Inks

WILLIE SCHUBERT Letters

STEVE OLIFF Colors

JOSÉ LUIS GARCÍA-LÓPEZ Covers

Batman created by BOB KANE

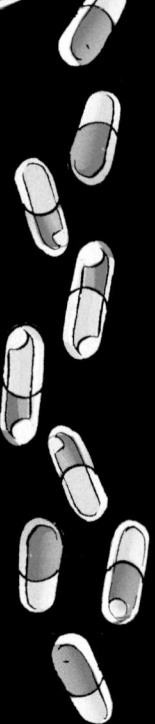

Andy Helfer **Kevin Dooley** Editors – Original Series
Robin Wildman Editor
Robbin Brosterman Design Director – Books

Eddie Berganza Executive Editor
Bob Harras VP – Editor-in-Chief

Diane Nelson President
Dan DiDio and **Jim Lee** Co-Publishers
Geoff Johns Chief Creative Officer
John Rood Executive VP – Sales, Marketing and Business Development
Amy Genkins Senior VP – Business and Legal Affairs
Nairi Gardiner Senior VP – Finance
Jeff Boison VP – Publishing Operations
Mark Chiarello VP – Art Direction and Design
John Cunningham VP – Marketing
Terri Cunningham VP – Talent Relations and Services
Alison Gill Senior VP – Manufacturing and Operations
David Hyde VP – Publicity
Hank Kanalz Senior VP – Digital
Jay Kogan VP – Business and Legal Affairs, Publishing
Jack Mahan VP – Business Affairs, Talent
Nick Napolitano VP – Manufacturing Administration
Sue Pohja VP – Book Sales
Courtney Simmons Senior VP – Publicity
Bob Wayne Senior VP – Sales

DC Comics, 1700 Broadway, New York, NY 10019
A Warner Bros. Entertainment Company.
Printed by RR Donnelley, Salem, VA, USA. 3/16/12. First Printing.
ISBN: 978-1-4012-3383-9

SUSTAINABLE FORESTRY INITIATIVE
Certified Chain of Custody
At Least 25% Certified Forest Content
www.sfiprogram.org
SFI-01042
APPLIES TO TEXT STOCK ONLY

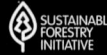

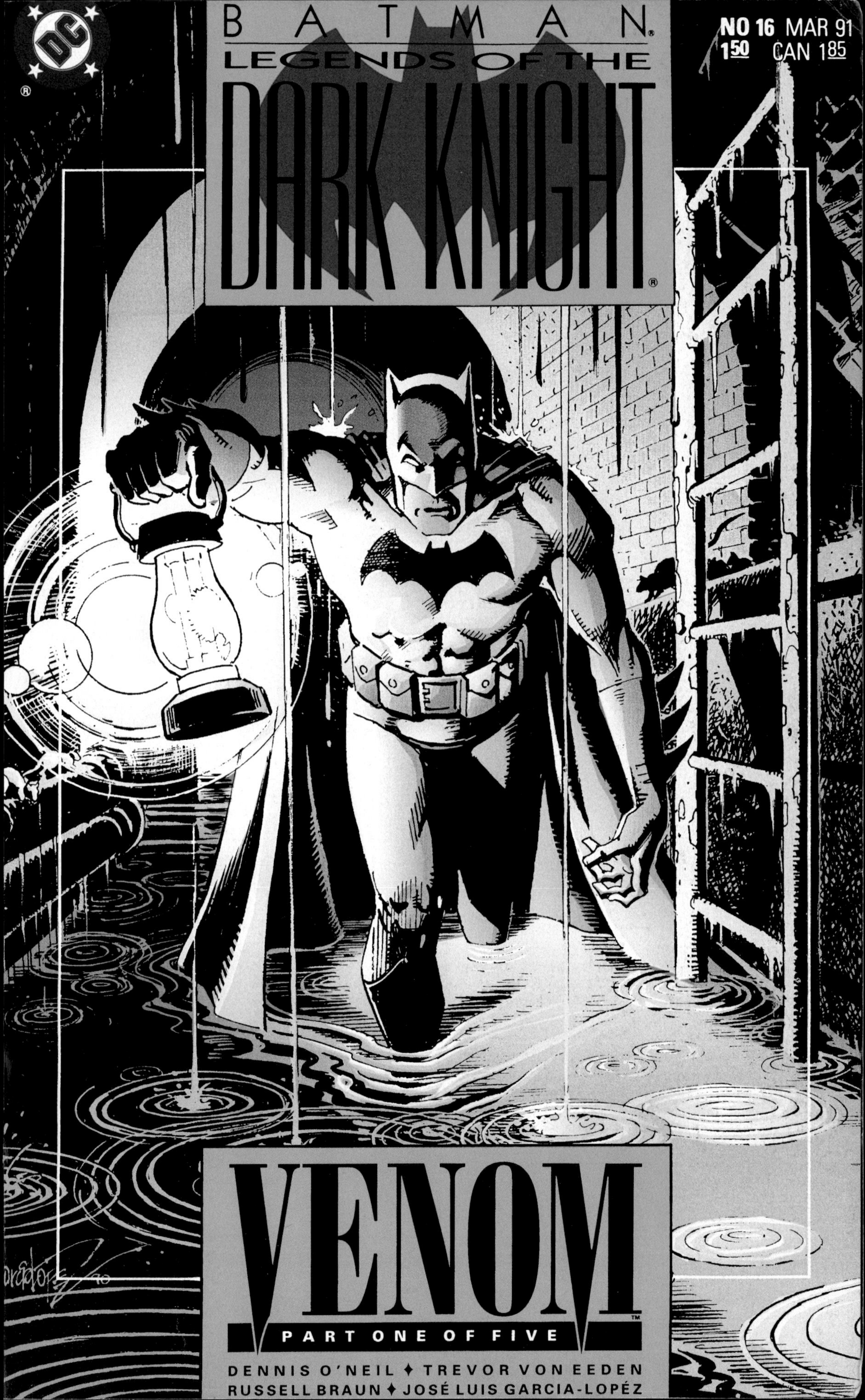

BATMAN
LEGENDS OF THE
DARK KNIGHT
NO 16 MAR 91
1.50 CAN 1.85
VENOM
PART ONE OF FIVE
DENNIS O'NEIL ♦ TREVOR VON EEDEN
RUSSELL BRAUN ♦ JOSÉ LUIS GARCIA-LOPÉZ

VENOM: PART ONE

IT HAPPENED YEARS AGO, BUT WHEN HE CLOSES HIS EYES HE CAN STILL EXPERIENCE IT...NOT ONLY THE GLEAM OF WET SURFACES, BUT THE NIGHTMARISH LIGHT FROM THE FLARES AND THE PATTER AND THE HISS OF TIRES ON PAVEMENT AND THE GRUFF, URGENT VOICE OF THE WATER COMPANY FOREMAN--

--CAN'T GO IN THERE. THERE'S BEEN A WATER MAIN BREAK AND THE TUNNEL'S FLOODING. THAT AIN'T ALL--

--THE WHOLE DAMN THING'S ABOUT TO CAVE IN. WATER'S WEAKENED THE--

A CHILD'S DOWN THERE.

I DUNNO WHAT TO SAY--

SMELLS, TOO. MOLD AND EARTH AND STENCH.

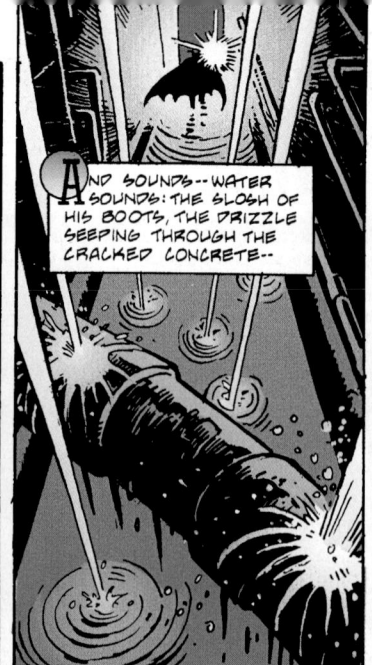

AND SOUNDS--WATER SOUNDS: THE SLOSH OF HIS BOOTS, THE DRIZZLE SEEPING THROUGH THE CRACKED CONCRETE--

--AND OTHER SOUNDS: CREAKS, CRUNCHES, SQUEAKS.

THE AIR IS THICK, OPPRESSIVE, COLD.

THE TUNNEL SEEMS ENDLESS.

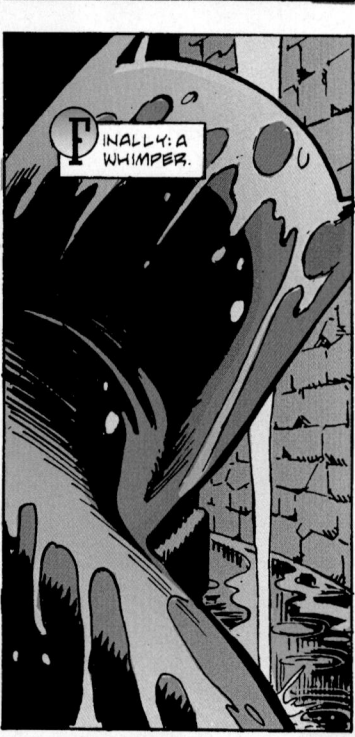

FINALLY: A WHIMPER.

A HUMAN VOICE.

A CHILD'S VOICE.

8

FOR A MOMENT THE WORLD IS A ROAR--

--AND THEN, A SILENCE, UNTIL GRADUALLY HE CAN AGAIN HEAR ALL THE OTHER SOUNDS AND HIS OWN HUSKY WORDS--

SISSY? SISSY PORTER?

MISTER?

YOU OKAY?

MISTER?

I'LL HAVE YOU OUT IN A MINUTE.
GIVE YOU MY WORD ON THAT.
MY PROMISE.
NEVER BREAK--
--A PROMISE.
ONE MORE PIECE.

NO GOOD. GOT TO TRY--

--ANOTHER GRIP.

11

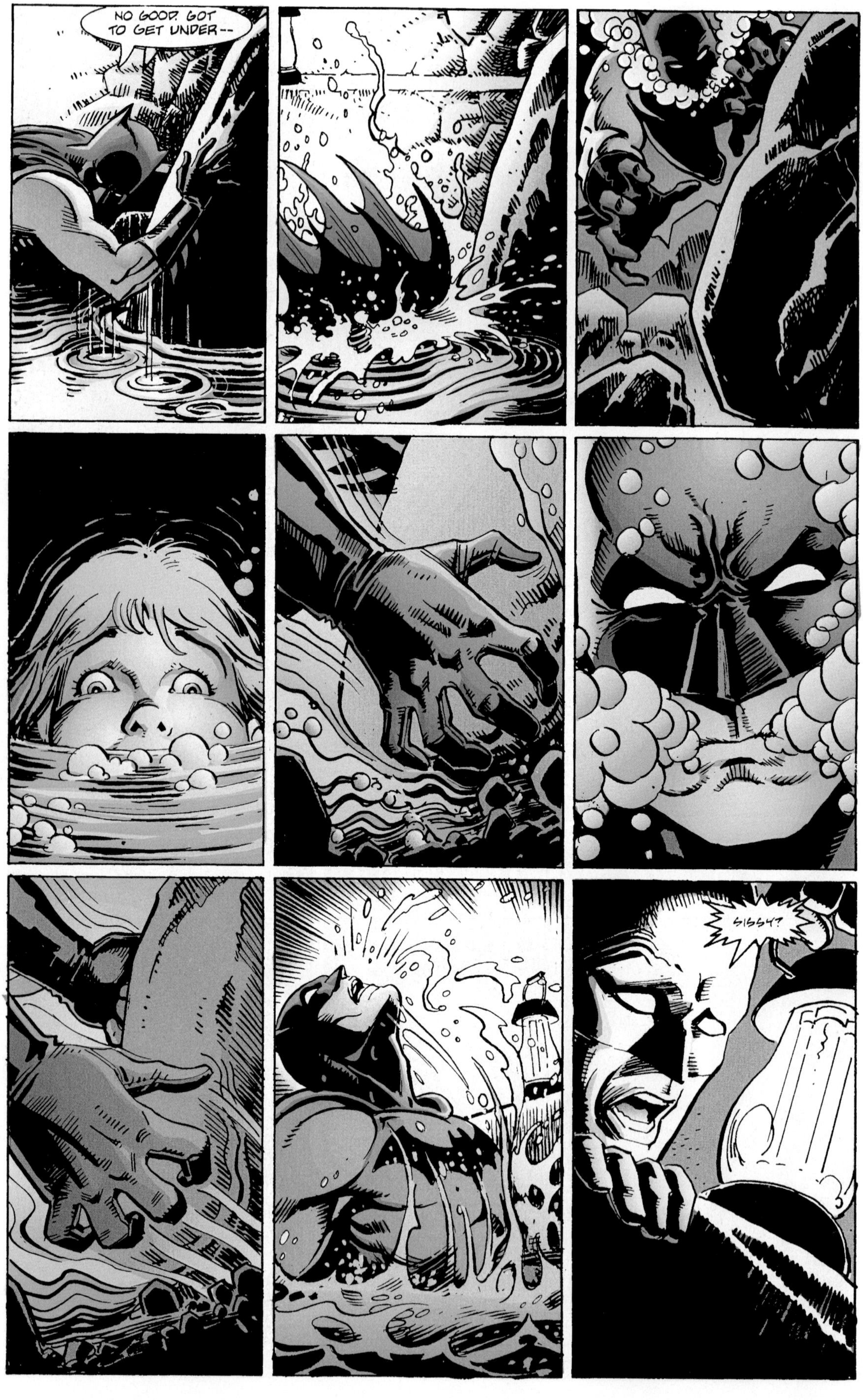
NO GOOD. GOT TO GET UNDER--
SISSY?

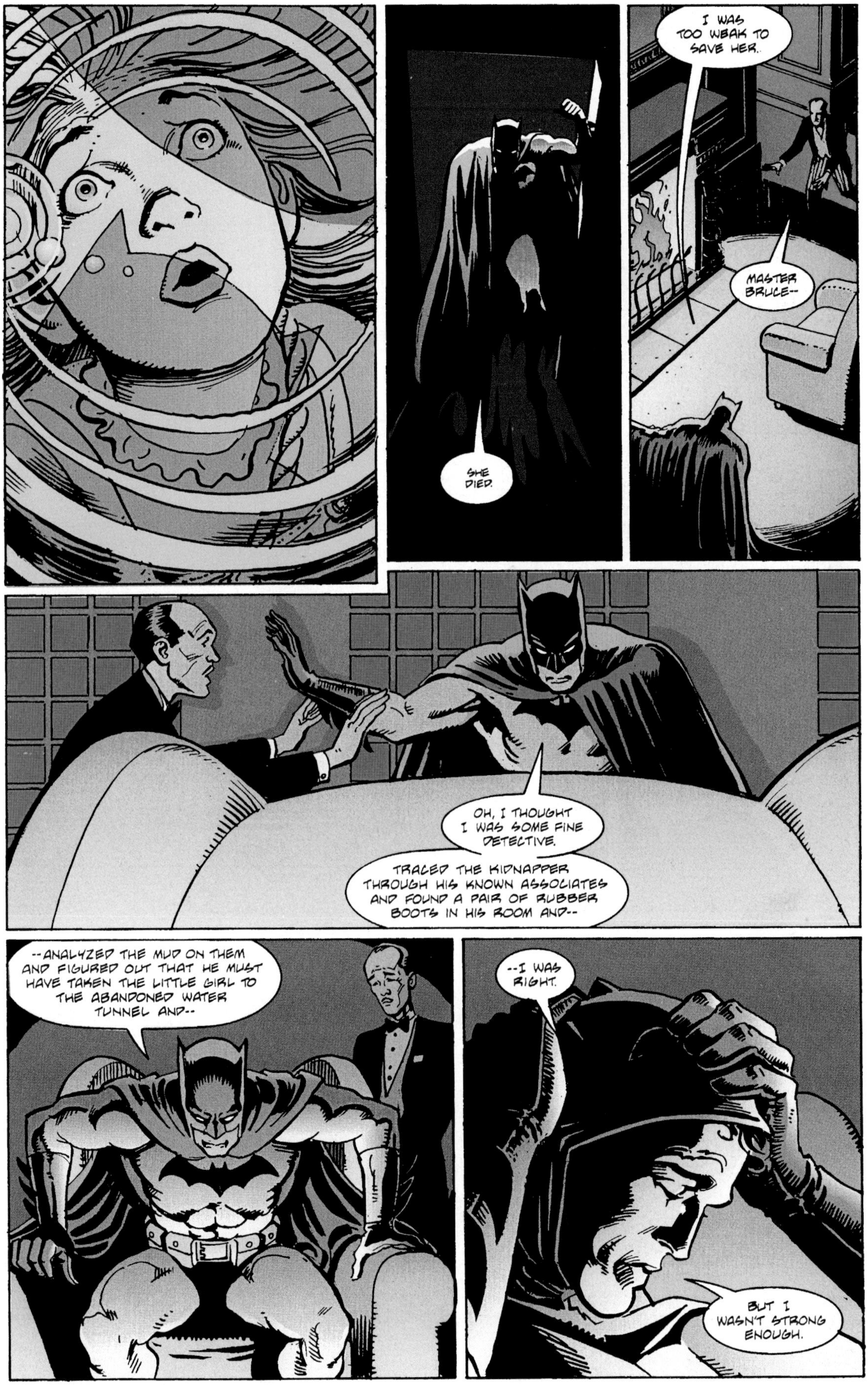
SHE DIED.
I WAS TOO WEAK TO SAVE HER..
MASTER BRUCE--
OH, I THOUGHT I WAS SOME FINE DETECTIVE.
TRACED THE KIDNAPPER THROUGH HIS KNOWN ASSOCIATES AND FOUND A PAIR OF RUBBER BOOTS IN HIS ROOM AND--
--ANALYZED THE MUD ON THEM AND FIGURED OUT THAT HE MUST HAVE TAKEN THE LITTLE GIRL TO THE ABANDONED WATER TUNNEL AND--
--I WAS RIGHT.
BUT I WASN'T STRONG ENOUGH.

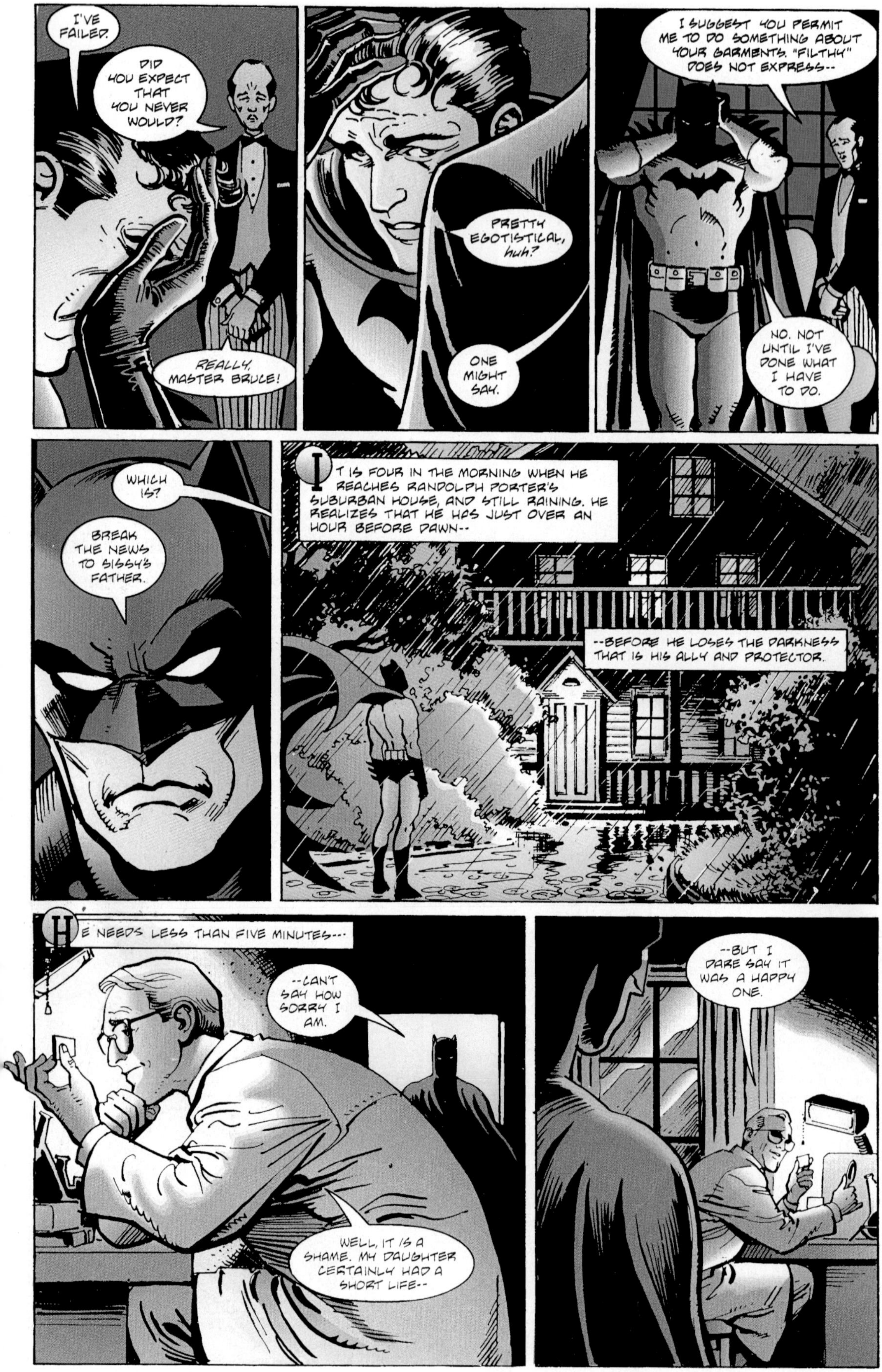
I'VE FAILED.
DID YOU EXPECT THAT YOU NEVER WOULD?
REALLY, MASTER BRUCE!
PRETTY EGOTISTICAL, huh?
ONE MIGHT SAY.
I SUGGEST YOU PERMIT ME TO DO SOMETHING ABOUT YOUR GARMENTS. "FILTHY" DOES NOT EXPRESS--
NO. NOT UNTIL I'VE DONE WHAT I HAVE TO DO.
WHICH IS?
BREAK THE NEWS TO SISSY'S FATHER.
IT IS FOUR IN THE MORNING WHEN HE REACHES RANDOLPH PORTER'S SUBURBAN HOUSE, AND STILL RAINING. HE REALIZES THAT HE HAS JUST OVER AN HOUR BEFORE DAWN--
--BEFORE HE LOSES THE DARKNESS THAT IS HIS ALLY AND PROTECTOR.
HE NEEDS LESS THAN FIVE MINUTES---
--CAN'T SAY HOW SORRY I AM.
WELL, IT IS A SHAME. MY DAUGHTER CERTAINLY HAD A SHORT LIFE--
--BUT I DARE SAY IT WAS A HAPPY ONE.

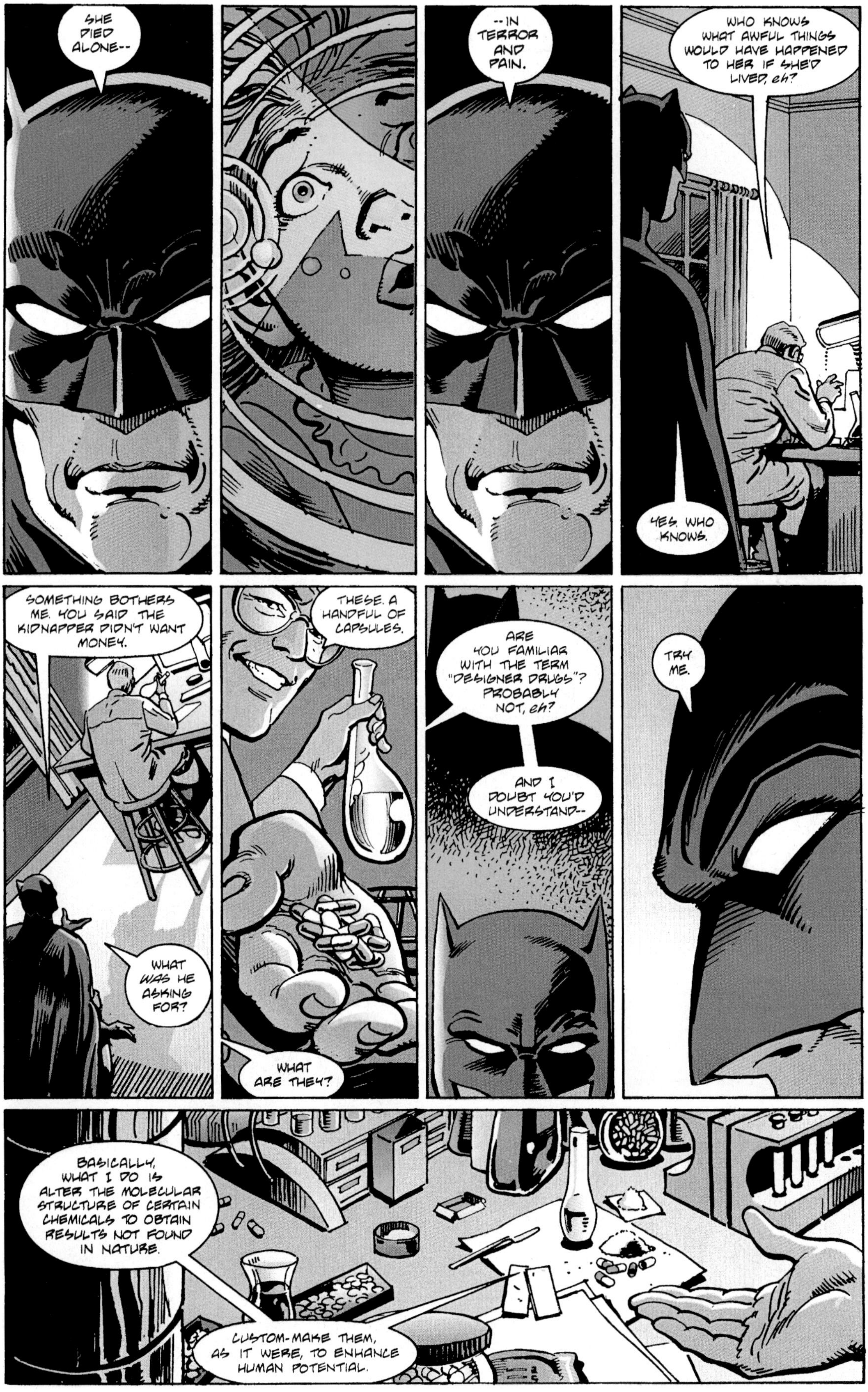
SHE DIED ALONE--
--IN TERROR AND PAIN.
WHO KNOWS WHAT AWFUL THINGS WOULD HAVE HAPPENED TO HER IF SHE'D LIVED, eh?
YES. WHO KNOWS.
SOMETHING BOTHERS ME. YOU SAID THE KIDNAPPER DIDN'T WANT MONEY.
WHAT WAS HE ASKING FOR?
THESE. A HANDFUL OF CAPSULES.
WHAT ARE THEY?
ARE YOU FAMILIAR WITH THE TERM "DESIGNER DRUGS"? PROBABLY NOT, eh?
AND I DOUBT YOU'D UNDERSTAND--
TRY ME.
BASICALLY, WHAT I DO IS ALTER THE MOLECULAR STRUCTURE OF CERTAIN CHEMICALS TO OBTAIN RESULTS NOT FOUND IN NATURE.
CUSTOM-MAKE THEM, AS IT WERE, TO ENHANCE HUMAN POTENTIAL.

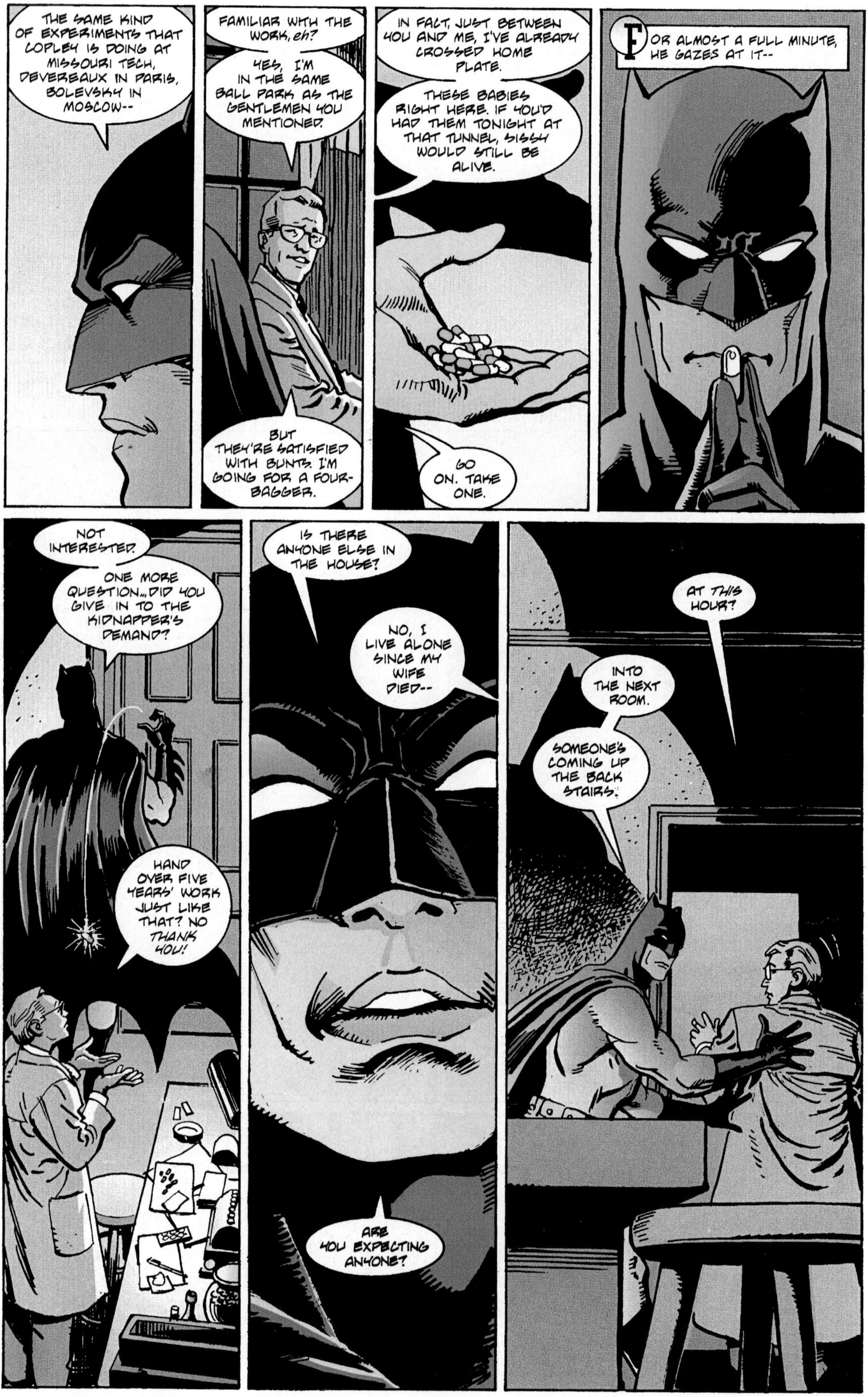
THE SAME KIND OF EXPERIMENTS THAT COPLEY IS DOING AT MISSOURI TECH, DEVEREAUX IN PARIS, BOLEVSKY IN MOSCOW--
FAMILIAR WITH THE WORK, eh?
YES, I'M IN THE SAME BALL PARK AS THE GENTLEMEN YOU MENTIONED.
BUT THEY'RE SATISFIED WITH BUNTS. I'M GOING FOR A FOUR-BAGGER.
IN FACT, JUST BETWEEN YOU AND ME, I'VE ALREADY CROSSED HOME PLATE.
THESE BABIES RIGHT HERE. IF YOU'D HAD THEM TONIGHT AT THAT TUNNEL, SISSY WOULD STILL BE ALIVE.
GO ON. TAKE ONE.
FOR ALMOST A FULL MINUTE, HE GAZES AT IT--
NOT INTERESTED.
ONE MORE QUESTION...DID YOU GIVE IN TO THE KIDNAPPER'S DEMAND?
HAND OVER FIVE YEARS' WORK JUST LIKE THAT? NO THANK YOU!
IS THERE ANYONE ELSE IN THE HOUSE?
NO, I LIVE ALONE SINCE MY WIFE DIED--
ARE YOU EXPECTING ANYONE?
AT THIS HOUR?
INTO THE NEXT ROOM.
SOMEONE'S COMING UP THE BACK STAIRS.

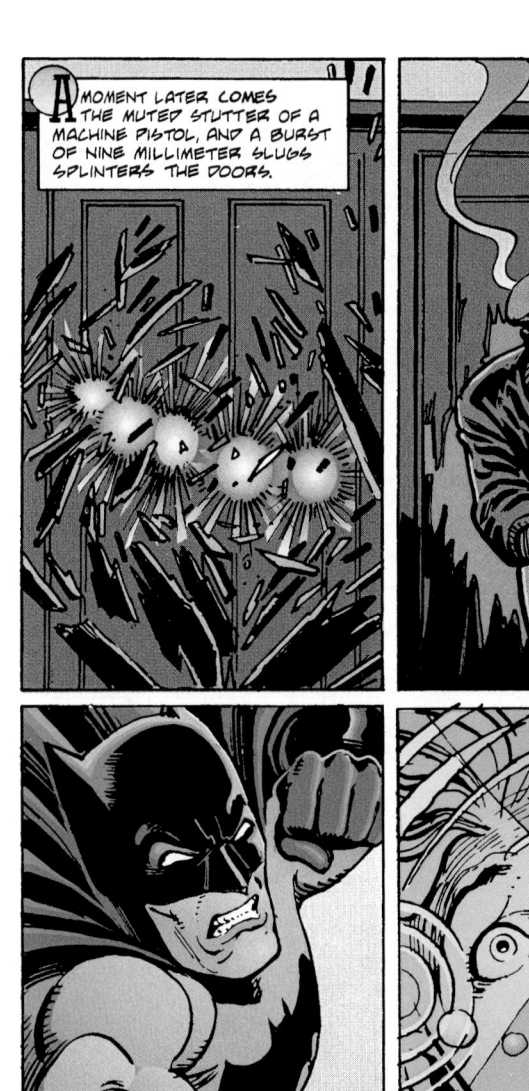

A MOMENT LATER COMES THE MUTED STUTTER OF A MACHINE PISTOL, AND A BURST OF NINE MILLIMETER SLUGS SPLINTERS THE DOORS.

OWWWW.

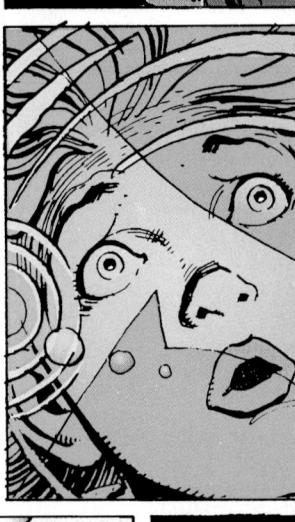

WHAT IN BLUE BLAZES--?

ONE OF THE KIDNAPPERS. CALL THE COPS.

I'M GOING AFTER HIS PARTNER.

17

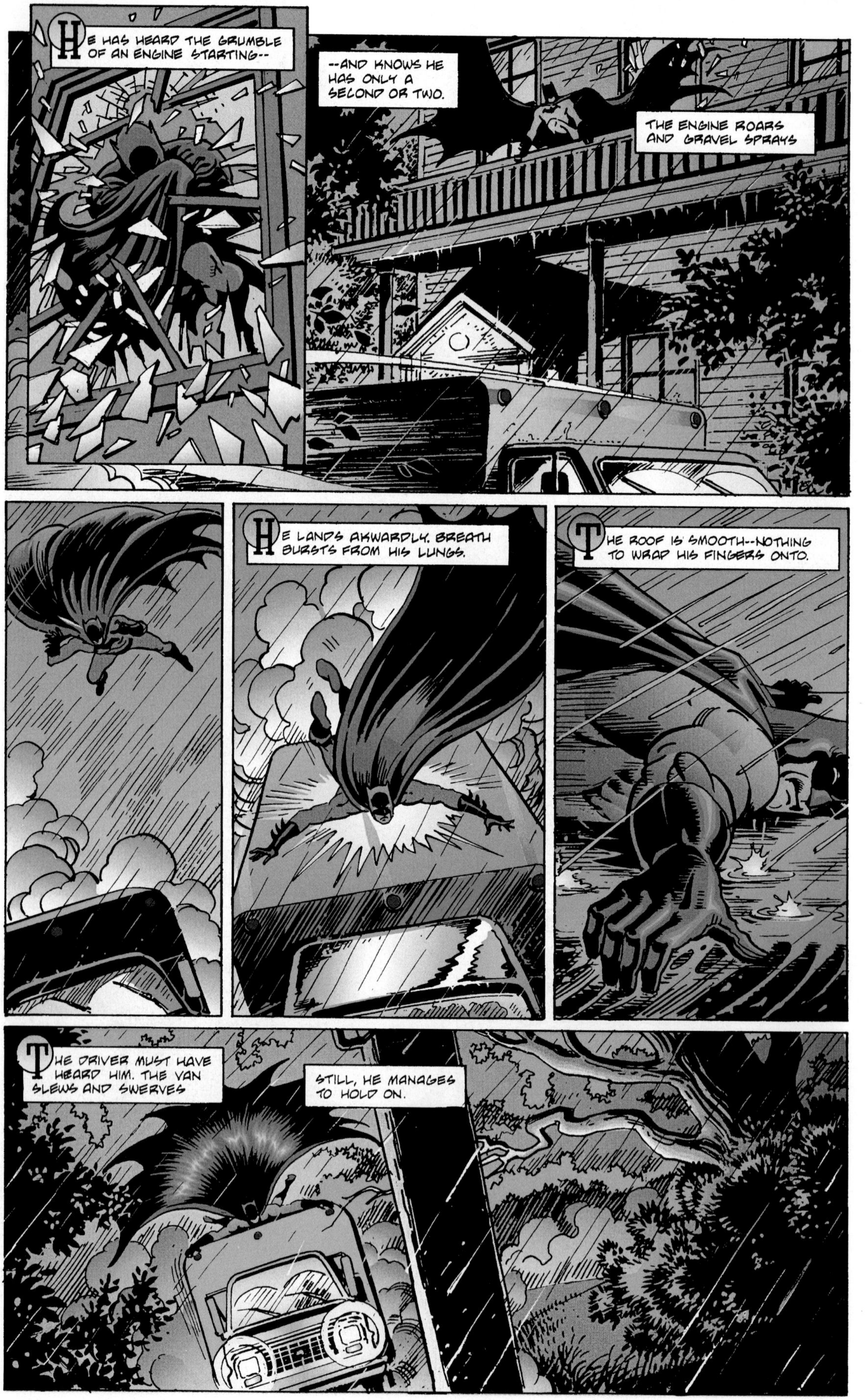
HE HAS HEARD THE GRUMBLE OF AN ENGINE STARTING--
--AND KNOWS HE HAS ONLY A SECOND OR TWO.
THE ENGINE ROARS AND GRAVEL SPRAYS
HE LANDS AWKWARDLY. BREATH BURSTS FROM HIS LUNGS.
THE ROOF IS SMOOTH--NOTHING TO WRAP HIS FINGERS ONTO.
THE DRIVER MUST HAVE HEARD HIM. THE VAN SLEWS AND SWERVES
STILL, HE MANAGES TO HOLD ON.

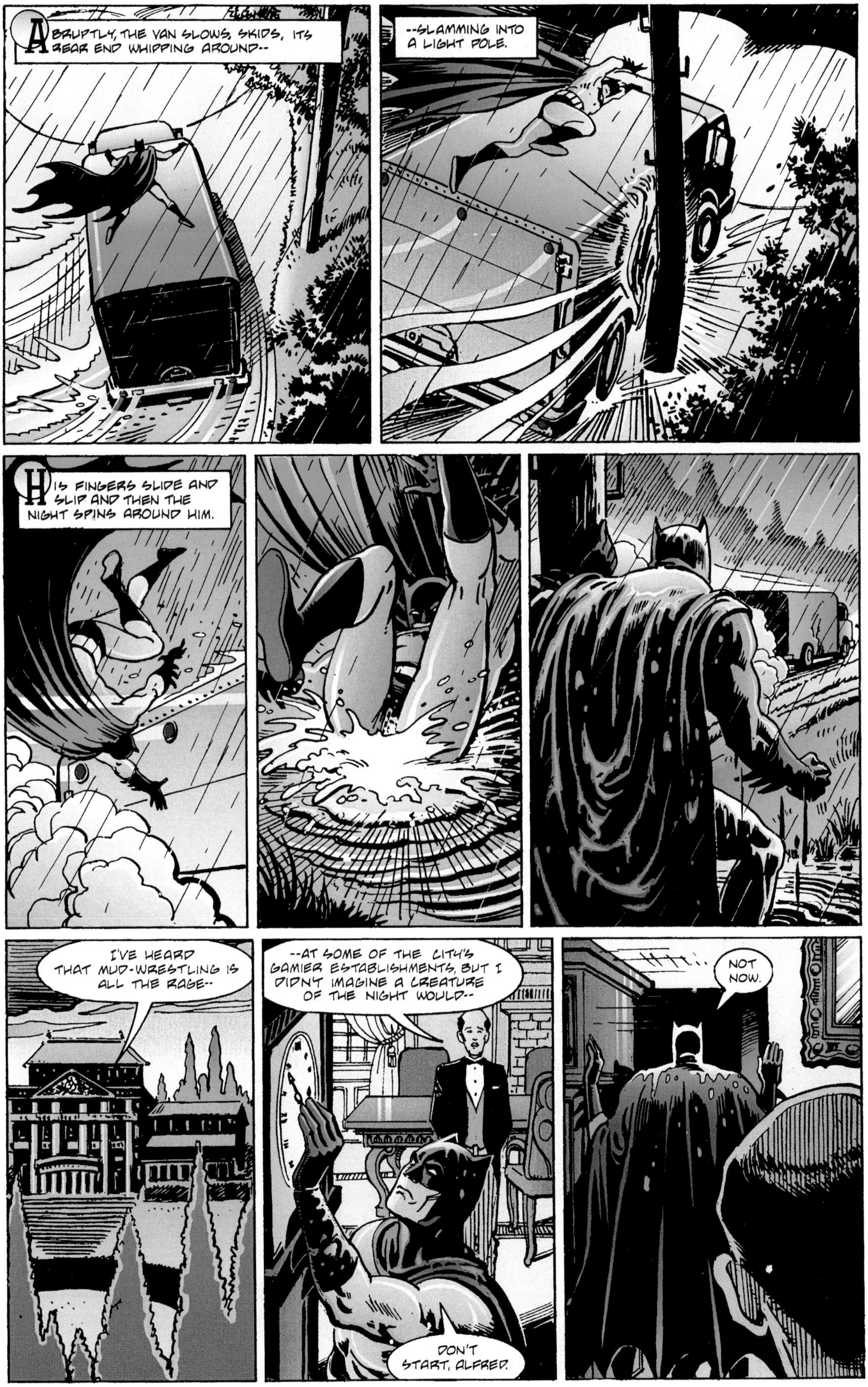
ABRUPTLY, THE VAN SLOWS, SKIDS, ITS REAR END WHIPPING AROUND--
--SLAMMING INTO A LIGHT POLE.
HIS FINGERS SLIDE AND SLIP AND THEN THE NIGHT SPINS AROUND HIM.
I'VE HEARD THAT MUD-WRESTLING IS ALL THE RAGE--
--AT SOME OF THE CITY'S GAMIER ESTABLISHMENTS, BUT I DIDN'T IMAGINE A CREATURE OF THE NIGHT WOULD--
DON'T START, ALFRED.
NOT NOW.

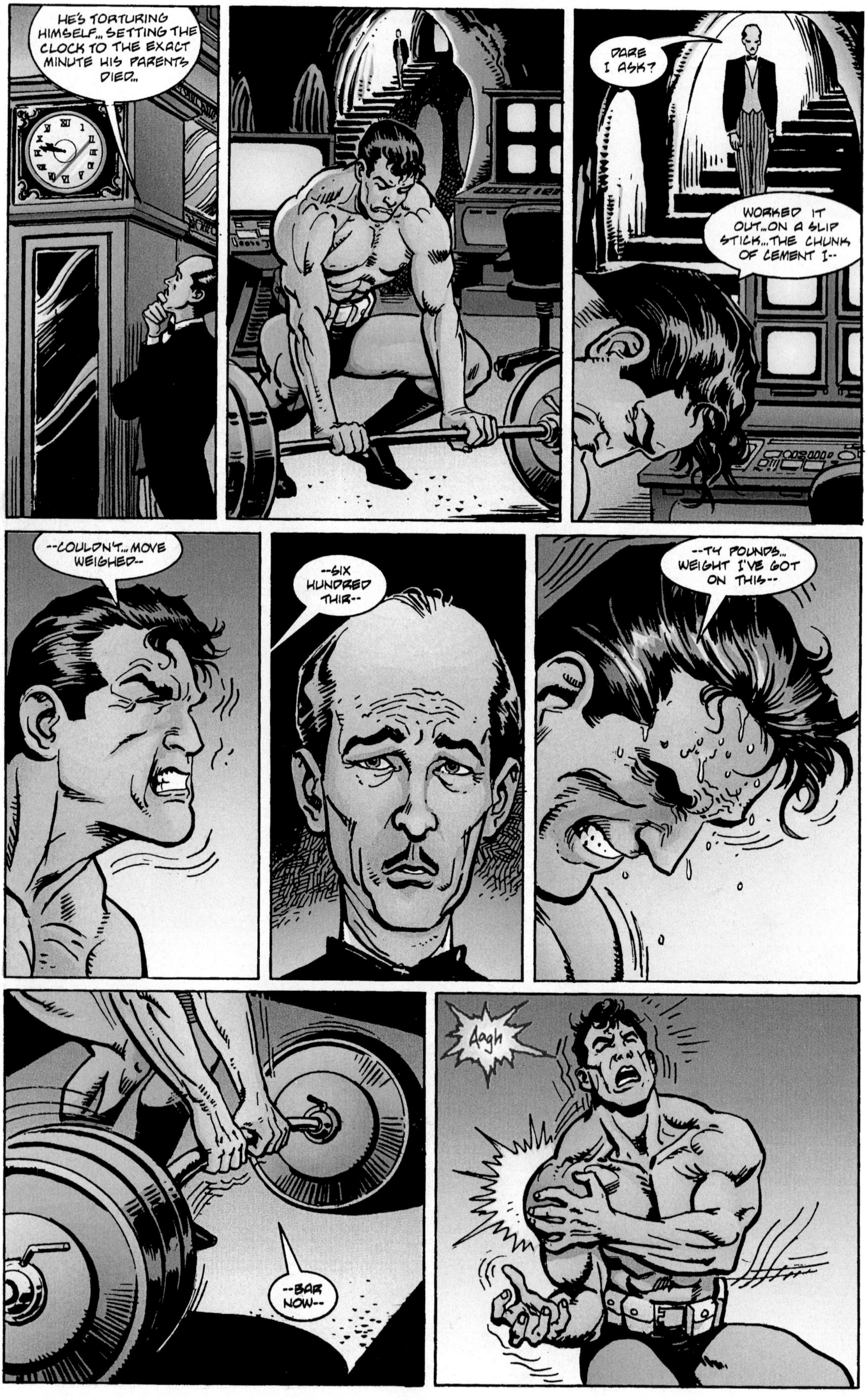
HE'S TORTURING HIMSELF... SETTING THE CLOCK TO THE EXACT MINUTE HIS PARENTS DIED...
DARE I ASK?
WORKED IT OUT...ON A SLIP STICK...THE CHUNK OF CEMENT I--
--COULDN'T...MOVE WEIGHED--
--SIX HUNDRED THIR--
--TY POUNDS... WEIGHT I'VE GOT ON THIS--
--BAR NOW--
Aagh

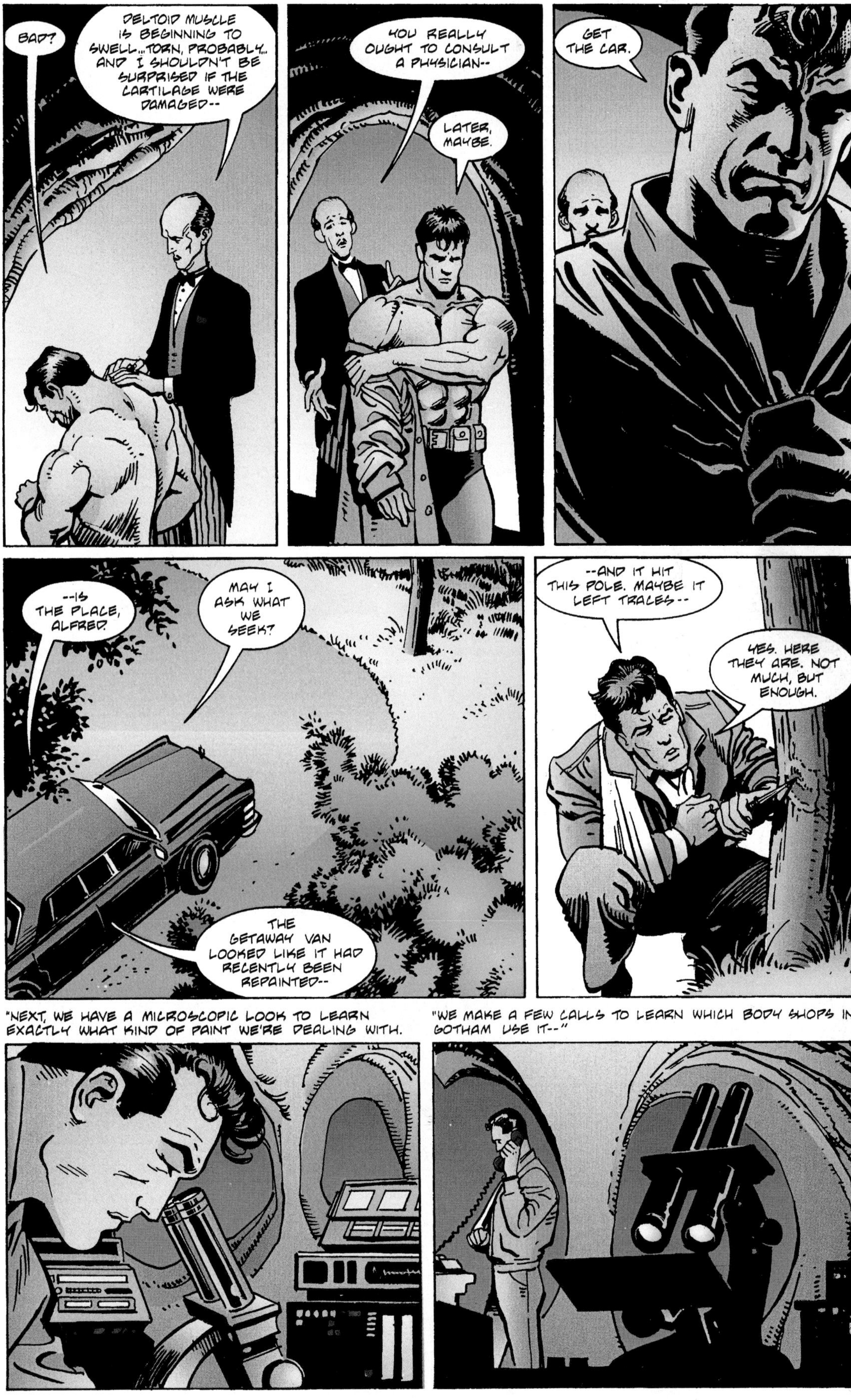
BAD?
DELTOID MUSCLE IS BEGINNING TO SWELL...TORN, PROBABLY... AND I SHOULDN'T BE SURPRISED IF THE CARTILAGE WERE DAMAGED--
YOU REALLY OUGHT TO CONSULT A PHYSICIAN--
LATER, MAYBE.
GET THE CAR.
--IS THE PLACE, ALFRED.
MAY I ASK WHAT WE SEEK?
THE GETAWAY VAN LOOKED LIKE IT HAD RECENTLY BEEN REPAINTED--
--AND IT HIT THIS POLE. MAYBE IT LEFT TRACES--
YES. HERE THEY ARE. NOT MUCH, BUT ENOUGH.
"NEXT, WE HAVE A MICROSCOPIC LOOK TO LEARN EXACTLY WHAT KIND OF PAINT WE'RE DEALING WITH.
"WE MAKE A FEW CALLS TO LEARN WHICH BODY SHOPS IN GOTHAM USE IT--"

"--AND THEN WE VISIT THE LIKELY ONES. WE MAKE A DONATION TO THE OWNERS' FAVORITE CHARITIES--

"--AND THEY VERY GENEROUSLY PERMIT US TO EXAMINE THEIR RECORDS."

--SEEING YOU, HARVEY.

HARVEY DENT--THE DISTRICT ATTORNEY...THE ONE I--BATMAN--HAVE A WORKING ARRANGEMENT WITH...

I AM FAMILIAR WITH YOUR RELATIONSHIP WITH MISTER DENT.

'COURSE YOU ARE. 'COURSE YOU ARE...WHERE WAS I?

OH, YEAH. DENT SAYS THAT ONE OF THE NAMES I GOT FROM THE BODY SHOP...THIS GUY HAS A RECORD...INCLUDES SUSPICION OF KIDNAPPING...WE'RE GONNA SEE HIM...

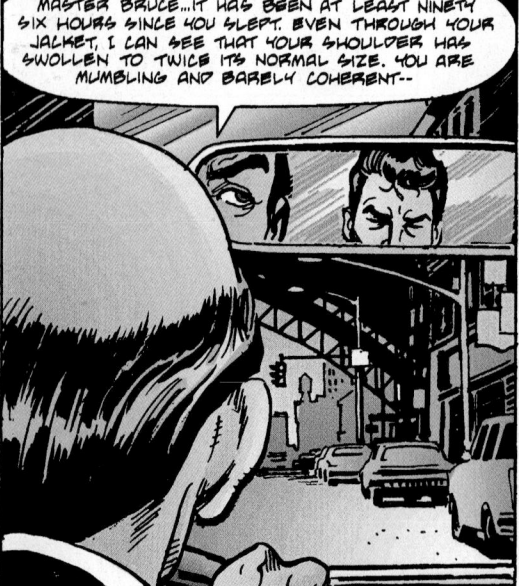

MASTER BRUCE...IT HAS BEEN AT LEAST NINETY SIX HOURS SINCE YOU SLEPT. EVEN THROUGH YOUR JACKET, I CAN SEE THAT YOUR SHOULDER HAS SWOLLEN TO TWICE ITS NORMAL SIZE. YOU ARE MUMBLING AND BARELY COHERENT--

--I REALLY MUST INSIST THAT YOU SEE A DOCTOR AND THEN RETIRE--

NO!

I COULDN'T SAVE THE GIRL... COULDN'T SAVE LITTLE SISSY PORTER... WATCHED SISSY PORTER DIE...BUT I CAN GET THE SCUM WHO KILLED HER...

22

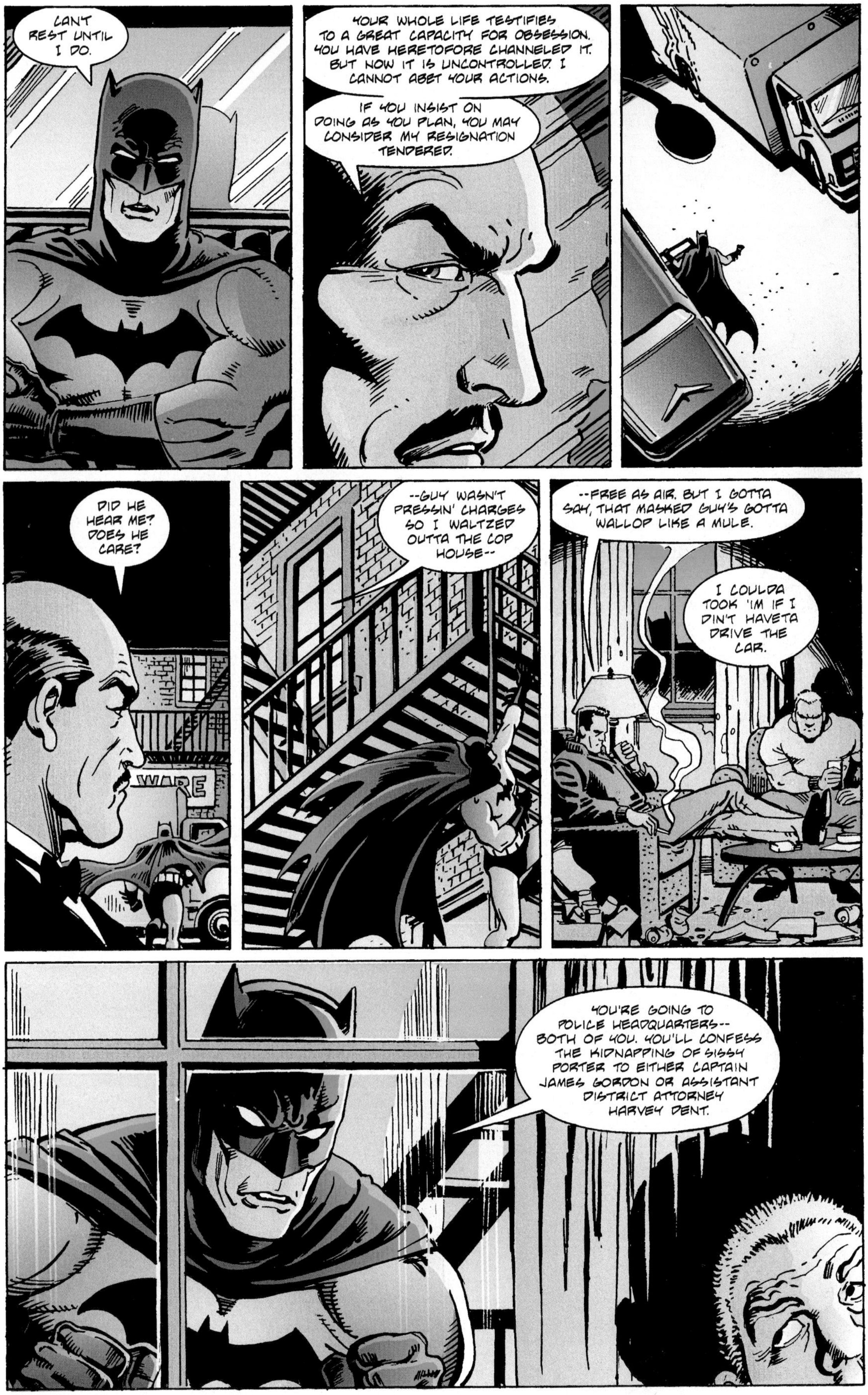
CAN'T REST UNTIL I DO.
YOUR WHOLE LIFE TESTIFIES TO A GREAT CAPACITY FOR OBSESSION. YOU HAVE HERETOFORE CHANNELED IT. BUT NOW IT IS UNCONTROLLED. I CANNOT ABET YOUR ACTIONS.
IF YOU INSIST ON DOING AS YOU PLAN, YOU MAY CONSIDER MY RESIGNATION TENDERED.
DID HE HEAR ME? DOES HE CARE?
WARE
--GUY WASN'T PRESSIN' CHARGES SO I WALTZED OUTTA THE COP HOUSE--
--FREE AS AIR. BUT I GOTTA SAY, THAT MASKED GUY'S GOTTA WALLOP LIKE A MULE.
I COULDA TOOK 'IM IF I DIN'T HAVETA DRIVE THE CAR.
YOU'RE GOING TO POLICE HEADQUARTERS--BOTH OF YOU. YOU'LL CONFESS THE KIDNAPPING OF SISSY PORTER TO EITHER CAPTAIN JAMES GORDON OR ASSISTANT DISTRICT ATTORNEY HARVEY DENT.

OR BOTH. PREFERABLY BOTH.

HEY, MAN, I GOT NO BEEF WITH YOU.

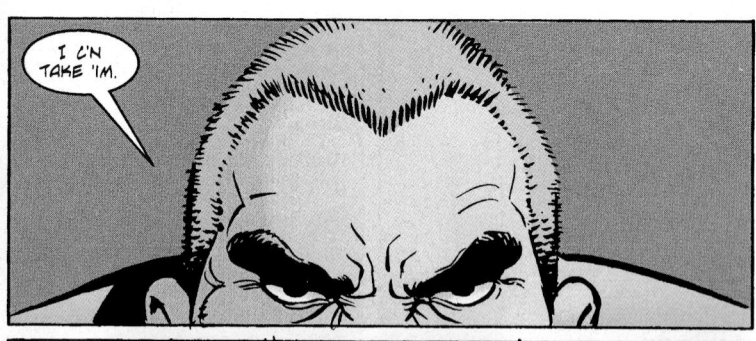

I C'N TAKE 'IM.

YOU'RE WELCOME TO TRY.

I'M TELLIN' YA, PATSY, HE CAN HIT!

I C'N TAKE 'IM.

Unnn

WHUUHF

ANNGH!

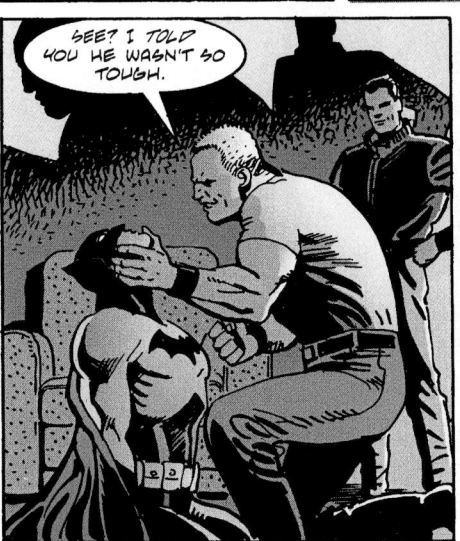

SEE? I *TOLD* YOU HE WASN'T SO TOUGH.

YOU HOLDIN' HIM, PATSY? REAL TIGHT? LIKE HE CAN'T GET LOOSE?

YEAH.

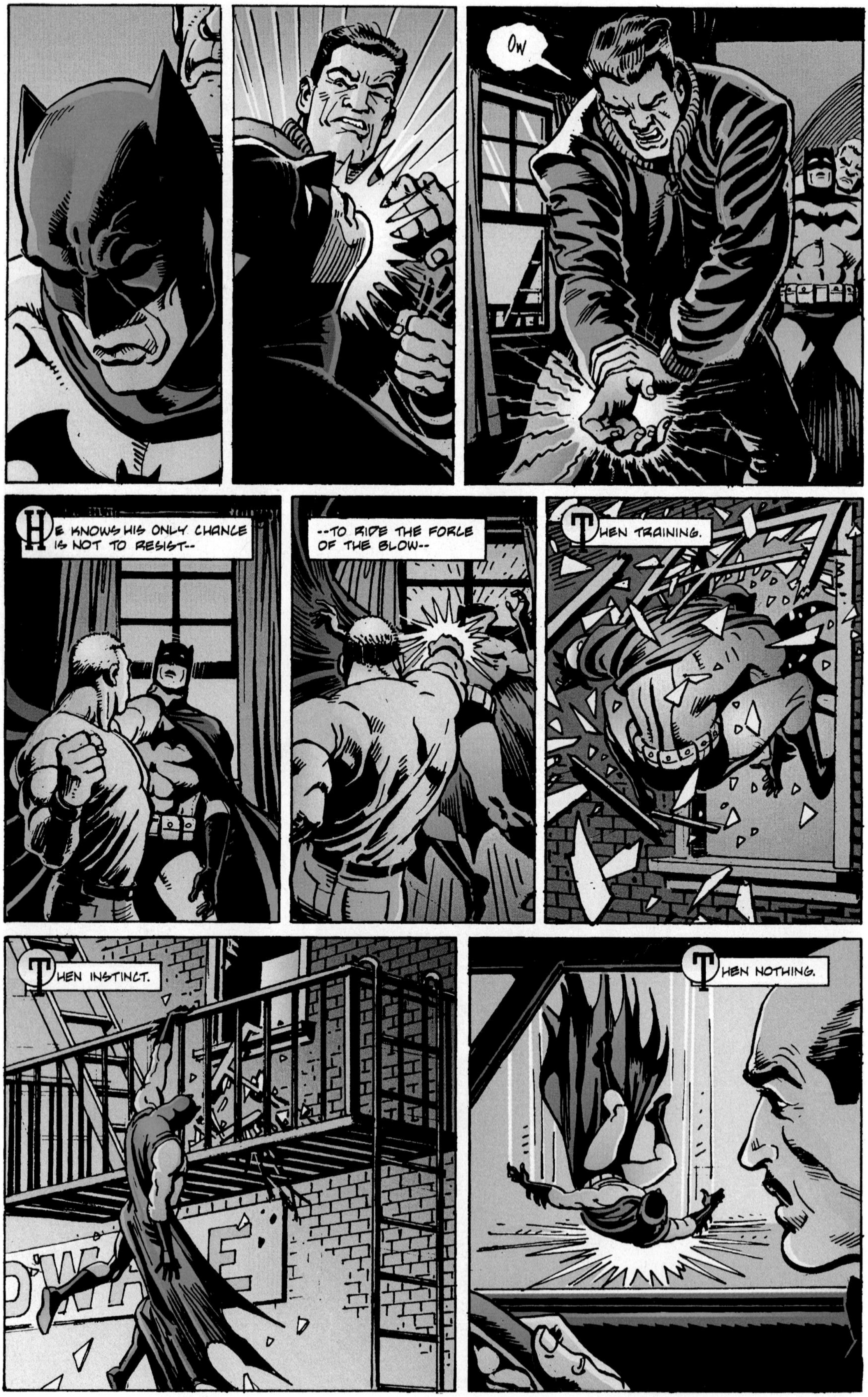
OW
HE KNOWS HIS ONLY CHANCE IS NOT TO RESIST--
--TO RIDE THE FORCE OF THE BLOW--
THEN TRAINING.
THEN INSTINCT.
THEN NOTHING.

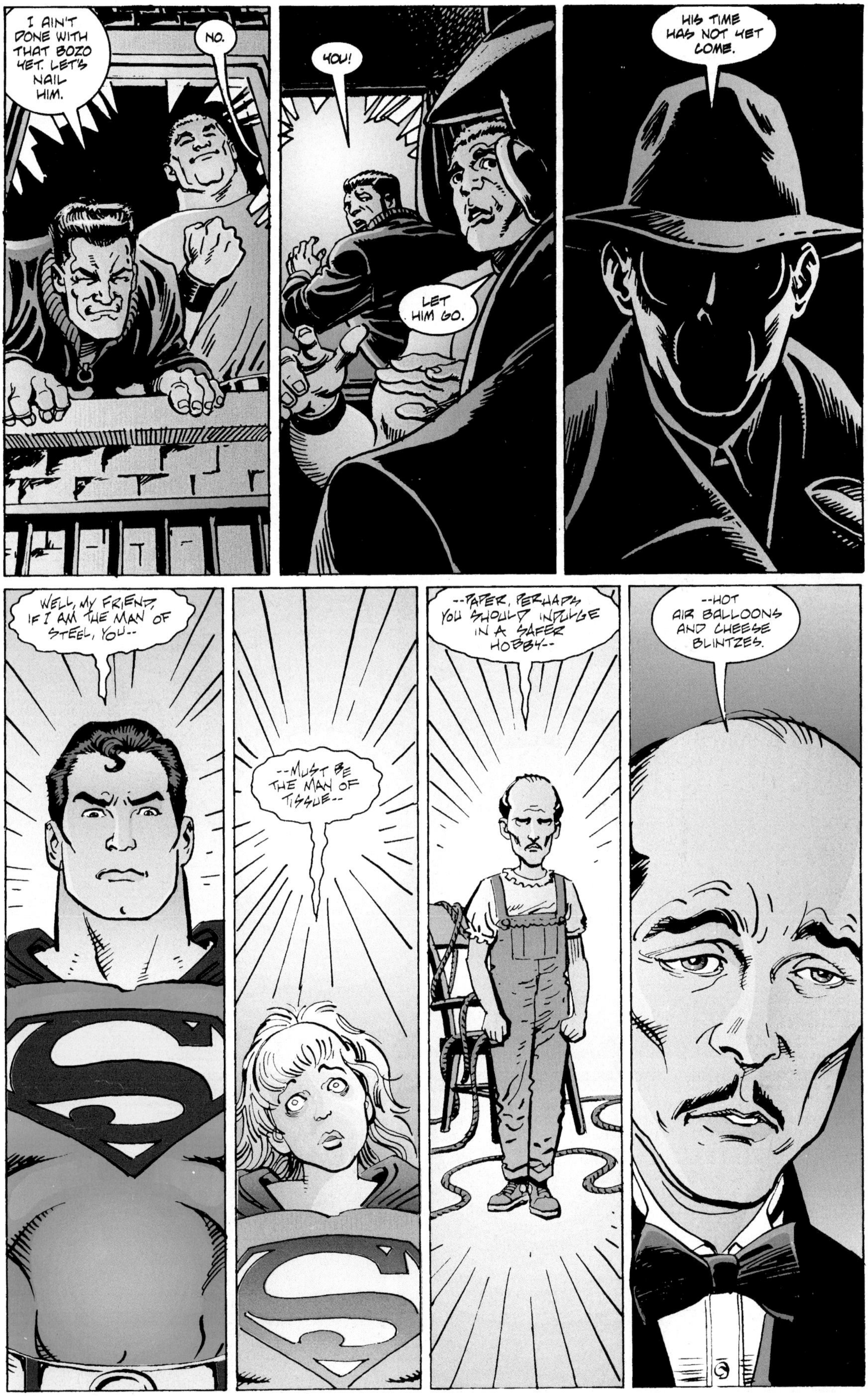
I AIN'T DONE WITH THAT BOZO YET. LET'S NAIL HIM.
NO.
YOU!
LET HIM GO.
HIS TIME HAS NOT YET COME.
WELL, MY FRIEND, IF I AM THE MAN OF STEEL, YOU--
--MUST BE THE MAN OF TISSUE--
--PAPER. PERHAPS YOU SHOULD INDULGE IN A SAFER HOBBY--
--HOT AIR BALLOONS AND CHEESE BLINTZES.

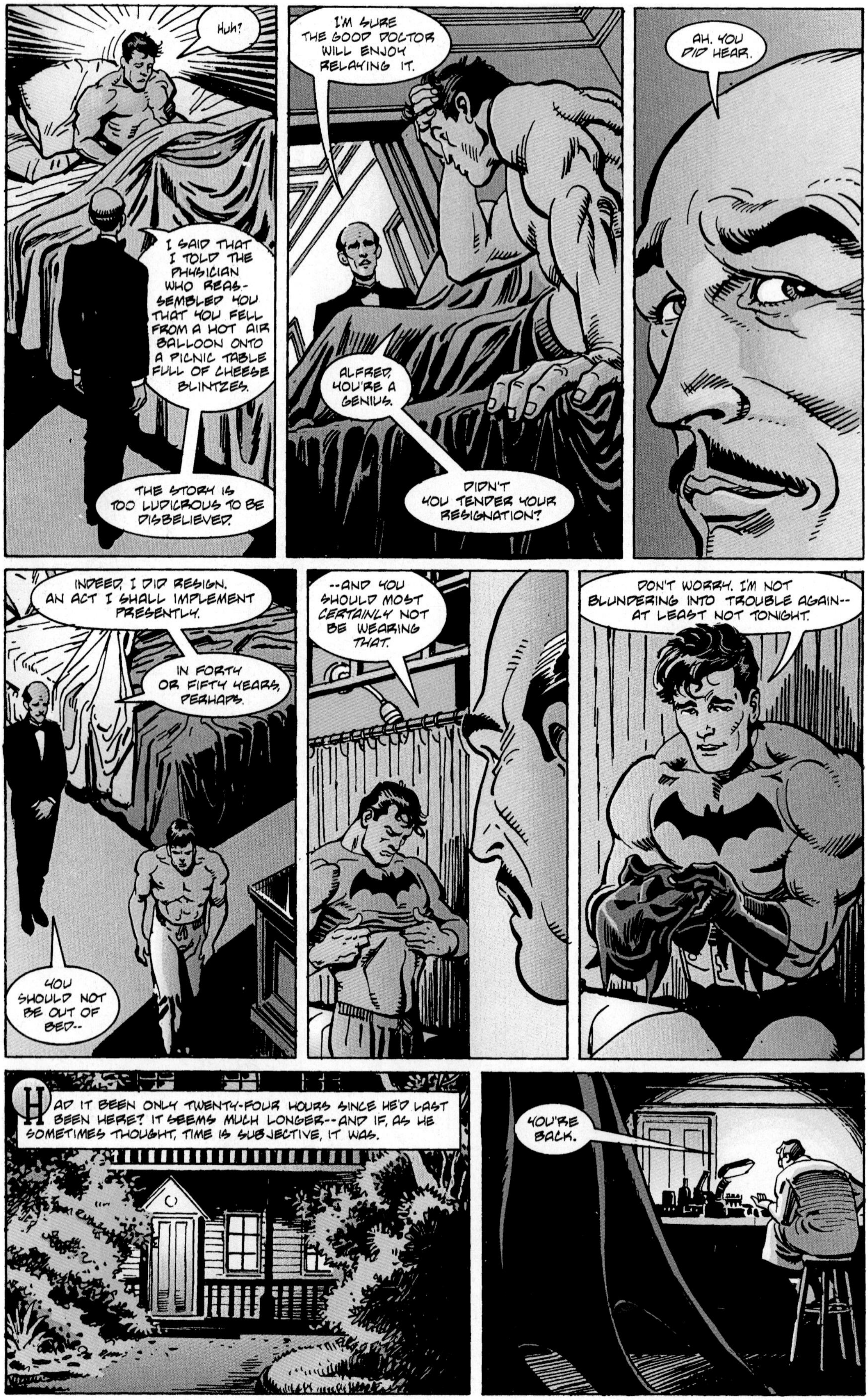
Huh?
I SAID THAT I TOLD THE PHYSICIAN WHO REAS-SEMBLED YOU THAT YOU FELL FROM A HOT AIR BALLOON ONTO A PICNIC TABLE FULL OF CHEESE BLINTZES.
THE STORY IS TOO LUDICROUS TO BE DISBELIEVED.
I'M SURE THE GOOD DOCTOR WILL ENJOY RELAYING IT.
ALFRED, YOU'RE A GENIUS.
DIDN'T YOU TENDER YOUR RESIGNATION?
AH. YOU DID HEAR.
INDEED, I DID RESIGN. AN ACT I SHALL IMPLEMENT PRESENTLY.
IN FORTY OR FIFTY YEARS, PERHAPS.
YOU SHOULD NOT BE OUT OF BED--
--AND YOU SHOULD MOST CERTAINLY NOT BE WEARING THAT.
DON'T WORRY. I'M NOT BLUNDERING INTO TROUBLE AGAIN-- AT LEAST NOT TONIGHT.
HAD IT BEEN ONLY TWENTY-FOUR HOURS SINCE HE'D LAST BEEN HERE? IT SEEMS MUCH LONGER--AND IF, AS HE SOMETIMES THOUGHT, TIME IS SUBJECTIVE, IT WAS.
YOU'RE BACK.

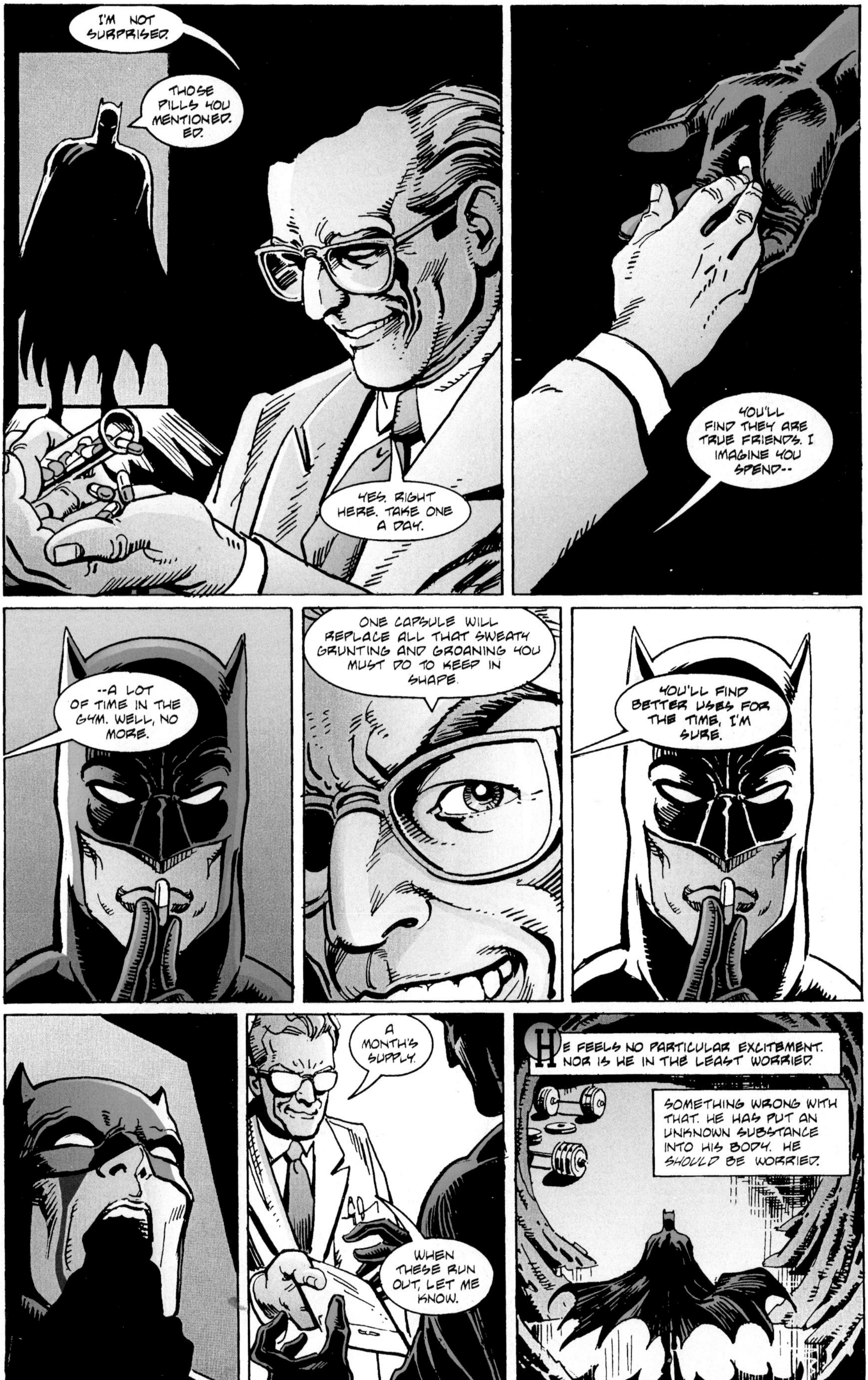
I'M NOT SURPRISED.
THOSE PILLS YOU MENTIONED, ED.
YES. RIGHT HERE. TAKE ONE A DAY.
YOU'LL FIND THEY ARE TRUE FRIENDS. I IMAGINE YOU SPEND--
--A LOT OF TIME IN THE GYM. WELL, NO MORE.
ONE CAPSULE WILL REPLACE ALL THAT SWEATY GRUNTING AND GROANING YOU MUST DO TO KEEP IN SHAPE.
YOU'LL FIND BETTER USES FOR THE TIME, I'M SURE.
A MONTH'S SUPPLY.
WHEN THESE RUN OUT, LET ME KNOW.
HE FEELS NO PARTICULAR EXCITEMENT. NOR IS HE IN THE LEAST WORRIED.
SOMETHING WRONG WITH THAT. HE HAS PUT AN UNKNOWN SUBSTANCE INTO HIS BODY. HE SHOULD BE WORRIED.

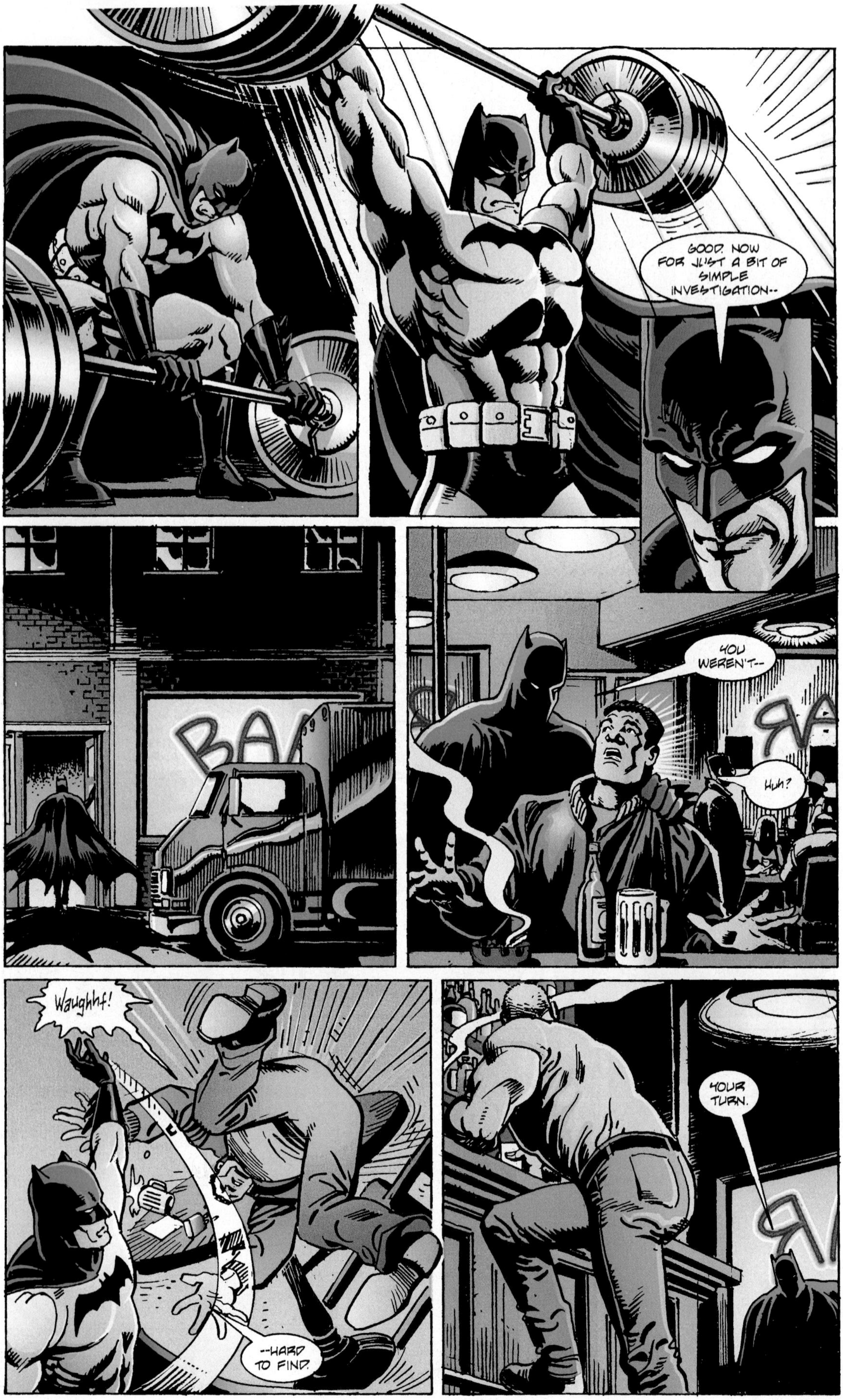
GOOD. NOW FOR JUST A BIT OF SIMPLE INVESTIGATION--
BA
YOU WEREN'T--
Huh?
Waughhf!
--HARD TO FIND.
YOUR TURN.

I C'N TAKE YOU.

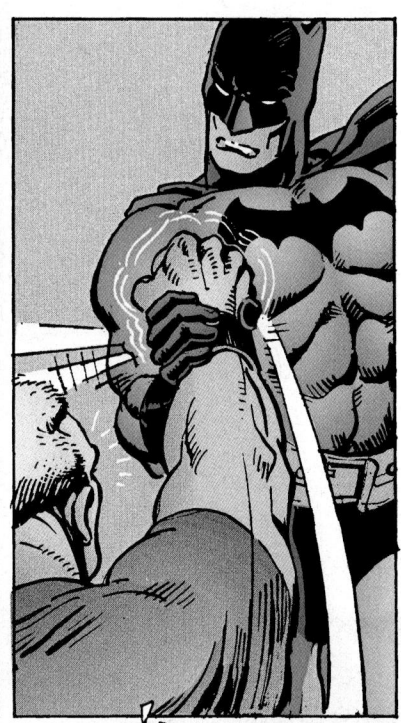

BAR

IT BEGINS AT THE BASE OF HIS SPINE--

--RISES THROUGH HIS CHEST AND LUNGS--

-- AND THEN HE CAN CONTAIN IT NO LONGER--

HAHAHAHAHAHAHAHAHA

--THE LAUGH THAT SOUNDS STRANGELY LIKE A SHRIEK...

Continued.

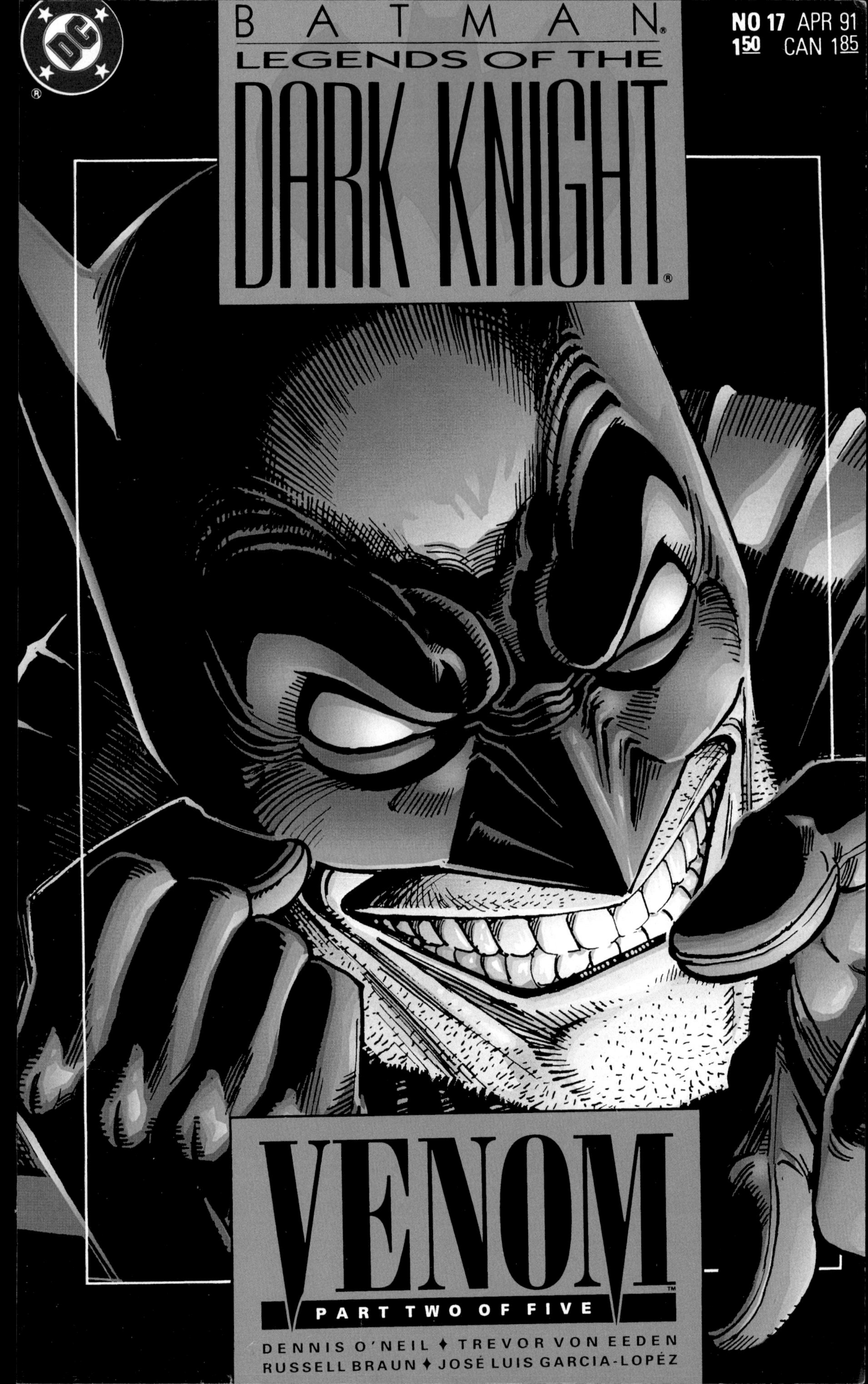
DC
BATMAN
LEGENDS OF THE
DARK KNIGHT
NO 17 APR 91
1.50 CAN 1.85
VENOM
PART TWO OF FIVE
DENNIS O'NEIL ♦ TREVOR VON EEDEN
RUSSELL BRAUN ♦ JOSÉ LUIS GARCIA-LOPÉZ

VENOM: PART TWO

"THE DOOR WAS EASY.

"THE FIRST TWO PUNKS WEREN'T ANYTHING TO SWEAT ABOUT, EITHER.

"AND THE THIRD--HE WAS GOING TO SING ME A WHOLE OPERA. ONLY HE DIDN'T KNOW THAT.

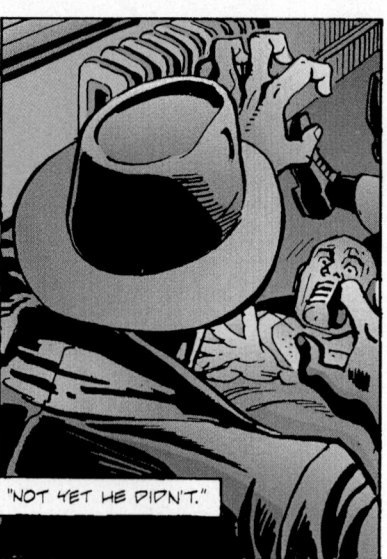

"NOT YET HE DIDN'T."

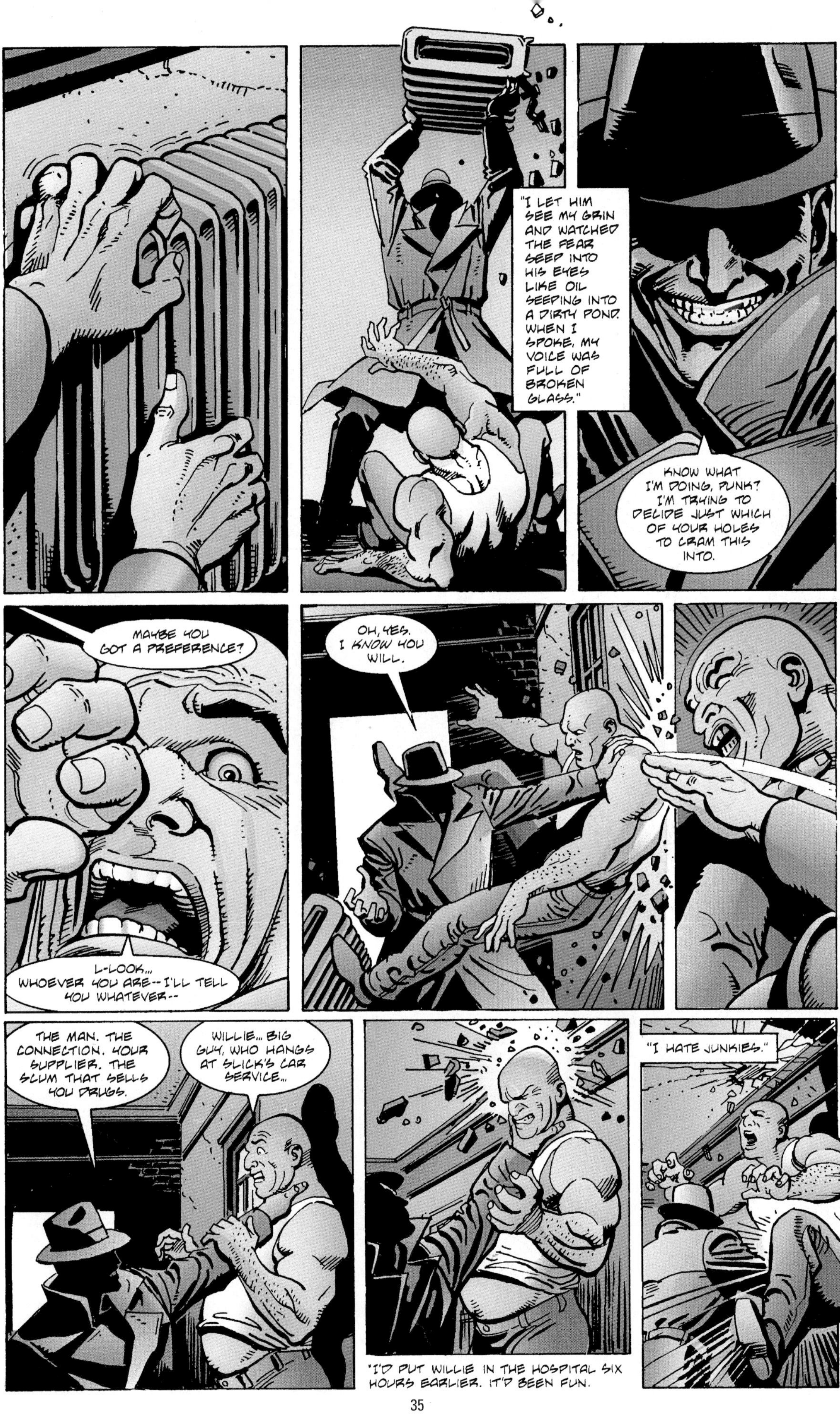
"I LET HIM SEE MY GRIN AND WATCHED THE FEAR SEEP INTO HIS EYES LIKE OIL SEEPING INTO A DIRTY POND. WHEN I SPOKE, MY VOICE WAS FULL OF BROKEN GLASS."
KNOW WHAT I'M DOING, PUNK? I'M TRYING TO DECIDE JUST WHICH OF YOUR HOLES TO CRAM THIS INTO.
MAYBE YOU GOT A PREFERENCE?
L-LOOK... WHOEVER YOU ARE--I'LL TELL YOU WHATEVER--
OH, YES. I KNOW YOU WILL.
THE MAN. THE CONNECTION. YOUR SUPPLIER. THE SCUM THAT SELLS YOU DRUGS.
WILLIE... BIG GUY, WHO HANGS AT SLICK'S CAR SERVICE...
"I'D PUT WILLIE IN THE HOSPITAL SIX HOURS EARLIER. IT'D BEEN FUN.
"I HATE JUNKIES."

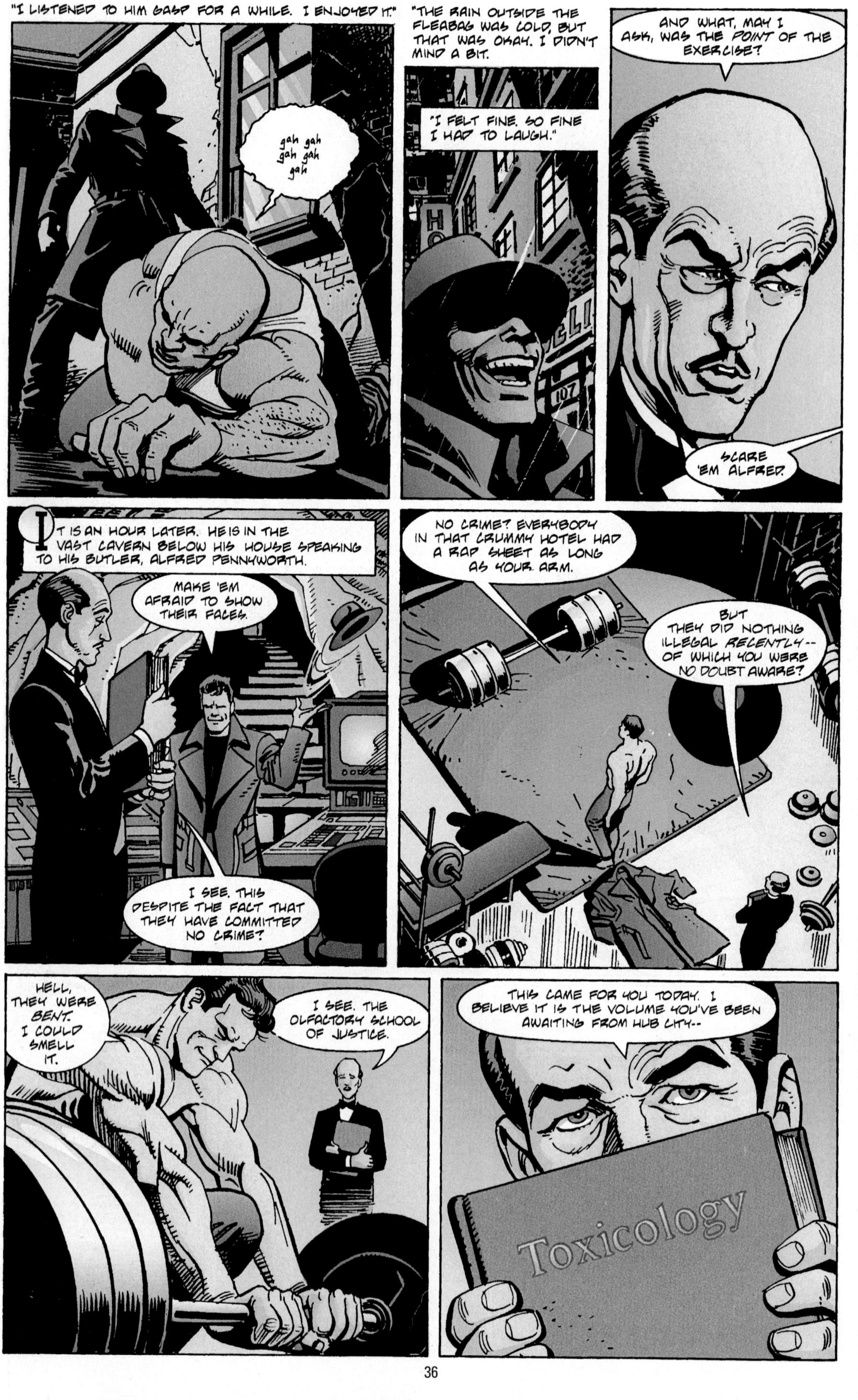
"I LISTENED TO HIM GASP FOR A WHILE. I ENJOYED IT."
gah gah gah gah gah
"THE RAIN OUTSIDE THE FLEABAG WAS COLD, BUT THAT WAS OKAY. I DIDN'T MIND A BIT.
"I FELT FINE. SO FINE I HAD TO LAUGH."
AND WHAT, MAY I ASK, WAS THE POINT OF THE EXERCISE?
SCARE 'EM ALFRED.
IT IS AN HOUR LATER. HE IS IN THE VAST CAVERN BELOW HIS HOUSE SPEAKING TO HIS BUTLER, ALFRED PENNYWORTH.
MAKE 'EM AFRAID TO SHOW THEIR FACES.
I SEE. THIS DESPITE THE FACT THAT THEY HAVE COMMITTED NO CRIME?
NO CRIME? EVERYBODY IN THAT CRUMMY HOTEL HAD A RAP SHEET AS LONG AS YOUR ARM.
BUT THEY DID NOTHING ILLEGAL RECENTLY-- OF WHICH YOU WERE NO DOUBT AWARE?
HELL, THEY WERE BENT. I COULD SMELL IT.
I SEE. THE OLFACTORY SCHOOL OF JUSTICE.
THIS CAME FOR YOU TODAY. I BELIEVE IT IS THE VOLUME YOU'VE BEEN AWAITING FROM HUB CITY--
Toxicology

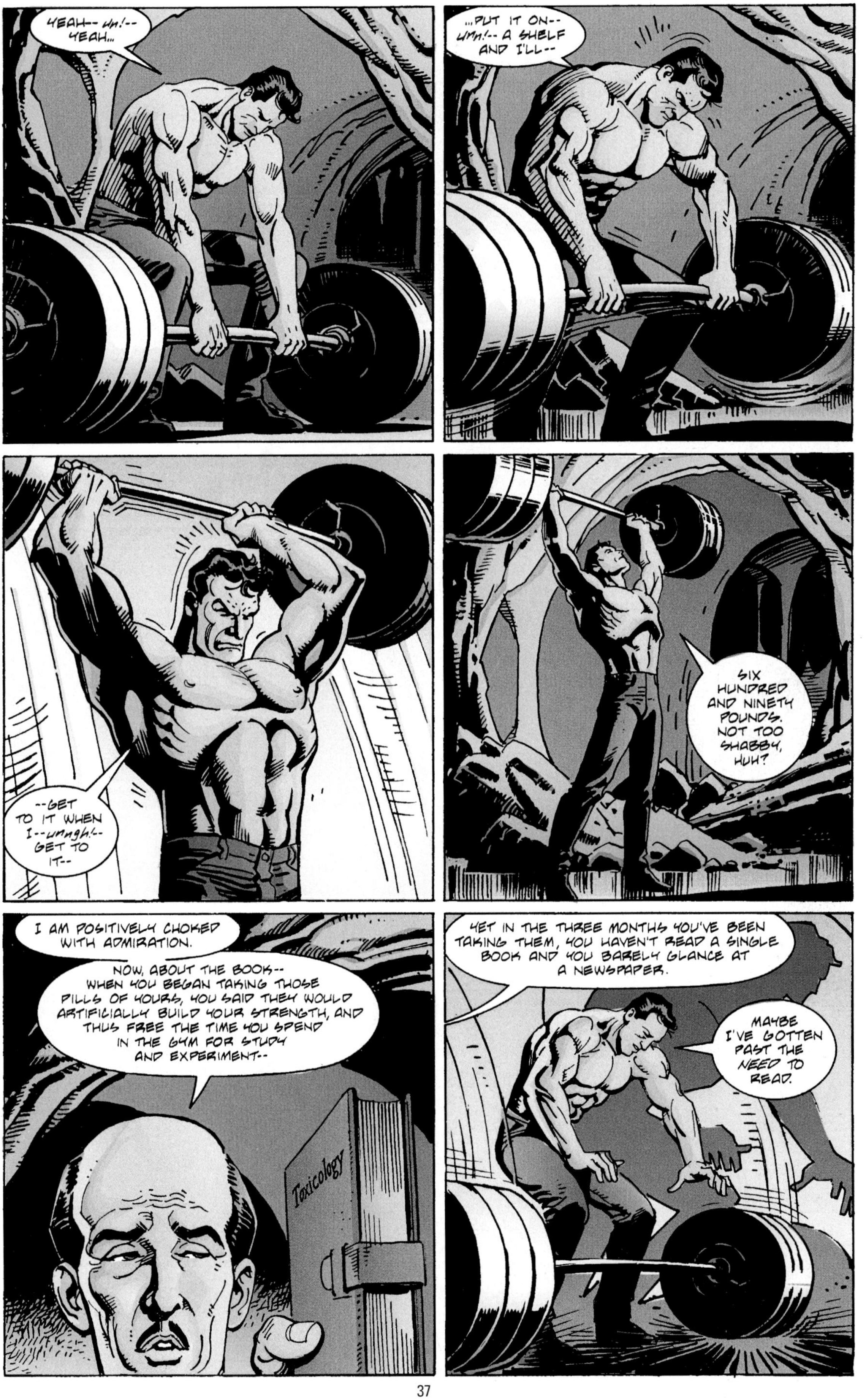
YEAH-- UH!-- YEAH...
...PUT IT ON-- UMM!-- A SHELF AND I'LL--
--GET TO IT WHEN I--UMMGH!-- GET TO IT--
SIX HUNDRED AND NINETY POUNDS. NOT TOO SHABBY, HUH?
I AM POSITIVELY CHOKED WITH ADMIRATION.
NOW, ABOUT THE BOOK-- WHEN YOU BEGAN TAKING THOSE PILLS OF YOURS, YOU SAID THEY WOULD ARTIFICIALLY BUILD YOUR STRENGTH, AND THUS FREE THE TIME YOU SPEND IN THE GYM FOR STUDY AND EXPERIMENT--
Toxicology
YET IN THE THREE MONTHS YOU'VE BEEN TAKING THEM, YOU HAVEN'T READ A SINGLE BOOK AND YOU BARELY GLANCE AT A NEWSPAPER.
MAYBE I'VE GOTTEN PAST THE NEED TO READ.

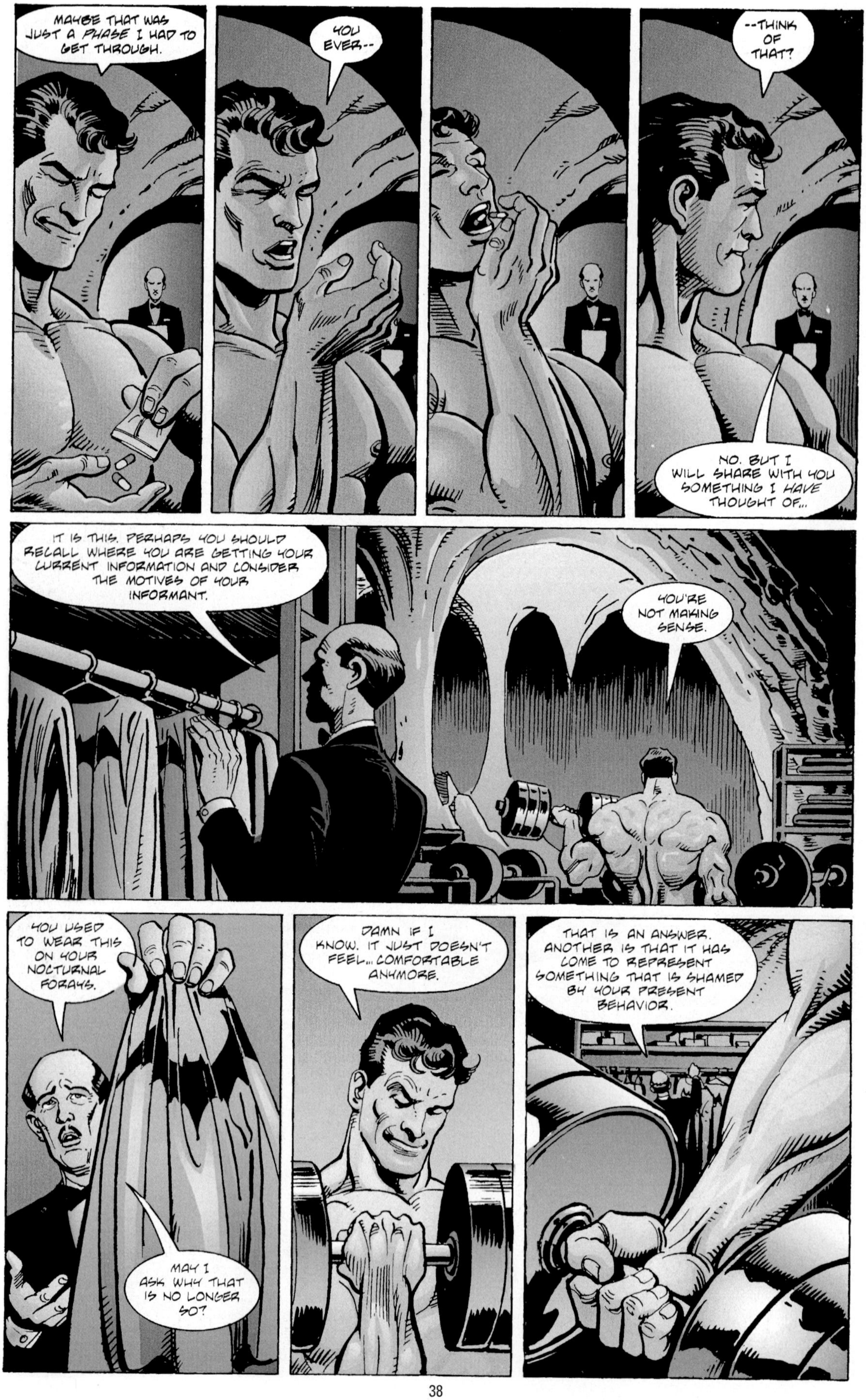
MAYBE THAT WAS JUST A *PHASE* I HAD TO GET THROUGH.
YOU EVER--
--THINK OF THAT?
NO. BUT I WILL SHARE WITH YOU SOMETHING I *HAVE* THOUGHT OF...
IT IS THIS. PERHAPS YOU SHOULD RECALL WHERE YOU ARE GETTING YOUR CURRENT INFORMATION AND CONSIDER THE MOTIVES OF YOUR INFORMANT.
YOU'RE NOT MAKING SENSE.
YOU USED TO WEAR THIS ON YOUR NOCTURNAL FORAYS.
MAY I ASK WHY THAT IS NO LONGER SO?
DAMN IF I KNOW. IT JUST DOESN'T FEEL... COMFORTABLE ANYMORE.
THAT IS AN ANSWER. ANOTHER IS THAT IT HAS COME TO REPRESENT SOMETHING THAT IS SHAMED BY YOUR PRESENT BEHAVIOR.

I'VE GOT NOTHING TO BE ASHAMED OF. GET THAT LOUD AND CLEAR-- *NOTHING!*

AND IF YOU THINK I DO... MAYBE YOU'RE ONE OF *THEM!*

ONE OF WHOM?

THE WEAKLINGS. THE SNIVELERS WHO'VE LET THE CITY BECOME A SEWER BECAUSE THEY'RE AFRAID TO DO WHAT HAS TO BE DONE.

WHERE ARE YOU GOING?

AWAY FROM YOU.

MAYBE YOU SHOULD *KEEP* WALKING

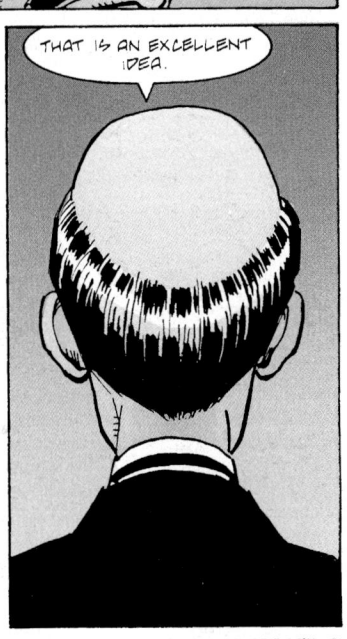

THAT IS AN EXCELLENT IDEA.

"SHAMED," HE SAID.

I'LL SHOW HIM.

OF COURSE, MAYBE I WAS A LITTLE ROUGH ON HIM...

GOOD TO SEE YOU AGAIN.

DOCTOR RANDOLPH PORTER IS SMOOTH AND AVUNCULAR, AS ALWAYS.

39

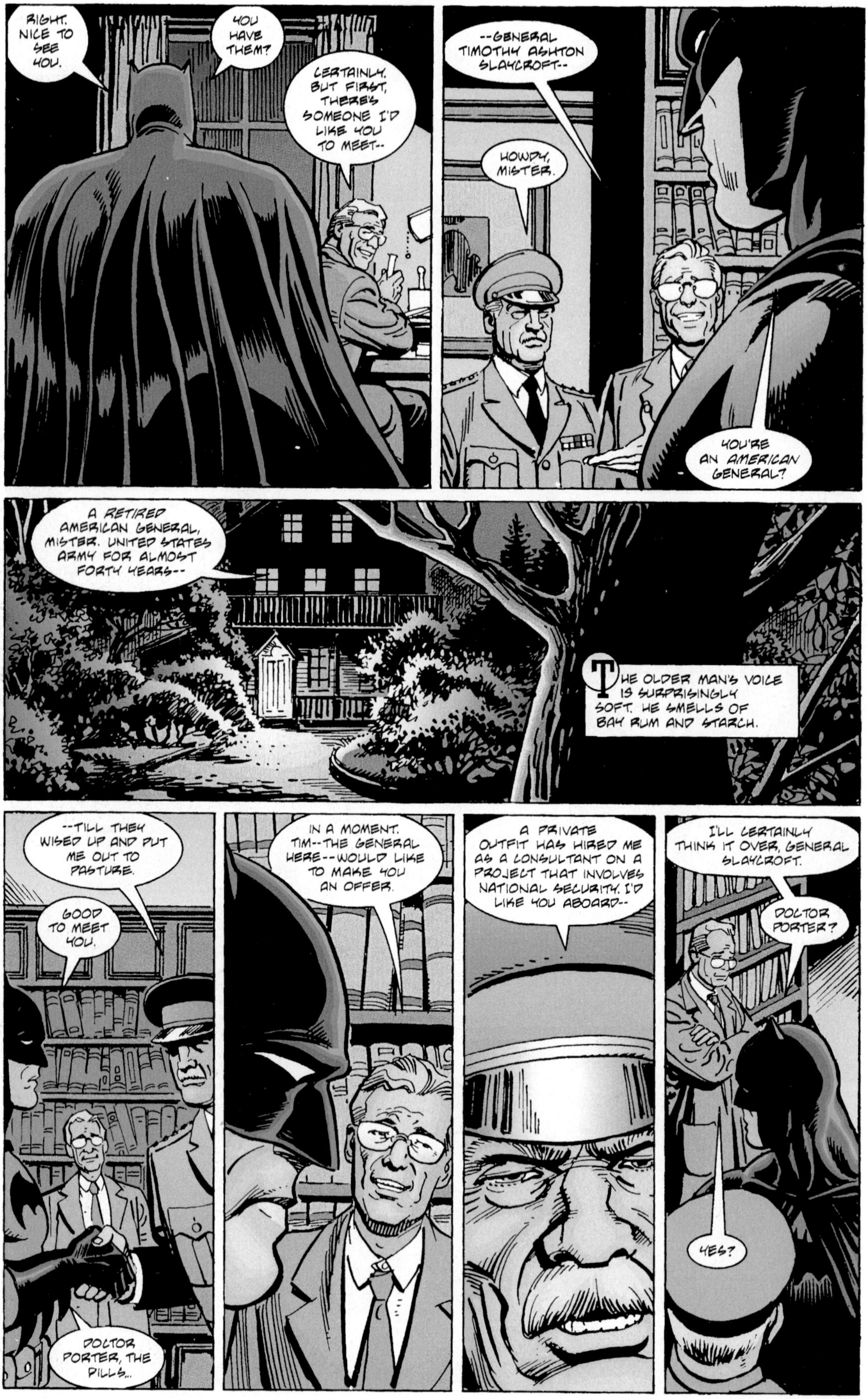
RIGHT. NICE TO SEE YOU.
YOU HAVE THEM?
CERTAINLY. BUT FIRST, THERE'S SOMEONE I'D LIKE YOU TO MEET--
--GENERAL TIMOTHY ASHTON SLAYCROFT--
HOWDY, MISTER.
YOU'RE AN AMERICAN GENERAL?
A RETIRED AMERICAN GENERAL, MISTER. UNITED STATES ARMY FOR ALMOST FORTY YEARS--
THE OLDER MAN'S VOICE IS SURPRISINGLY SOFT. HE SMELLS OF BAY RUM AND STARCH.
--TILL THEY WISED UP AND PUT ME OUT TO PASTURE.
GOOD TO MEET YOU.
DOCTOR PORTER, THE PILLS...
IN A MOMENT. TIM--THE GENERAL HERE--WOULD LIKE TO MAKE YOU AN OFFER.
A PRIVATE OUTFIT HAS HIRED ME AS A CONSULTANT ON A PROJECT THAT INVOLVES NATIONAL SECURITY. I'D LIKE YOU ABOARD--
I'LL CERTAINLY THINK IT OVER, GENERAL SLAYCROFT.
DOCTOR PORTER?
YES?

OH, THESE! YOU WANT THESE!

THANK YOU.

UH... DOCTOR PORTER?

YES?

THERE ARE ONLY FOUR.

I'VE BEEN BUSY-- DIDN'T HAVE TIME TO MAKE UP ANY MORE. THAT'S NOT A PROBLEM IS IT?

NO... OF COURSE NOT.

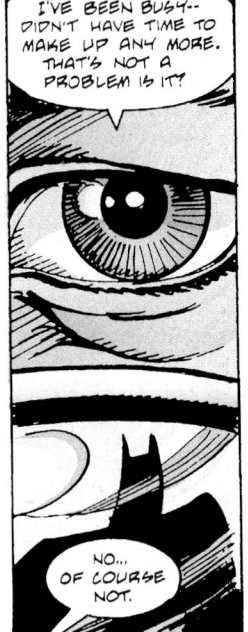

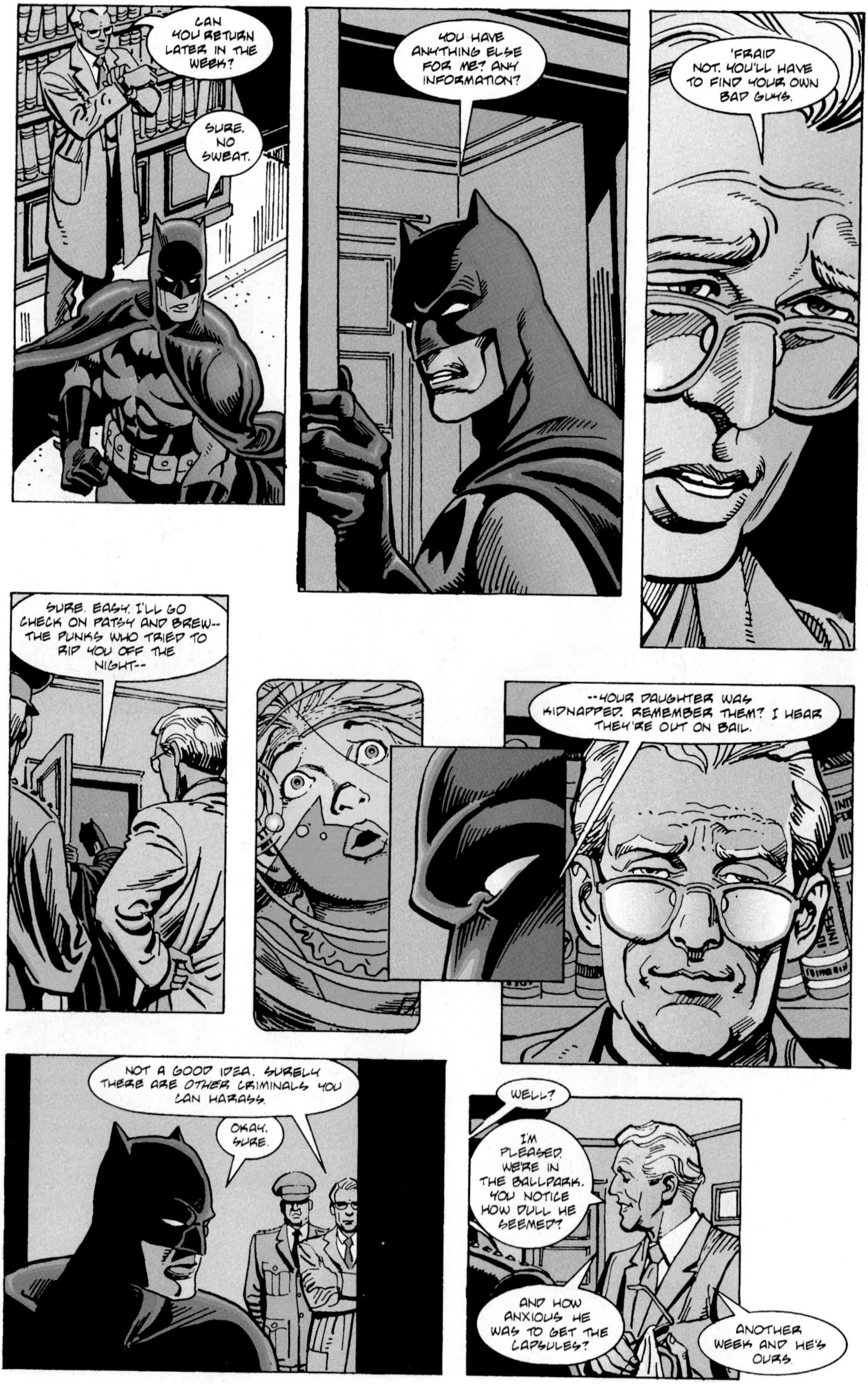
CAN YOU RETURN LATER IN THE WEEK?
SURE. NO SWEAT.
YOU HAVE ANYTHING ELSE FOR ME? ANY INFORMATION?
'FRAID NOT. YOU'LL HAVE TO FIND YOUR OWN BAD GUYS.
SURE. EASY. I'LL GO CHECK ON PATSY AND BREW-- THE PUNKS WHO TRIED TO RIP YOU OFF THE NIGHT--
--YOUR DAUGHTER WAS KIDNAPPED. REMEMBER THEM? I HEAR THEY'RE OUT ON BAIL.
NOT A GOOD IDEA. SURELY THERE ARE OTHER CRIMINALS YOU CAN HARASS.
OKAY. SURE.
WELL?
I'M PLEASED. WE'RE IN THE BALLPARK. YOU NOTICE HOW DULL HE SEEMED?
AND HOW ANXIOUS HE WAS TO GET THE CAPSULES?
ANOTHER WEEK AND HE'S OURS.

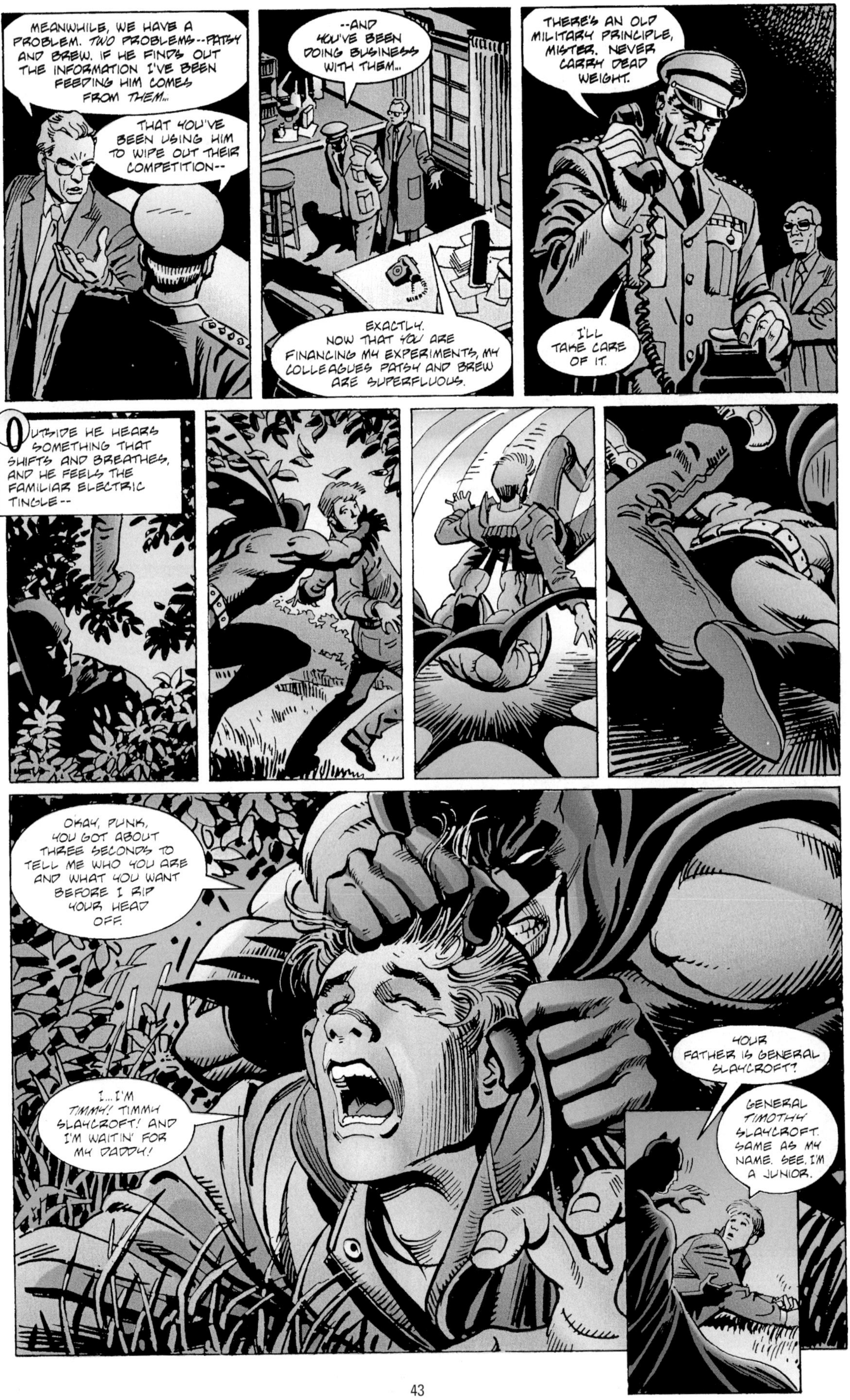
MEANWHILE, WE HAVE A PROBLEM. TWO PROBLEMS--PATSY AND BREW. IF HE FINDS OUT THE INFORMATION I'VE BEEN FEEDING HIM COMES FROM THEM...
THAT YOU'VE BEEN USING HIM TO WIPE OUT THEIR COMPETITION--
--AND YOU'VE BEEN DOING BUSINESS WITH THEM...
EXACTLY. NOW THAT YOU ARE FINANCING MY EXPERIMENTS, MY COLLEAGUES PATSY AND BREW ARE SUPERFLUOUS.
THERE'S AN OLD MILITARY PRINCIPLE, MISTER. NEVER CARRY DEAD WEIGHT.
I'LL TAKE CARE OF IT.
OUTSIDE HE HEARS SOMETHING THAT SHIFTS AND BREATHES, AND HE FEELS THE FAMILIAR ELECTRIC TINGLE--
OKAY, PUNK, YOU GOT ABOUT THREE SECONDS TO TELL ME WHO YOU ARE AND WHAT YOU WANT BEFORE I RIP YOUR HEAD OFF.
I...I'M TIMMY! TIMMY SLAYCROFT! AND I'M WAITIN' FOR MY DADDY!
YOUR FATHER IS GENERAL SLAYCROFT?
GENERAL TIMOTHY SLAYCROFT. SAME AS MY NAME. SEE, I'M A JUNIOR.

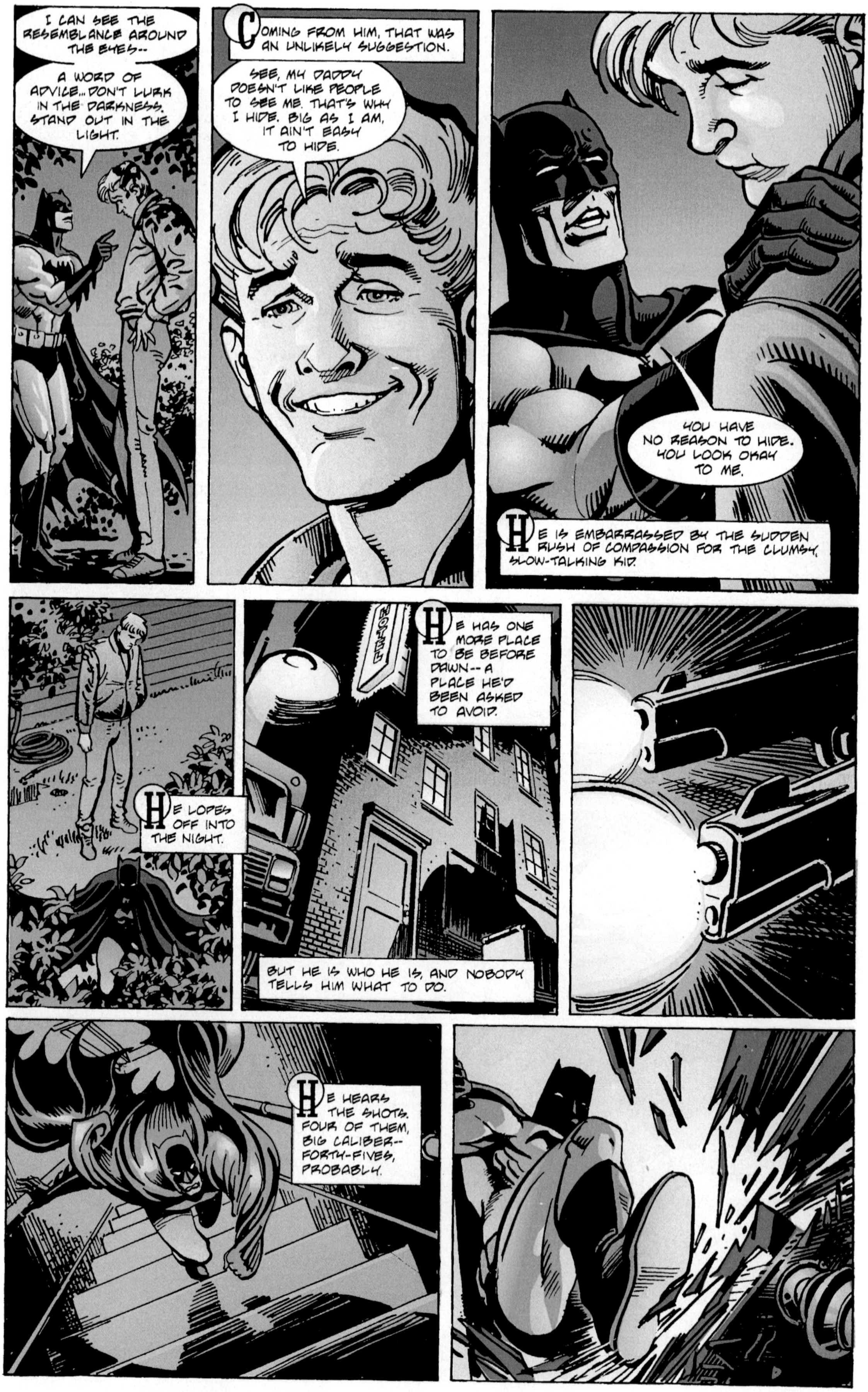

I CAN SEE THE RESEMBLANCE AROUND THE EYES--
A WORD OF ADVICE... DON'T LURK IN THE DARKNESS. STAND OUT IN THE LIGHT.
COMING FROM HIM, THAT WAS AN UNLIKELY SUGGESTION.
SEE, MY DADDY DOESN'T LIKE PEOPLE TO SEE ME. THAT'S WHY I HIDE. BIG AS I AM, IT AIN'T EASY TO HIDE.
YOU HAVE NO REASON TO HIDE. YOU LOOK OKAY TO ME.
HE IS EMBARRASSED BY THE SUDDEN RUSH OF COMPASSION FOR THE CLUMSY, SLOW-TALKING KID.
HE LOPES OFF INTO THE NIGHT.
HOTEL
HE HAS ONE MORE PLACE TO BE BEFORE DAWN-- A PLACE HE'D BEEN ASKED TO AVOID.
BUT HE IS WHO HE IS, AND NOBODY TELLS HIM WHAT TO DO.
HE HEARS THE SHOTS. FOUR OF THEM, BIG CALIBER-- FORTY-FIVES, PROBABLY.

ONE GLANCE IS ENOUGH.

HE HEARS FOOTSTEPS IN THE ALLEY BELOW THE WINDOW.

HE SEES TWO MEN RUNNING FOR A CAR. NO WAY TO CATCH THEM.

BUT STOP THEM? YES, MAYBE.

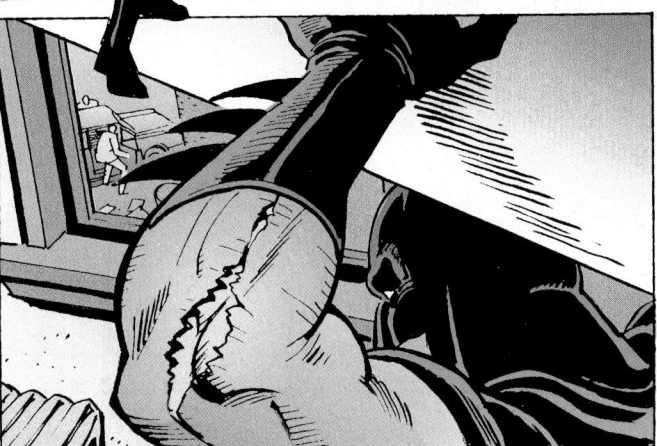

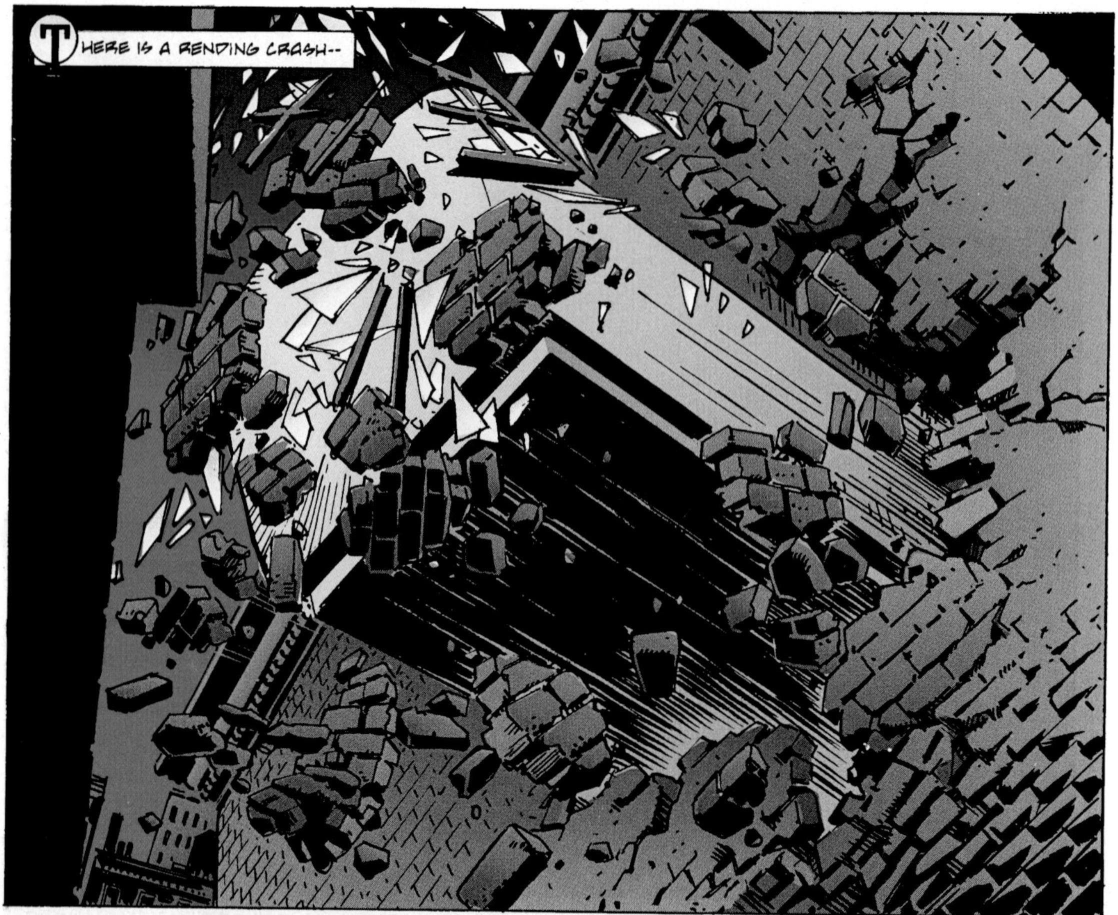
THERE IS A RENDING CRASH--

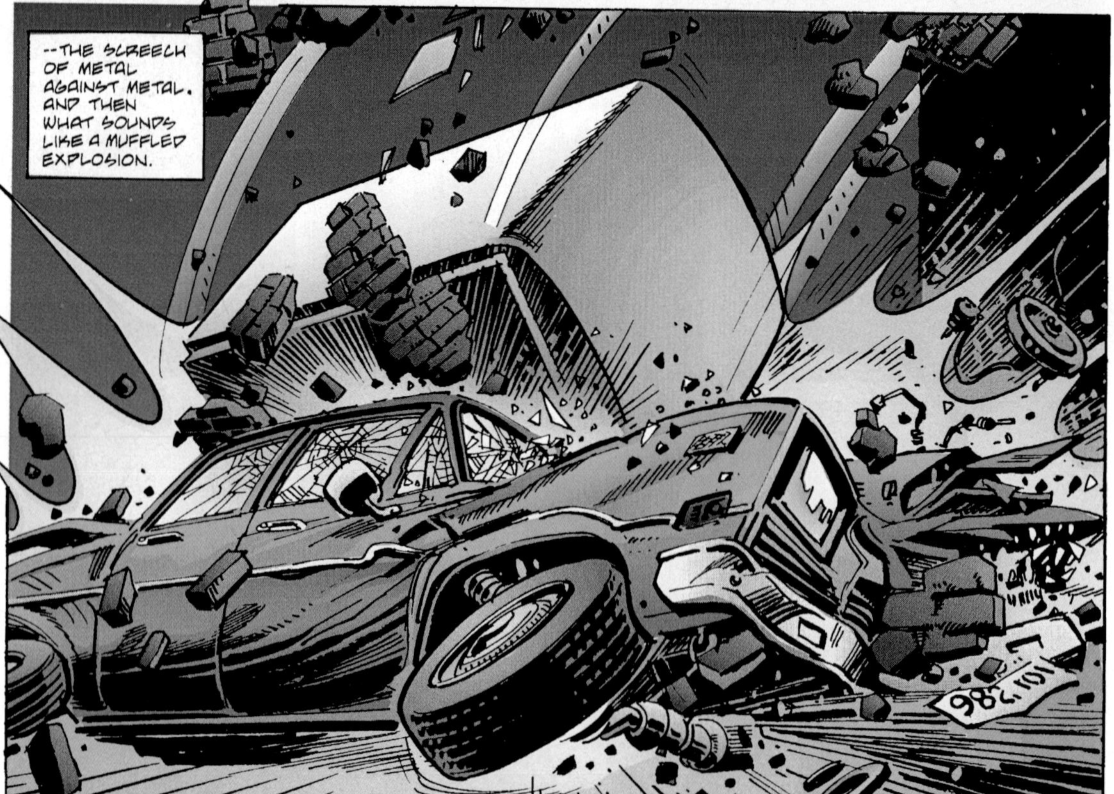
--THE SCREECH OF METAL AGAINST METAL. AND THEN WHAT SOUNDS LIKE A MUFFLED EXPLOSION.

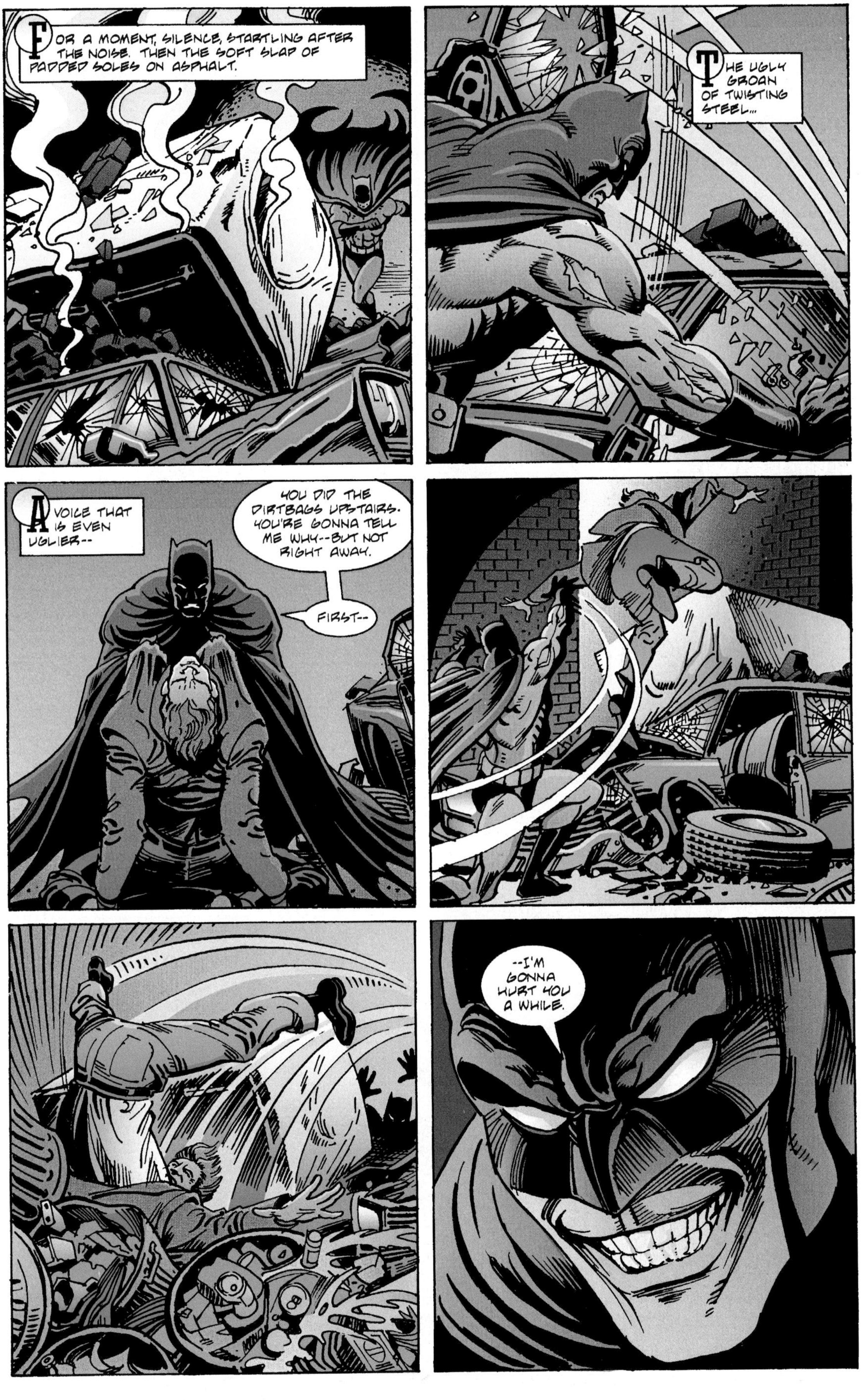
FOR A MOMENT, SILENCE, STARTLING AFTER THE NOISE. THEN THE SOFT SLAP OF PADDED SOLES ON ASPHALT.
THE UGLY GROAN OF TWISTING STEEL...
A VOICE THAT IS EVEN UGLIER--
YOU DID THE DIRTBAGS UPSTAIRS. YOU'RE GONNA TELL ME WHY--BUT NOT RIGHT AWAY.
FIRST--
--I'M GONNA HURT YOU A WHILE.

I'M GONNA BREAK A FEW BONES.

LISTEN TO YOU WHIMPER...

MISTER... WATCH OUT!

He sees the ripple of light on the blue-steel barrel.

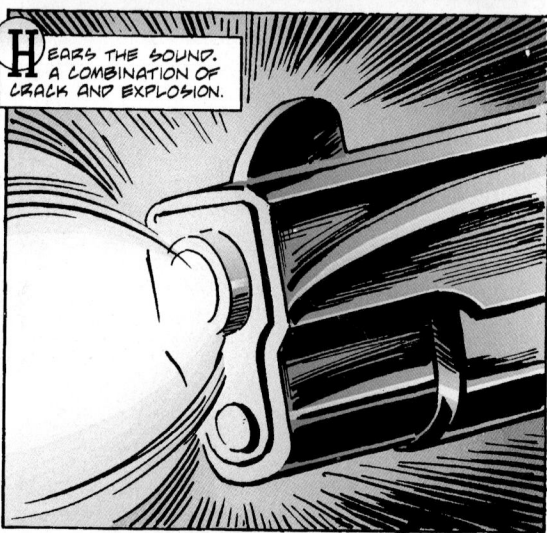

Hears the sound. A combination of crack and explosion.

Feels the man in his hands jerk as he stops the slug.

Hears more gunfire-- this time the chattering of an Uzi.

The killer's gasp stops abruptly as he dies.

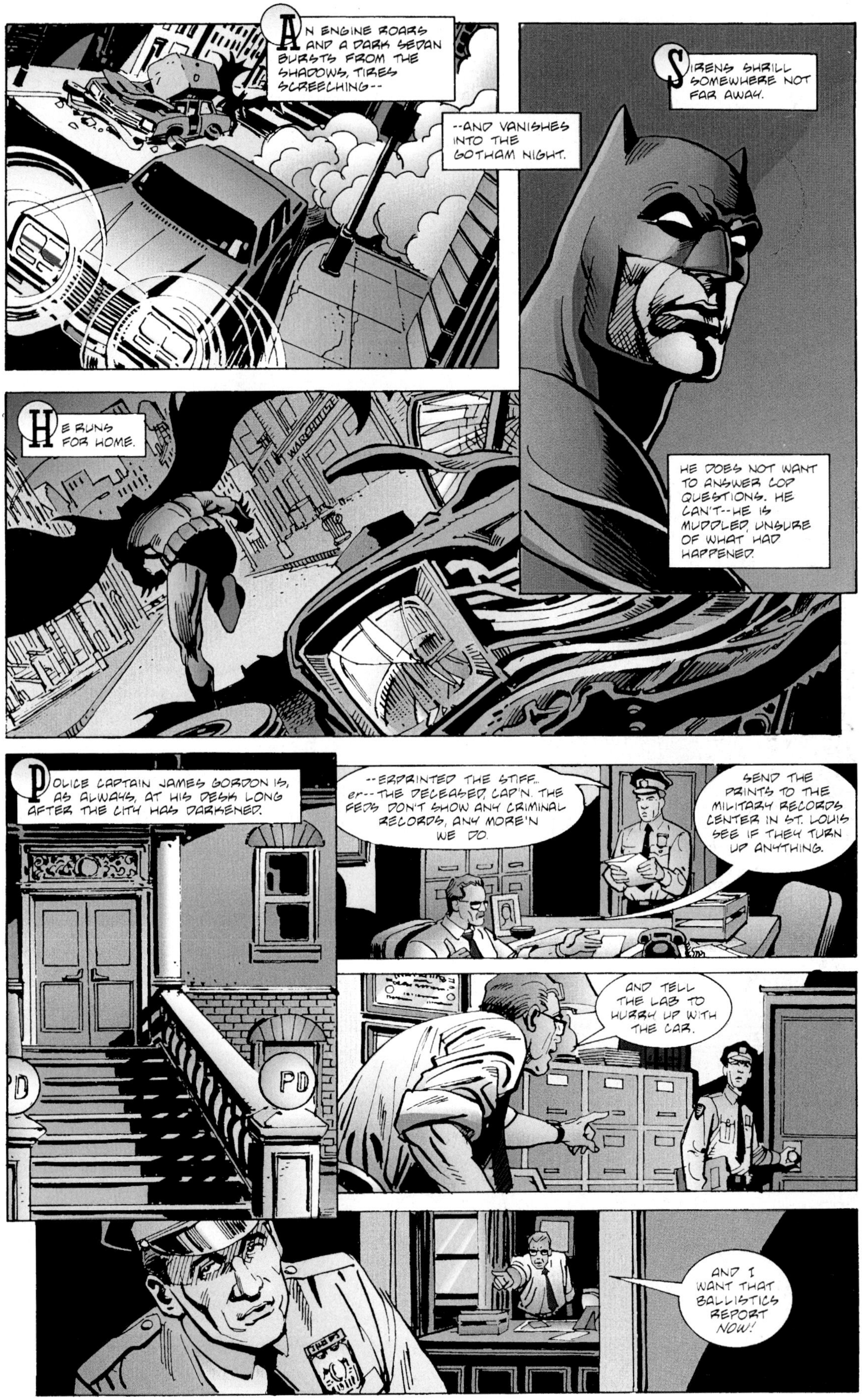
AN ENGINE ROARS AND A DARK SEDAN BURSTS FROM THE SHADOWS, TIRES SCREECHING--
--AND VANISHES INTO THE GOTHAM NIGHT.
SIRENS SHRILL SOMEWHERE NOT FAR AWAY.
HE DOES NOT WANT TO ANSWER COP QUESTIONS. HE CAN'T--HE IS MUDDLED, UNSURE OF WHAT HAD HAPPENED.
HE RUNS FOR HOME.
WAREHOUSE
POLICE CAPTAIN JAMES GORDON IS, AS ALWAYS, AT HIS DESK LONG AFTER THE CITY HAS DARKENED.
--ERPRINTED THE STIFF... er-- THE DECEASED, CAP'N. THE FEDS DON'T SHOW ANY CRIMINAL RECORDS, ANY MORE'N WE DO.
SEND THE PRINTS TO THE MILITARY RECORDS CENTER IN ST. LOUIS SEE IF THEY TURN UP ANYTHING.
PD
PD
AND TELL THE LAB TO HURRY UP WITH THE CAR.
AND I WANT THAT BALLISTICS REPORT NOW!

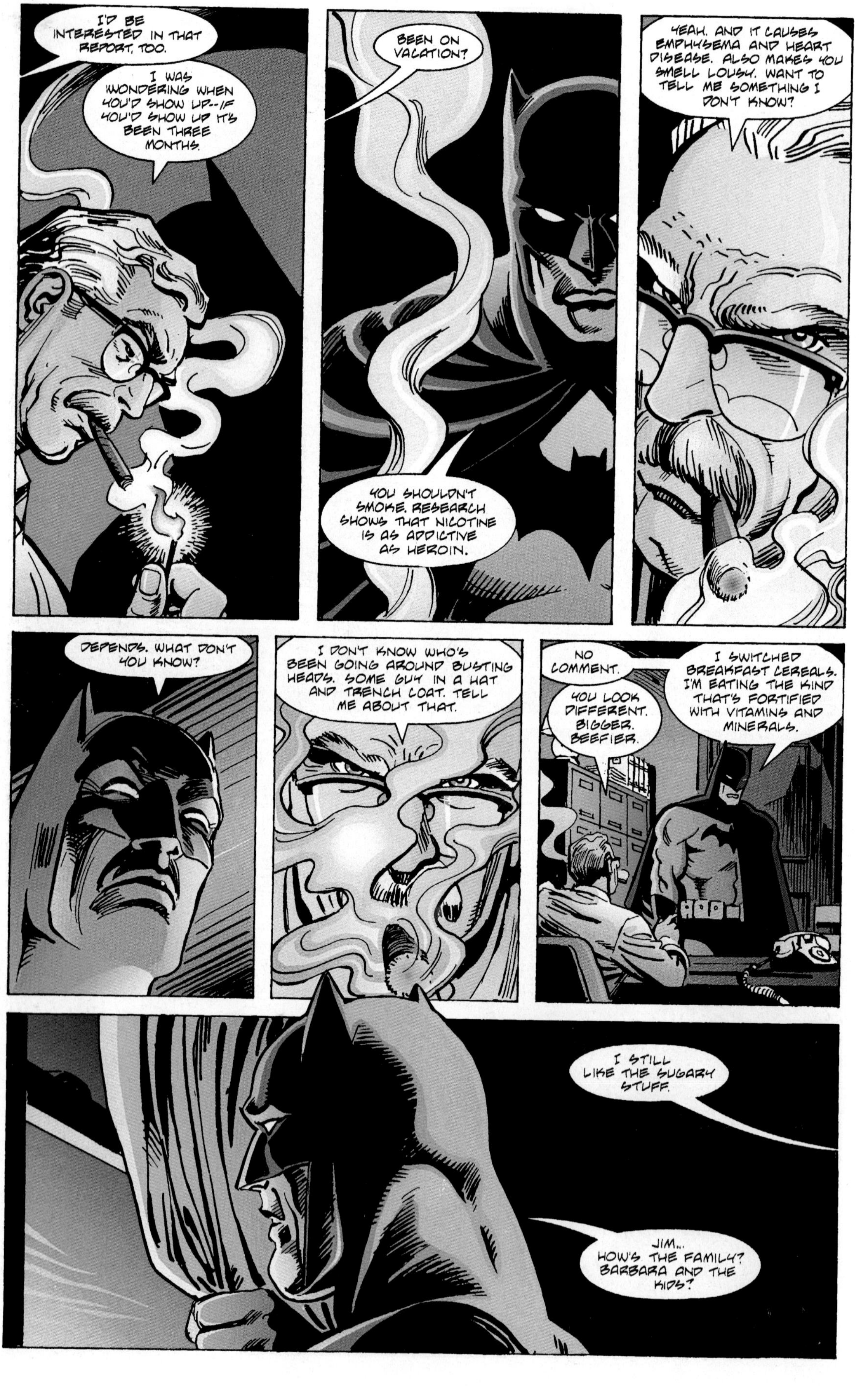
I'D BE INTERESTED IN THAT REPORT, TOO.
I WAS WONDERING WHEN YOU'D SHOW UP--IF YOU'D SHOW UP. IT'S BEEN THREE MONTHS.
BEEN ON VACATION?
YOU SHOULDN'T SMOKE. RESEARCH SHOWS THAT NICOTINE IS AS ADDICTIVE AS HEROIN.
YEAH. AND IT CAUSES EMPHYSEMA AND HEART DISEASE. ALSO MAKES YOU SMELL LOUSY. WANT TO TELL ME SOMETHING I DON'T KNOW?
DEPENDS. WHAT DON'T YOU KNOW?
I DON'T KNOW WHO'S BEEN GOING AROUND BUSTING HEADS. SOME GUY IN A HAT AND TRENCH COAT. TELL ME ABOUT THAT.
NO COMMENT.
YOU LOOK DIFFERENT. BIGGER. BEEFIER.
I SWITCHED BREAKFAST CEREALS. I'M EATING THE KIND THAT'S FORTIFIED WITH VITAMINS AND MINERALS.
I STILL LIKE THE SUGARY STUFF.
JIM... HOW'S THE FAMILY? BARBARA AND THE KIDS?

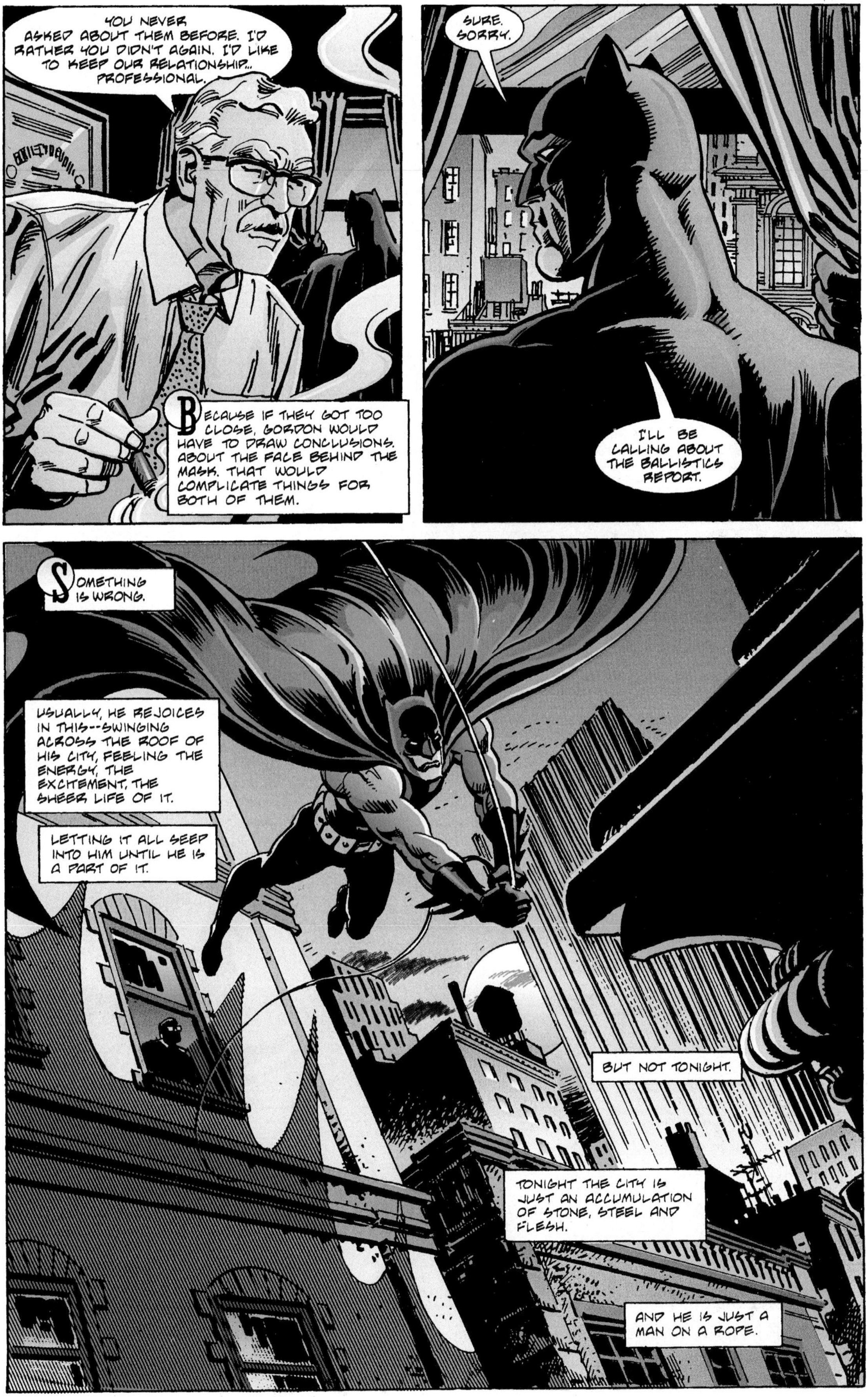
YOU NEVER ASKED ABOUT THEM BEFORE. I'D RATHER YOU DIDN'T AGAIN. I'D LIKE TO KEEP OUR RELATIONSHIP... PROFESSIONAL.
BECAUSE IF THEY GOT TOO CLOSE, GORDON WOULD HAVE TO DRAW CONCLUSIONS ABOUT THE FACE BEHIND THE MASK. THAT WOULD COMPLICATE THINGS FOR BOTH OF THEM.
SURE. SORRY.
I'LL BE CALLING ABOUT THE BALLISTICS REPORT.
SOMETHING IS WRONG.
USUALLY, HE REJOICES IN THIS--SWINGING ACROSS THE ROOF OF HIS CITY, FEELING THE ENERGY, THE EXCITEMENT, THE SHEER LIFE OF IT.
LETTING IT ALL SEEP INTO HIM UNTIL HE IS A PART OF IT.
BUT NOT TONIGHT.
TONIGHT THE CITY IS JUST AN ACCUMULATION OF STONE, STEEL AND FLESH.
AND HE IS JUST A MAN ON A ROPE.

DOCTOR RANDOLPH PORTER AND GENERAL TIMOTHY SLAYCROFT AREN'T PARTICULARLY EARLY RISERS, SO THEY DON'T MEET UNTIL ALMOST NOON--

--FRIEND IN ST. LOUIS FIELDED AN INQUIRY FROM A COP NAMED GORDON.

MY CONTACTS DOWNTOWN TELL ME GORDON WON'T QUIT AND CAN'T BE BOUGHT.

THAT'S BAD?

EXTREMELY. EVENTUALLY HE'LL LEARN THAT THE TWO DEAD MEN SERVED UNDER ME IN 'NAM. HE'LL TRACE THEIR MOVEMENTS--

--AND ONE FINE DAY HE'LL ARRIVE WITH WARRANTS.

HE WON'T BE ABLE TO PROVE YOU FIRED THAT SUBMACHINE GUN LAST NIGHT--AND EVEN IF HE DOES, YOU DID IT TO SAVE BATMAN'S LIFE.

THAT WILL NOT BE RELEVANT.

SPEAKING OF THE MASKED MAN...IS HE READY FOR THE NEXT PHASE OF HIS... AH-- DEVELOPMENT?

HE'S SWALLOWED THE HOOK. ALL I HAVE TO DO IS GIVE IT A LITTLE TUG AND REEL HIM IN.

ANY TIME I WANT.

ALFRED! ALFRED!

WHERE THE HELL IS THE BUTLER?

OH, I FORGOT--

HE'S NOT HERE.
LEFT A NOTE.
QUIT.

NOBODY TO TALK TO, DAMMIT. NEED SOMEBODY TO TALK TO.
MAYBE I CAN TALK TO THEM--

--THE BATS. THEY WON'T ANSWER ME--

--BUT THEY WILL LISTEN. THAT'S ALL ALFRED WOULD'VE DONE ANYWAY.
OKAY, LAST NIGHT. SOMEBODY YELLED JUST BEFORE THE SHOOTING. SAW HIM. RECOGNIZED HIM.

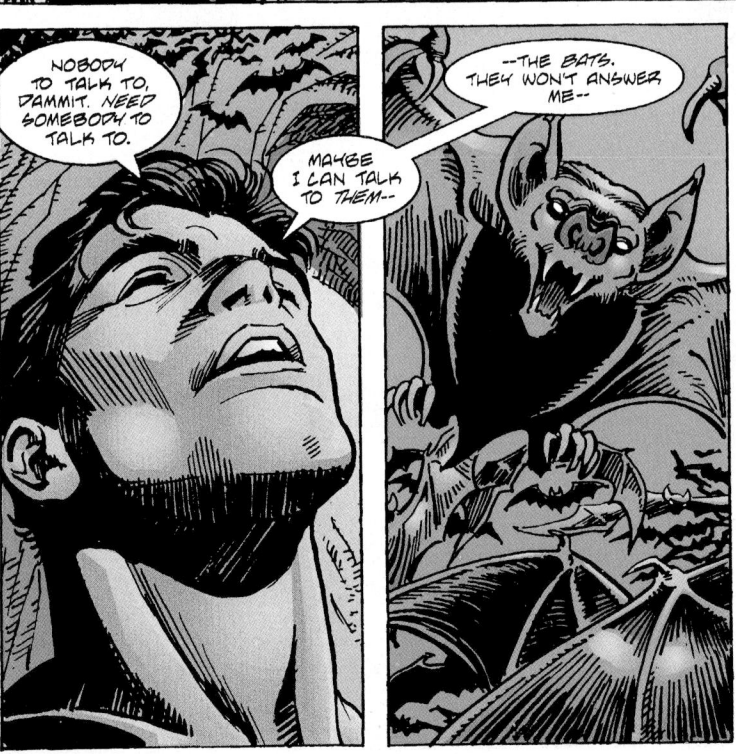

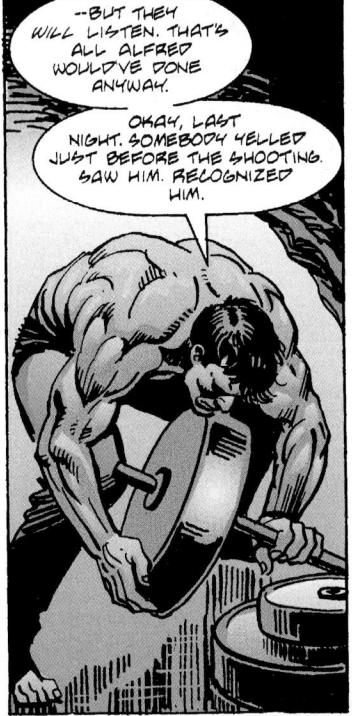

--THAT KID, THAT SLAYCROFT KID, TIMMY. HE YELLED. HE SAID, "THEY'RE GONNA SHOOT." SOMETHING LIKE THAT.

BUT WHAT WAS HE DOING THERE? WHERE'D HE GO? INTO--

--THAT CAR THAT DROVE OFF?

"HE"...

"SAVED"...

"MY"...

"LIFE"...

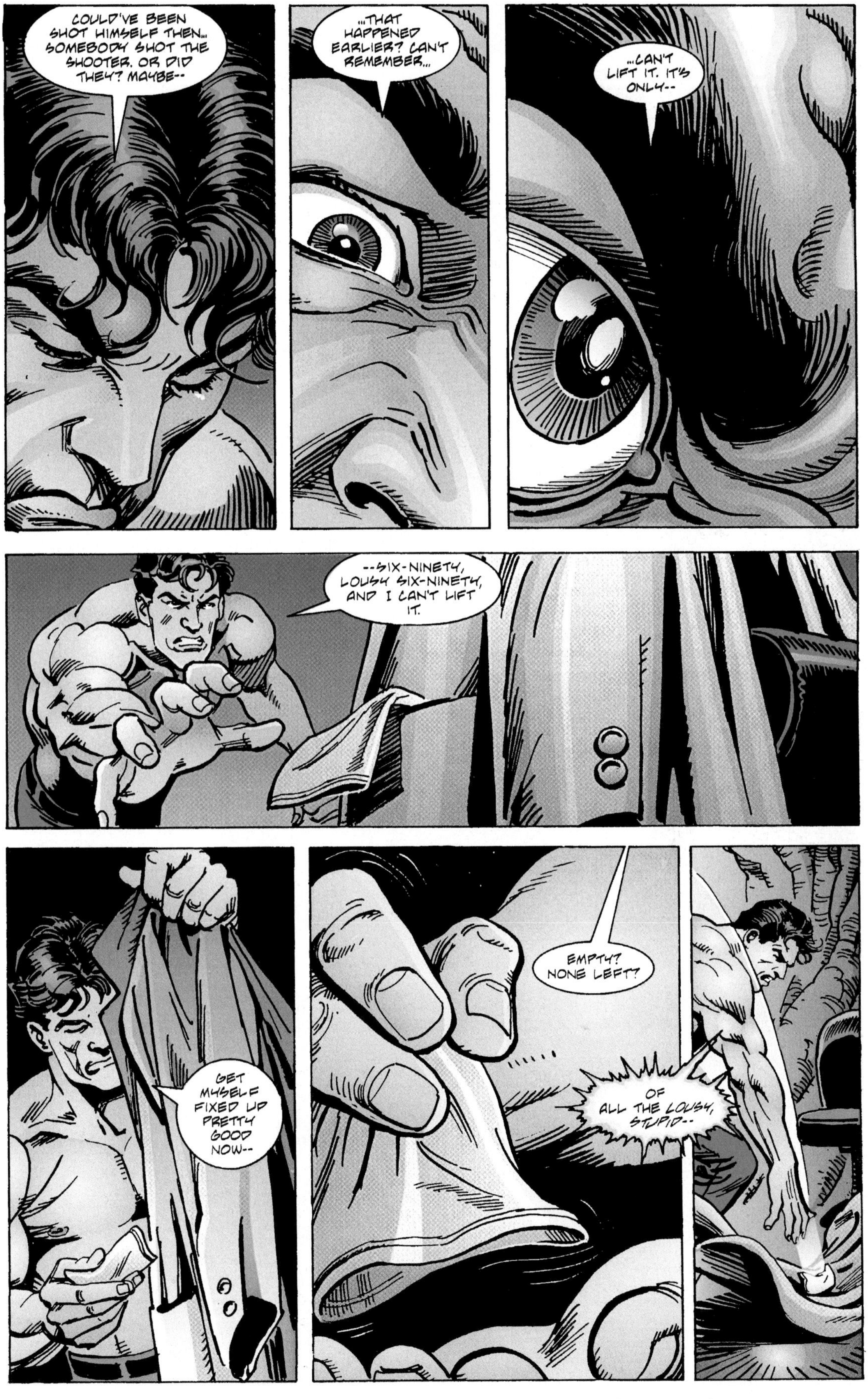
COULD'VE BEEN SHOT HIMSELF THEN... SOMEBODY SHOT THE SHOOTER. OR DID THEY? MAYBE--
...THAT HAPPENED EARLIER? CAN'T REMEMBER...
...CAN'T LIFT IT. IT'S ONLY--
--SIX-NINETY, LOUSY SIX-NINETY, AND I CAN'T LIFT IT.
GET MYSELF FIXED UP PRETTY GOOD NOW--
EMPTY? NONE LEFT?
OF ALL THE LOUSY, STUPID--

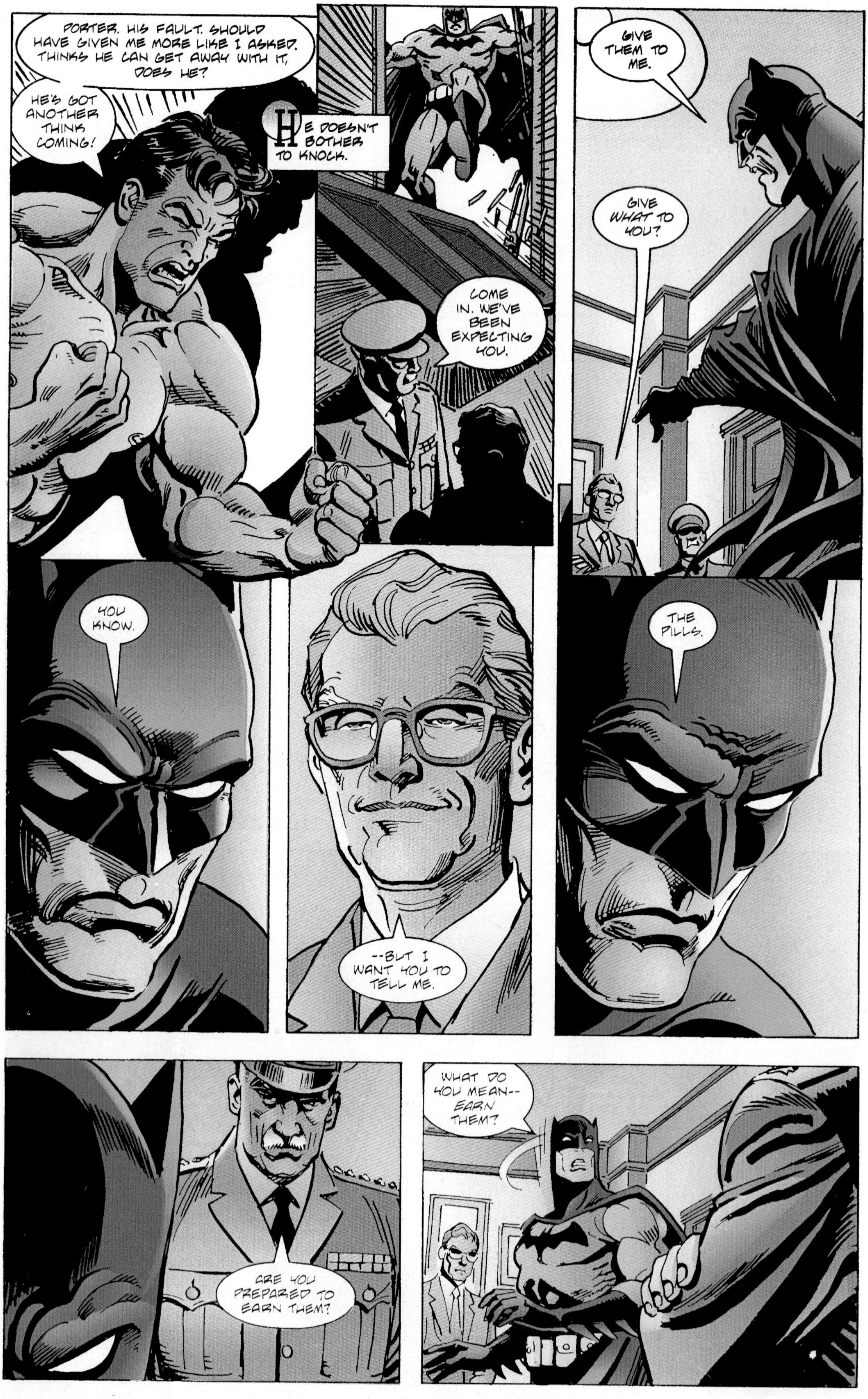
PORTER. HIS FAULT. SHOULD HAVE GIVEN ME MORE LIKE I ASKED. THINKS HE CAN GET AWAY WITH IT, DOES HE?
HE'S GOT ANOTHER THINK COMING!
HE DOESN'T BOTHER TO KNOCK.
COME IN. WE'VE BEEN EXPECTING YOU.
GIVE THEM TO ME.
GIVE WHAT TO YOU?
YOU KNOW.
--BUT I WANT YOU TO TELL ME.
THE PILLS.
ARE YOU PREPARED TO EARN THEM?
WHAT DO YOU MEAN-- EARN THEM?

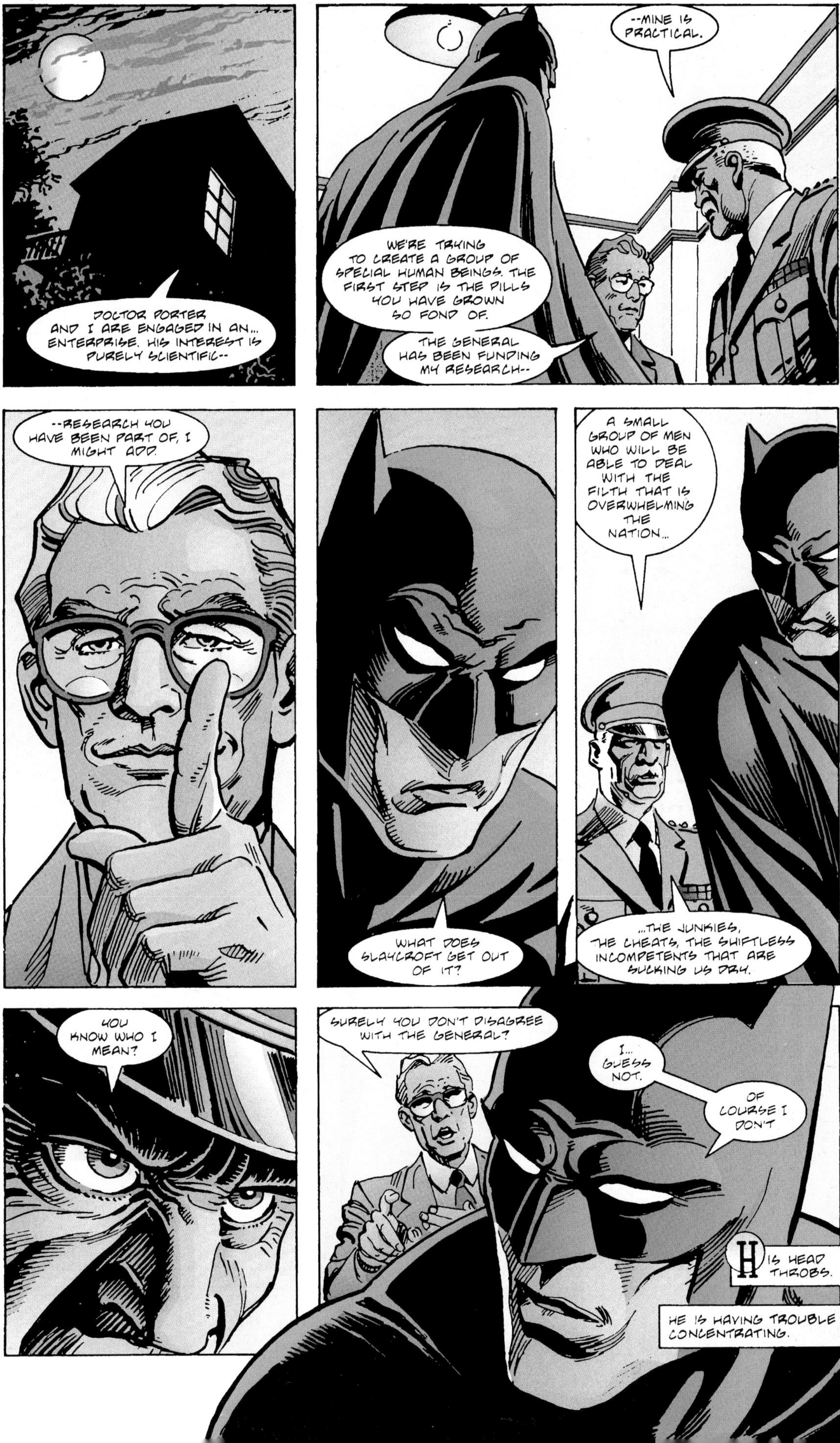
DOCTOR PORTER AND I ARE ENGAGED IN AN... ENTERPRISE. HIS INTEREST IS PURELY SCIENTIFIC--
--MINE IS PRACTICAL.
WE'RE TRYING TO CREATE A GROUP OF SPECIAL HUMAN BEINGS. THE FIRST STEP IS THE PILLS YOU HAVE GROWN SO FOND OF.
THE GENERAL HAS BEEN FUNDING MY RESEARCH--
--RESEARCH YOU HAVE BEEN PART OF, I MIGHT ADD.
WHAT DOES SLAYCROFT GET OUT OF IT?
A SMALL GROUP OF MEN WHO WILL BE ABLE TO DEAL WITH THE FILTH THAT IS OVERWHELMING THE NATION...
...THE JUNKIES, THE CHEATS, THE SHIFTLESS INCOMPETENTS THAT ARE SUCKING US DRY.
YOU KNOW WHO I MEAN?
SURELY YOU DON'T DISAGREE WITH THE GENERAL?
I... GUESS NOT.
OF COURSE I DON'T
HIS HEAD THROBS.
HE IS HAVING TROUBLE CONCENTRATING.

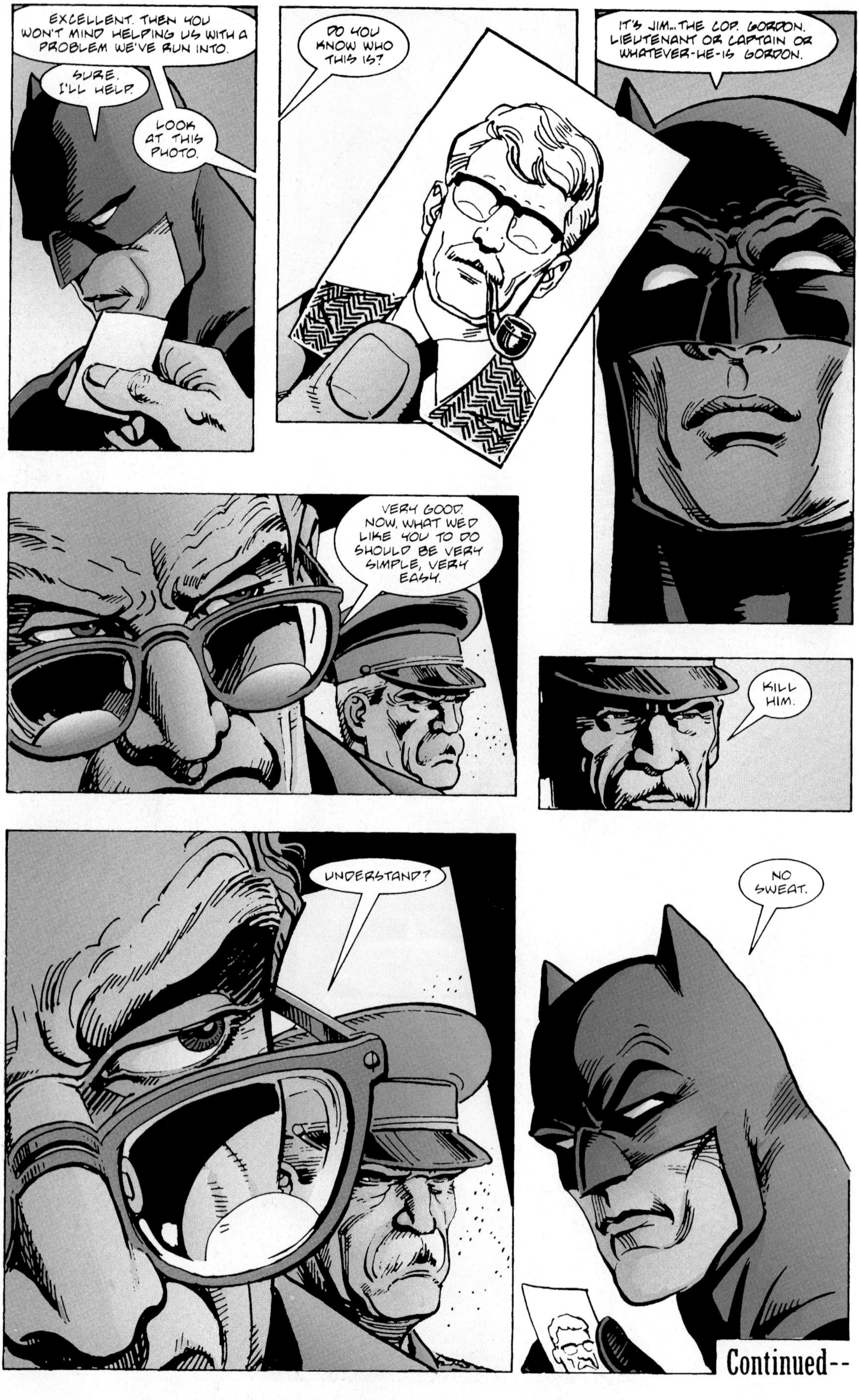
EXCELLENT. THEN YOU WON'T MIND HELPING US WITH A PROBLEM WE'VE RUN INTO.
SURE. I'LL HELP.
LOOK AT THIS PHOTO.
DO YOU KNOW WHO THIS IS?
IT'S JIM... THE COP. GORDON. LIEUTENANT OR CAPTAIN OR WHATEVER-HE-IS GORDON.
VERY GOOD. NOW, WHAT WED LIKE YOU TO DO SHOULD BE VERY SIMPLE, VERY EASY.
KILL HIM.
UNDERSTAND?
NO SWEAT.
Continued--

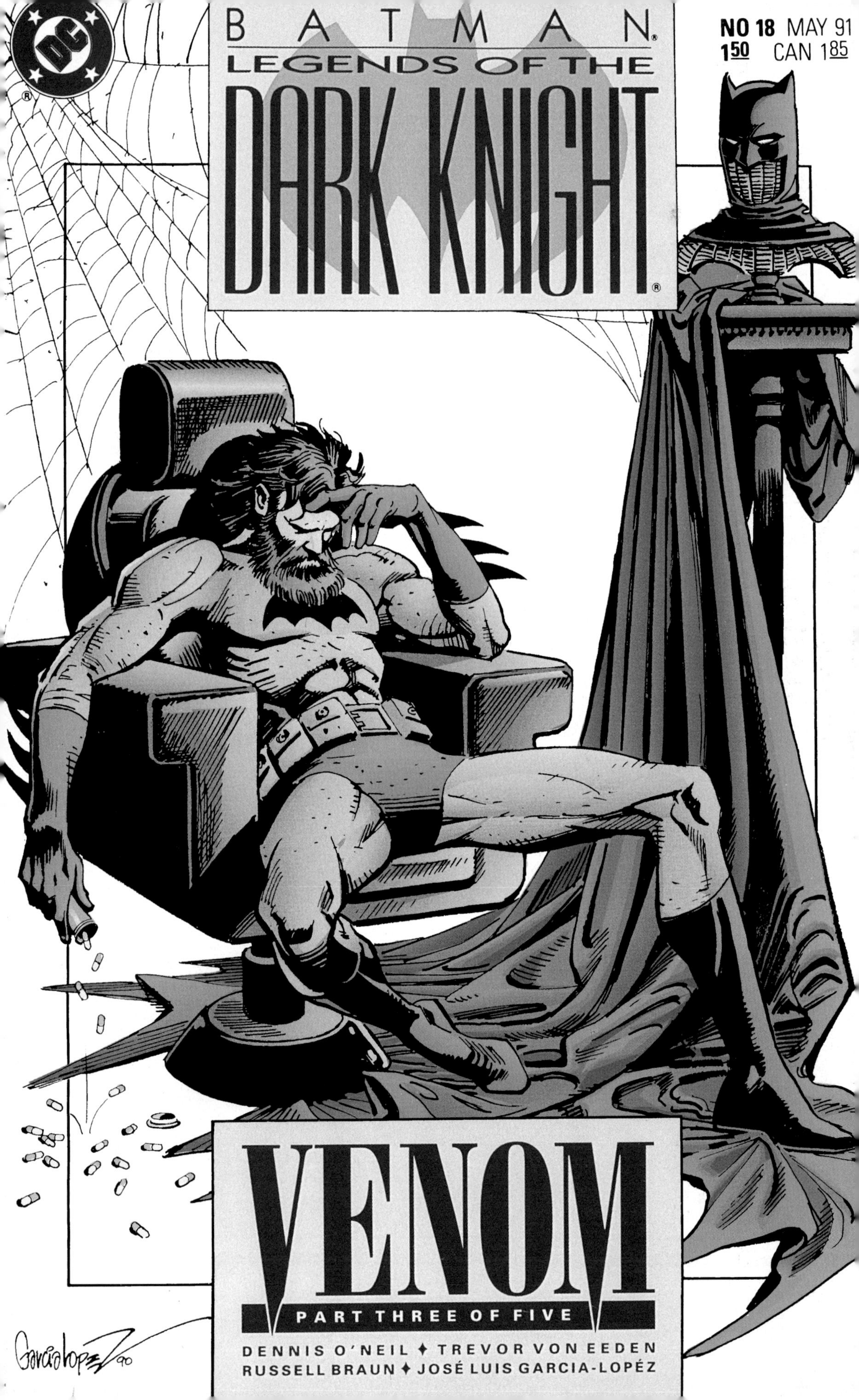
DC
BATMAN
LEGENDS OF THE
DARK KNIGHT
NO 18 MAY 91
1.50 CAN 1.85
VENOM
PART THREE OF FIVE
DENNIS O'NEIL ♦ TREVOR VON EEDEN
RUSSELL BRAUN ♦ JOSÉ LUIS GARCIA-LOPÉZ
GarciaLopez '90

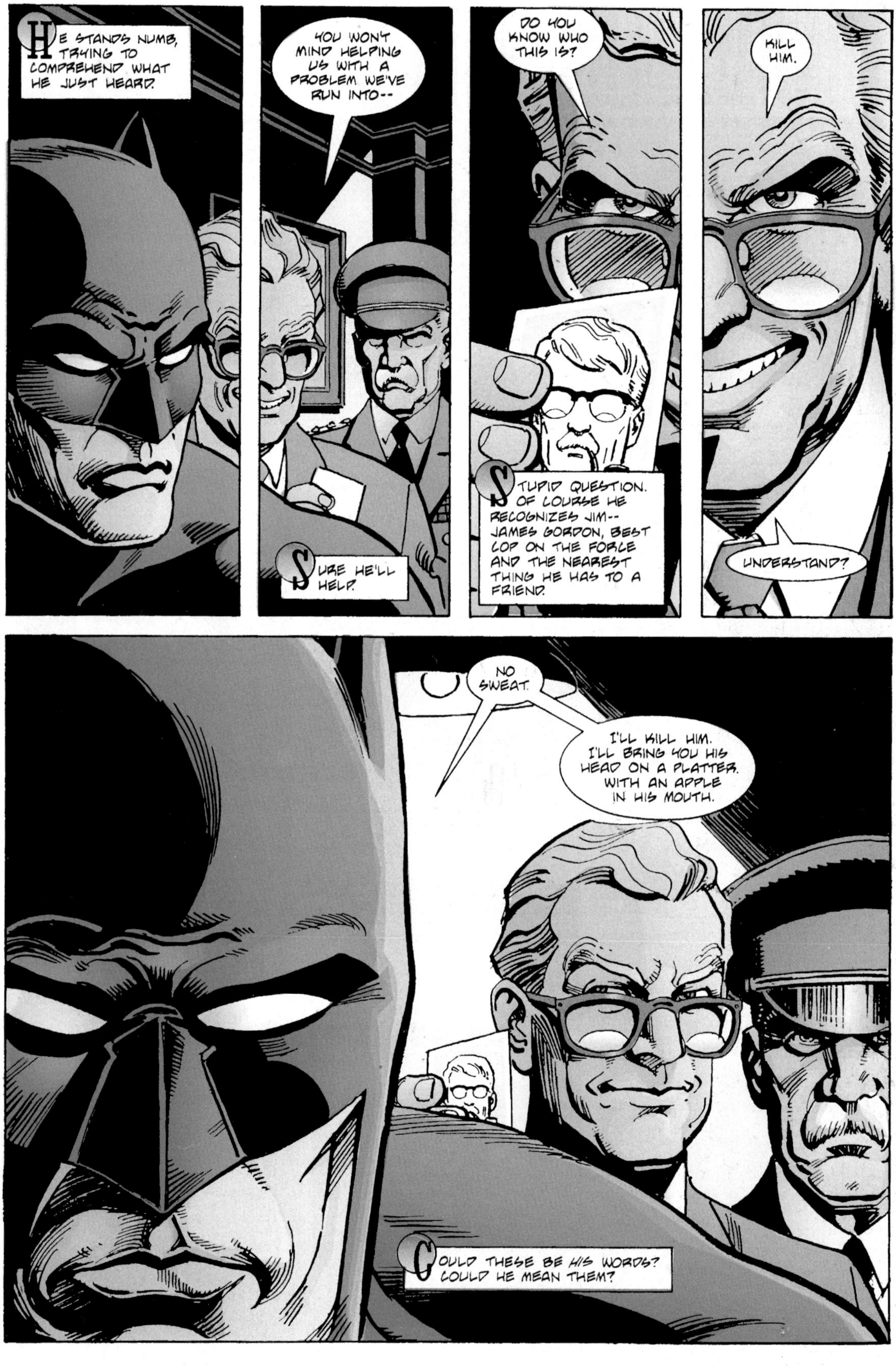
HE STANDS NUMB, TRYING TO COMPREHEND WHAT HE JUST HEARD.
YOU WON'T MIND HELPING US WITH A PROBLEM WE'VE RUN INTO--
SURE HE'LL HELP.
DO YOU KNOW WHO THIS IS?
STUPID QUESTION. OF COURSE HE RECOGNIZES JIM-- JAMES GORDON, BEST COP ON THE FORCE AND THE NEAREST THING HE HAS TO A FRIEND.
KILL HIM.
UNDERSTAND?
NO SWEAT.
I'LL KILL HIM. I'LL BRING YOU HIS HEAD ON A PLATTER. WITH AN APPLE IN HIS MOUTH.
COULD THESE BE *HIS* WORDS? COULD HE MEAN THEM?

VENOM: PART THREE

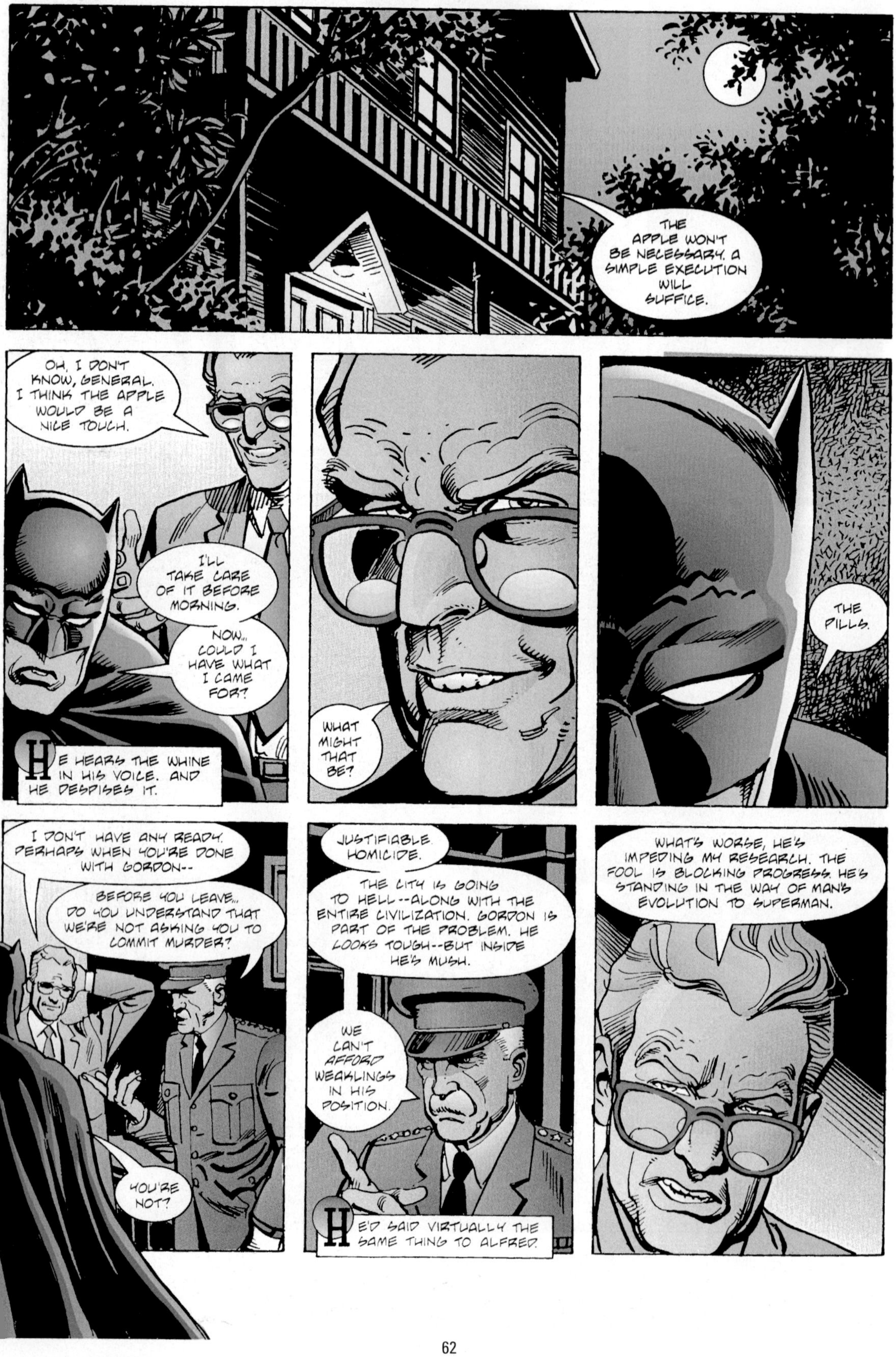
THE APPLE WON'T BE NECESSARY. A SIMPLE EXECUTION WILL SUFFICE.
OH, I DON'T KNOW, GENERAL. I THINK THE APPLE WOULD BE A NICE TOUCH.
I'LL TAKE CARE OF IT BEFORE MORNING.
NOW... COULD I HAVE WHAT I CAME FOR?
HE HEARS THE WHINE IN HIS VOICE. AND HE DESPISES IT.
WHAT MIGHT THAT BE?
THE PILLS.
I DON'T HAVE ANY READY. PERHAPS WHEN YOU'RE DONE WITH GORDON--
BEFORE YOU LEAVE... DO YOU UNDERSTAND THAT WE'RE NOT ASKING YOU TO COMMIT MURDER?
YOU'RE NOT?
JUSTIFIABLE HOMICIDE.
THE CITY IS GOING TO HELL--ALONG WITH THE ENTIRE CIVILIZATION. GORDON IS PART OF THE PROBLEM. HE LOOKS TOUGH--BUT INSIDE HE'S MUSH.
WE CAN'T AFFORD WEAKLINGS IN HIS POSITION.
HE'D SAID VIRTUALLY THE SAME THING TO ALFRED.
WHAT'S WORSE, HE'S IMPEDING MY RESEARCH. THE FOOL IS BLOCKING PROGRESS. HE'S STANDING IN THE WAY OF MAN'S EVOLUTION TO SUPERMAN.

I'LL BE BACK.

IT IS ALMOST FOUR WHEN HE REACHES GORDON'S SUBURBAN STREET. HE SEES HIS QUARRY IMMEDIATELY.

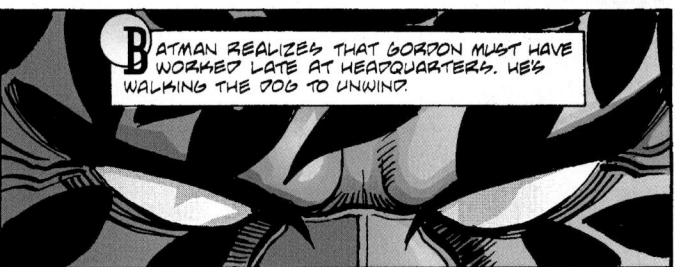

BATMAN REALIZES THAT GORDON MUST HAVE WORKED LATE AT HEADQUARTERS. HE'S WALKING THE DOG TO UNWIND.

UNWIND? NOT A CHANCE. HE'S STIFF, HIS SHOULDERS ARE TENSED. HIS EYES CONSTANTLY SWEEP THE STREET. HE CAN NEVER REALLY RELAX.

BUT ORDINARY KILLERS AREN'T TRAINED BY KIRIGI, DUCARD, TSUNETOMO AND THE REST.

HE'S ALL COP--ALWAYS EXPECTING TROUBLE. IF BATMAN WERE AN ORDINARY KILLER, GORDON WOULD BE AWARE OF HIM.

ORDINARY KILLERS HAVEN'T SPENT A LIFETIME PRACTICING WHAT BATMAN IS ABOUT TO DO--

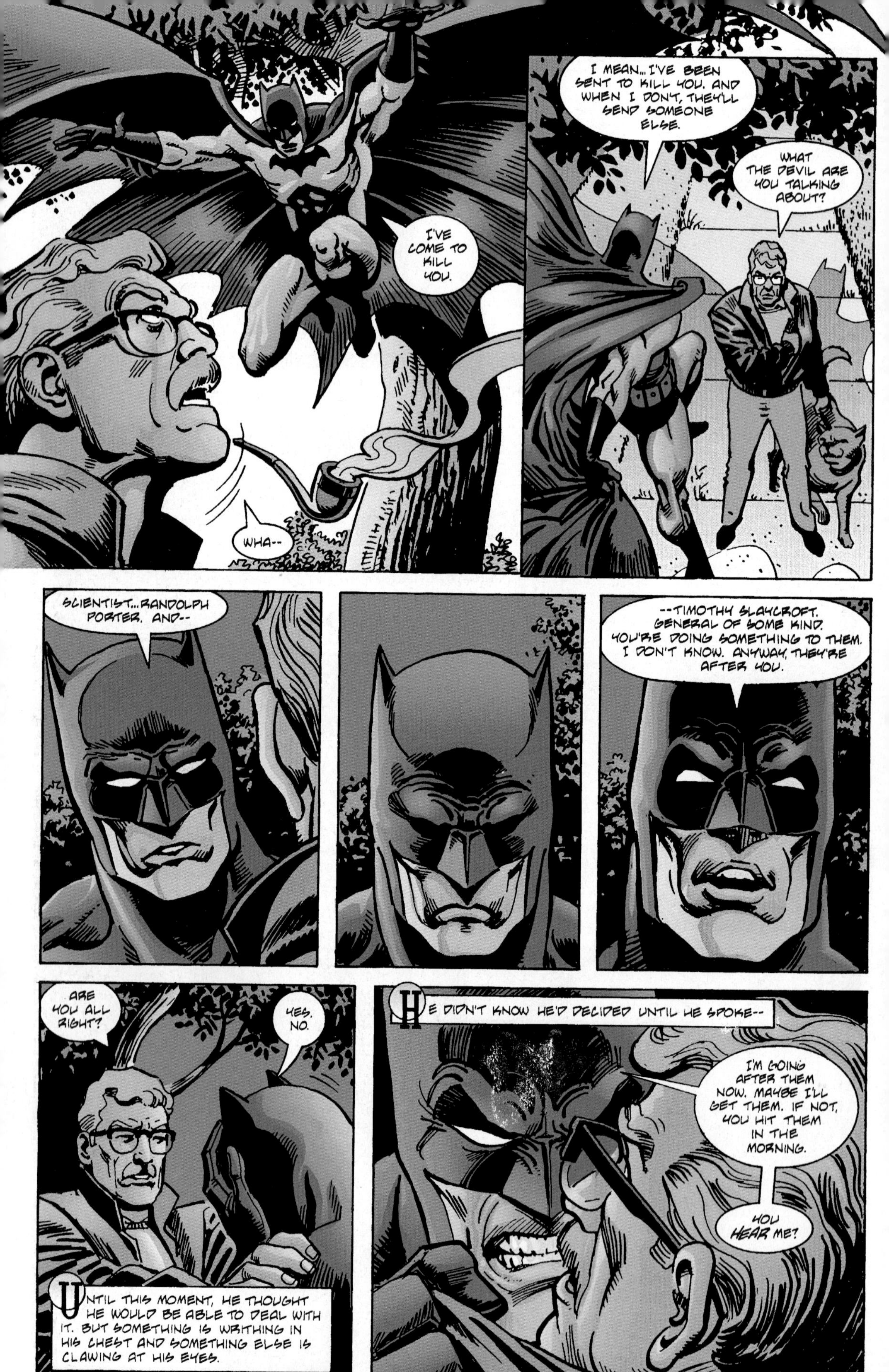
I'VE COME TO KILL YOU.
WHA--
I MEAN... I'VE BEEN SENT TO KILL YOU. AND WHEN I DON'T, THEY'LL SEND SOMEONE ELSE.
WHAT THE DEVIL ARE YOU TALKING ABOUT?
SCIENTIST... RANDOLPH PORTER. AND--
--TIMOTHY SLAYCROFT. GENERAL OF SOME KIND. YOU'RE DOING SOMETHING TO THEM. I DON'T KNOW. ANYWAY, THEY'RE AFTER YOU.
ARE YOU ALL RIGHT?
YES. NO.
UNTIL THIS MOMENT, HE THOUGHT HE WOULD BE ABLE TO DEAL WITH IT. BUT SOMETHING IS WRITHING IN HIS CHEST AND SOMETHING ELSE IS CLAWING AT HIS EYES.
HE DIDN'T KNOW HE'D DECIDED UNTIL HE SPOKE--
I'M GOING AFTER THEM NOW. MAYBE I'LL GET THEM. IF NOT, YOU HIT THEM IN THE MORNING.
YOU HEAR ME?

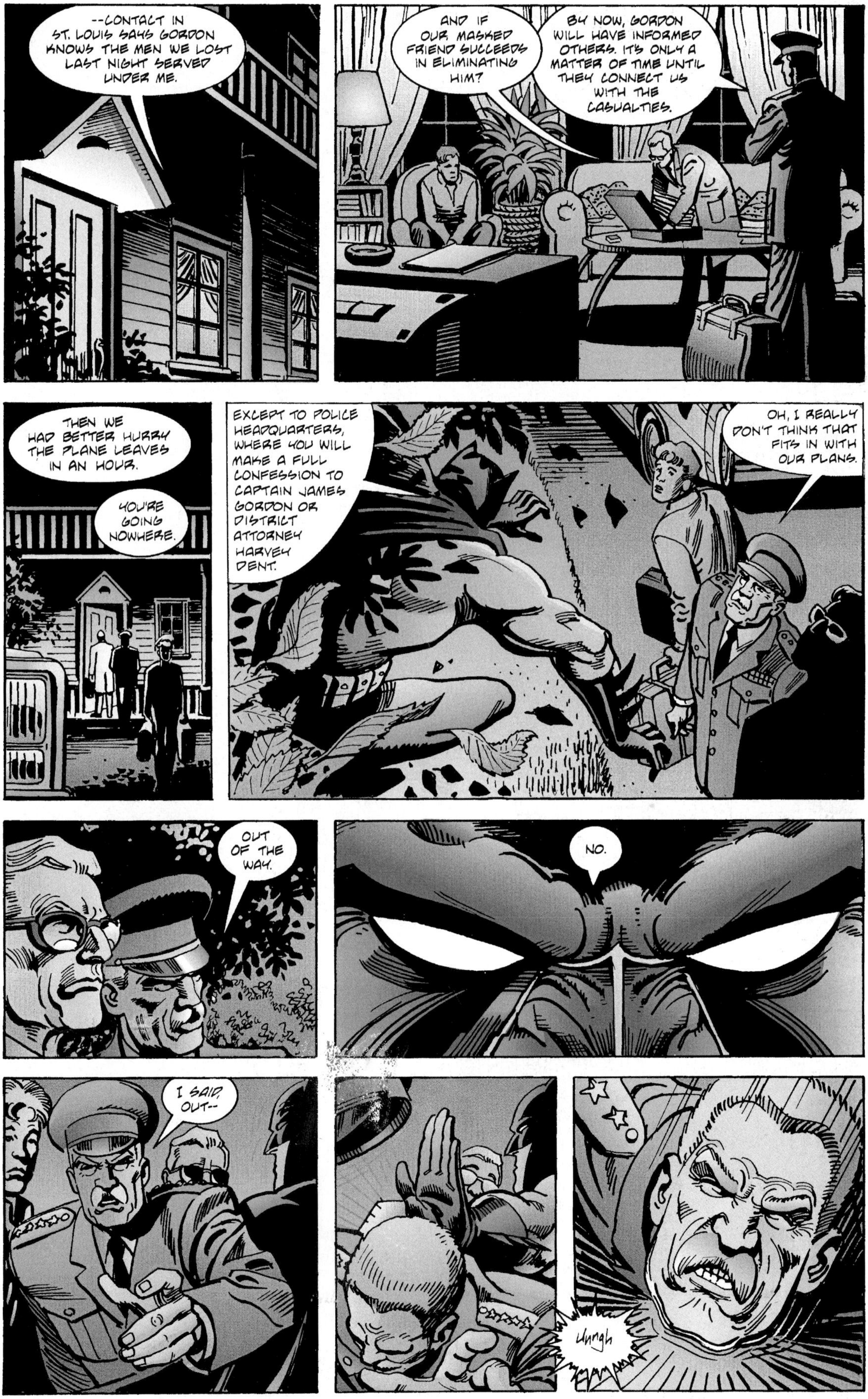
--CONTACT IN ST. LOUIS SAYS GORDON KNOWS THE MEN WE LOST LAST NIGHT SERVED UNDER ME.
AND IF OUR MASKED FRIEND SUCCEEDS IN ELIMINATING HIM?
BY NOW, GORDON WILL HAVE INFORMED OTHERS. IT'S ONLY A MATTER OF TIME UNTIL THEY CONNECT US WITH THE CASUALTIES.
THEN WE HAD BETTER HURRY. THE PLANE LEAVES IN AN HOUR.
YOU'RE GOING NOWHERE.
EXCEPT TO POLICE HEADQUARTERS, WHERE YOU WILL MAKE A FULL CONFESSION TO CAPTAIN JAMES GORDON OR DISTRICT ATTORNEY HARVEY DENT.
OH, I REALLY DON'T THINK THAT FITS IN WITH OUR PLANS.
OUT OF THE WAY.
NO.
I SAID, OUT--
Unngh

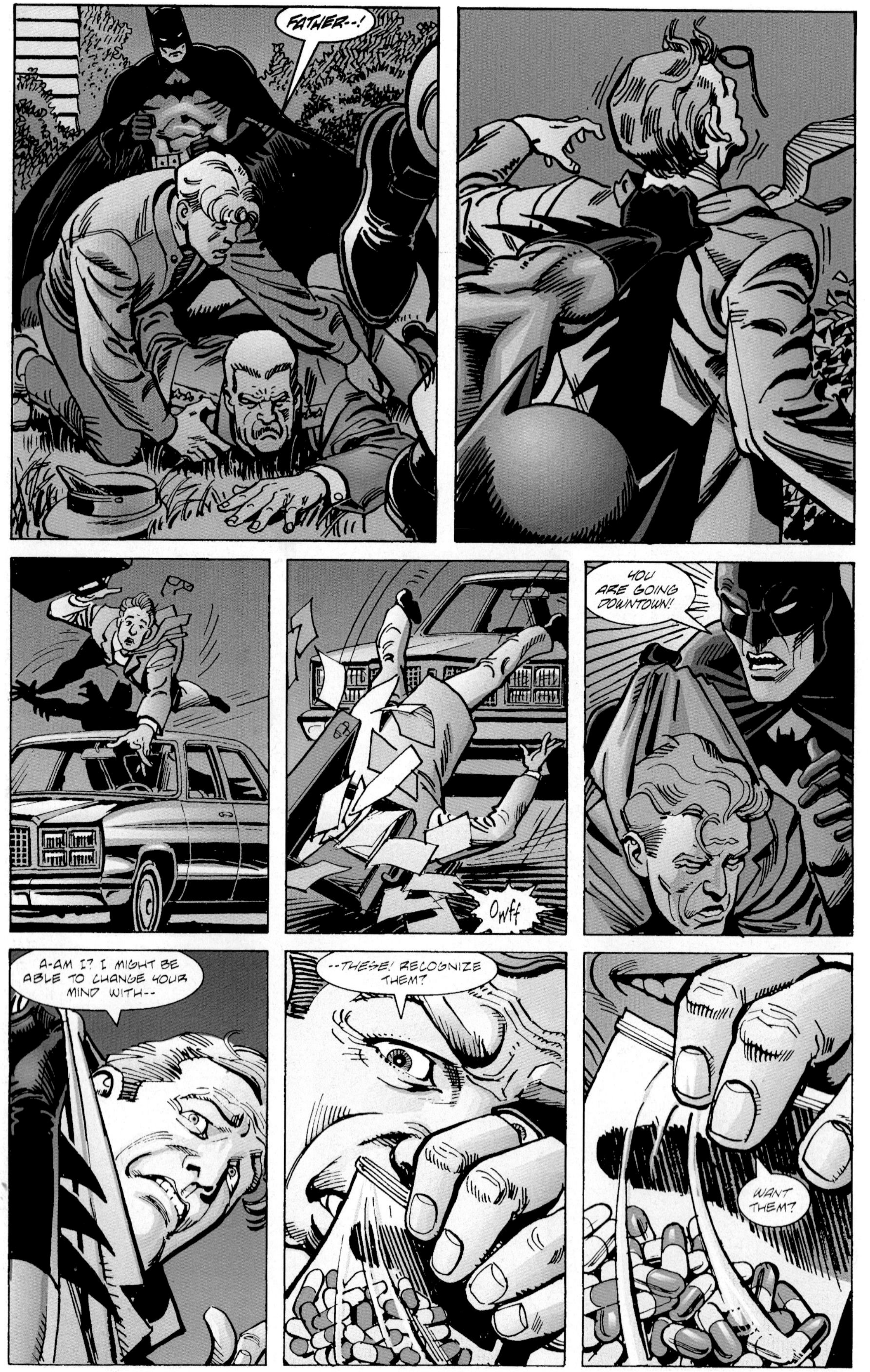
FATHER--!
YOU ARE GOING DOWNTOWN!
Owff
A-AM I? I MIGHT BE ABLE TO CHANGE YOUR MIND WITH--
--THESE! RECOGNIZE THEM?
WANT THEM?

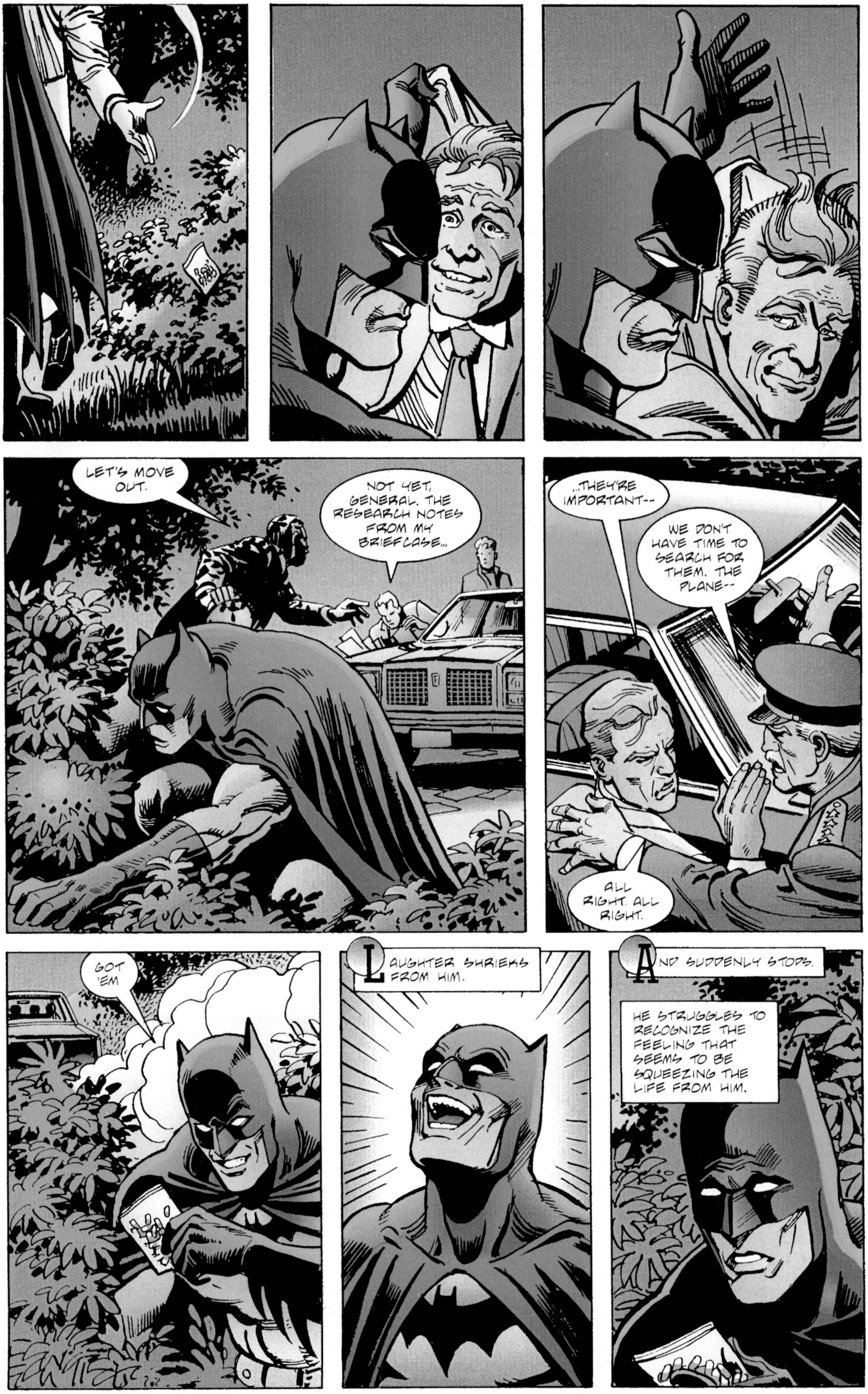

LET'S MOVE OUT.
NOT YET, GENERAL. THE RESEARCH NOTES FROM MY BRIEFCASE...
...THEY'RE IMPORTANT--
WE DON'T HAVE TIME TO SEARCH FOR THEM. THE PLANE--
ALL RIGHT. ALL RIGHT.
GOT 'EM
LAUGHTER SHRIEKS FROM HIM.
AND SUDDENLY STOPS.
HE STRUGGLES TO RECOGNIZE THE FEELING THAT SEEMS TO BE SQUEEZING THE LIFE FROM HIM.

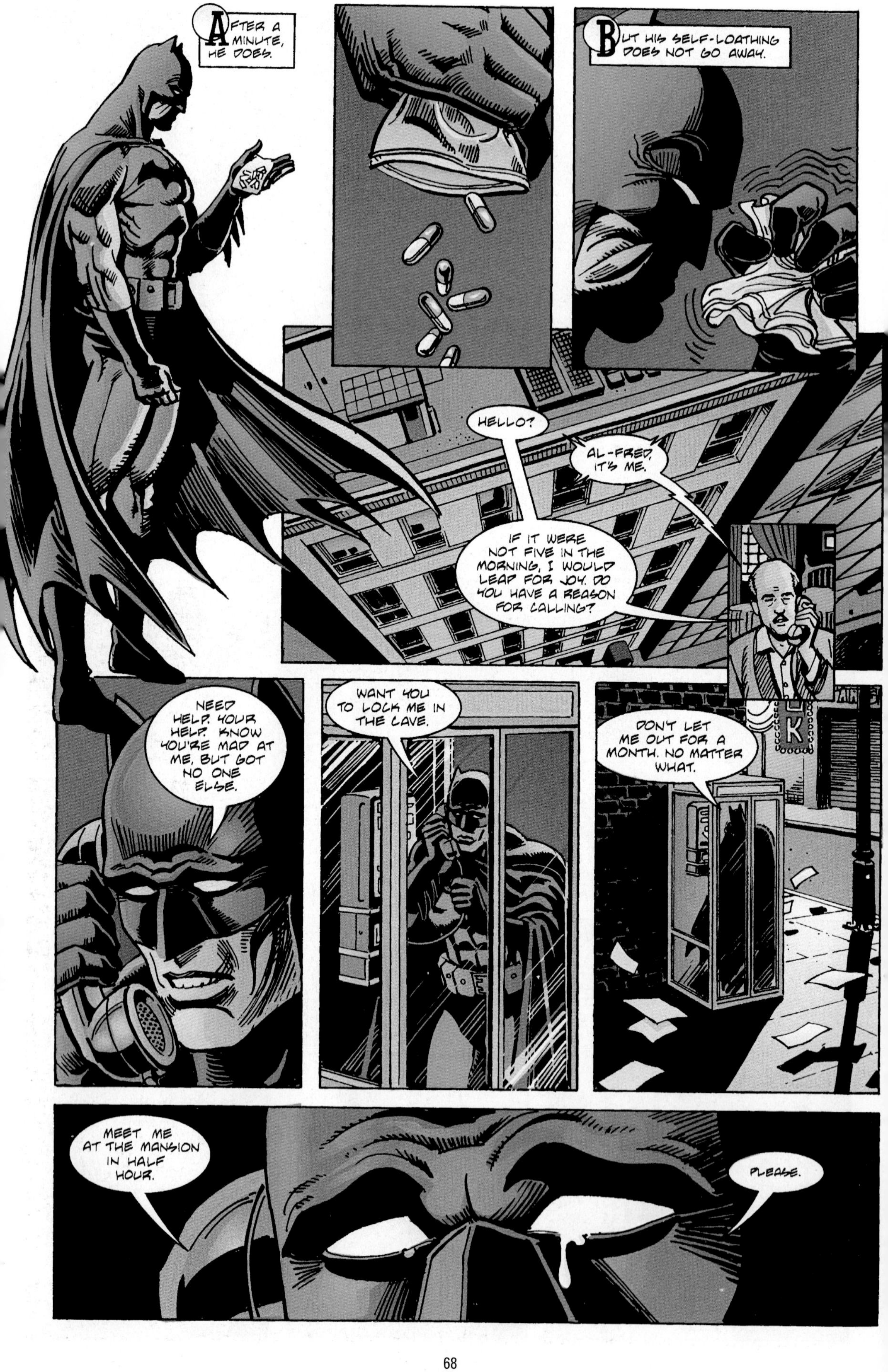
AFTER A MINUTE, HE DOES.
BUT HIS SELF-LOATHING DOES NOT GO AWAY.
HELLO?
AL-FRED, IT'S ME.
IF IT WERE NOT FIVE IN THE MORNING, I WOULD LEAP FOR JOY. DO YOU HAVE A REASON FOR CALLING?
NEED HELP. YOUR HELP. KNOW YOU'RE MAD AT ME, BUT GOT NO ONE ELSE.
WANT YOU TO LOCK ME IN THE CAVE.
DON'T LET ME OUT FOR A MONTH. NO MATTER WHAT.
MEET ME AT THE MANSION IN HALF HOUR.
PLEASE.

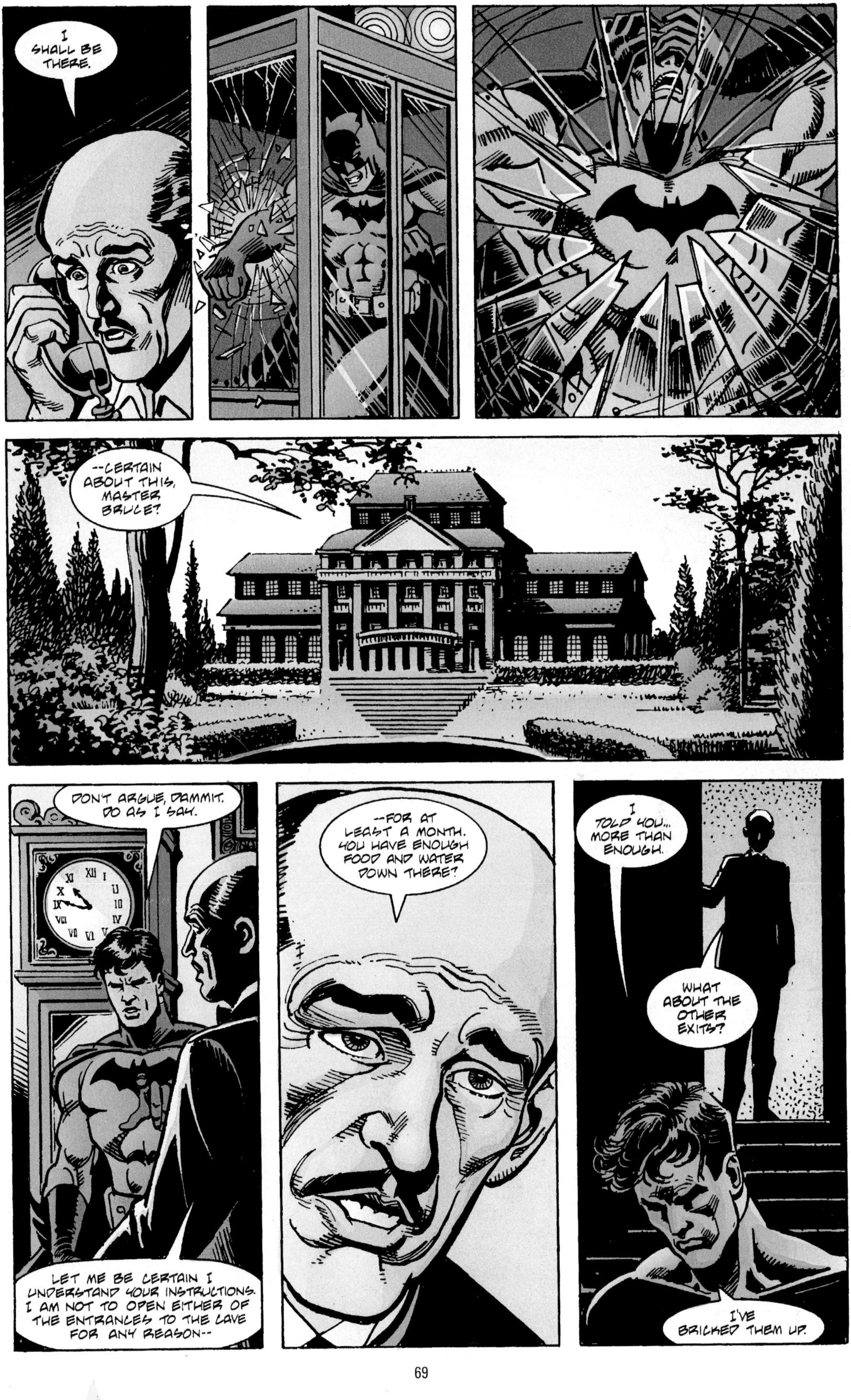
I SHALL BE THERE.
--CERTAIN ABOUT THIS, MASTER BRUCE?
DON'T ARGUE, DAMMIT. DO AS I SAY.
LET ME BE CERTAIN I UNDERSTAND YOUR INSTRUCTIONS. I AM NOT TO OPEN EITHER OF THE ENTRANCES TO THE CAVE FOR ANY REASON--
--FOR AT LEAST A MONTH. YOU HAVE ENOUGH FOOD AND WATER DOWN THERE?
I TOLD YOU... MORE THAN ENOUGH.
WHAT ABOUT THE OTHER EXITS?
I'VE BRICKED THEM UP.

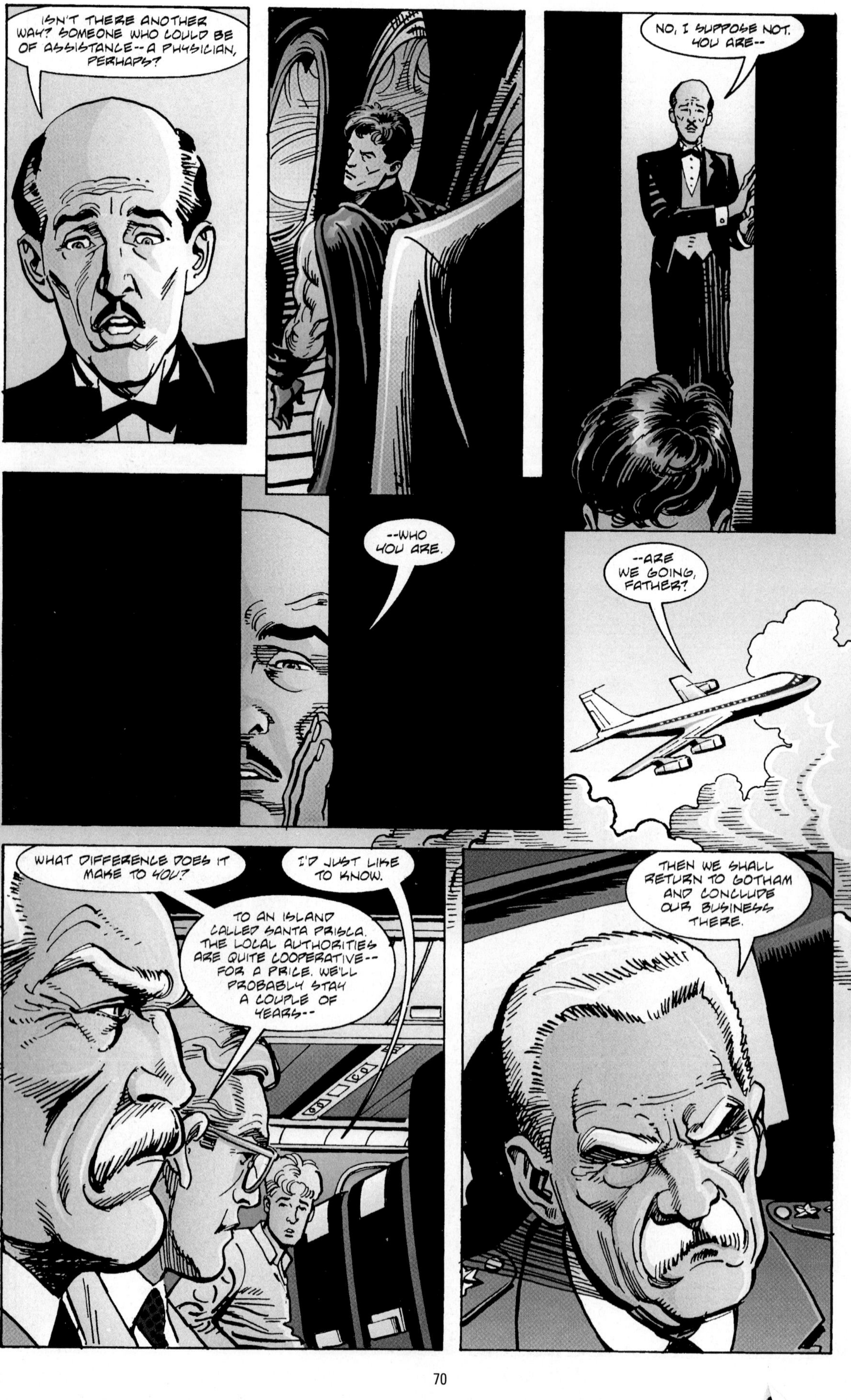
ISN'T THERE ANOTHER WAY? SOMEONE WHO COULD BE OF ASSISTANCE--A PHYSICIAN, PERHAPS?
NO, I SUPPOSE NOT. YOU ARE--
--WHO YOU ARE.
--ARE WE GOING, FATHER?
WHAT DIFFERENCE DOES IT MAKE TO YOU?
I'D JUST LIKE TO KNOW.
TO AN ISLAND CALLED SANTA PRISCA. THE LOCAL AUTHORITIES ARE QUITE COOPERATIVE--FOR A PRICE. WE'LL PROBABLY STAY A COUPLE OF YEARS--
THEN WE SHALL RETURN TO GOTHAM AND CONCLUDE OUR BUSINESS THERE.

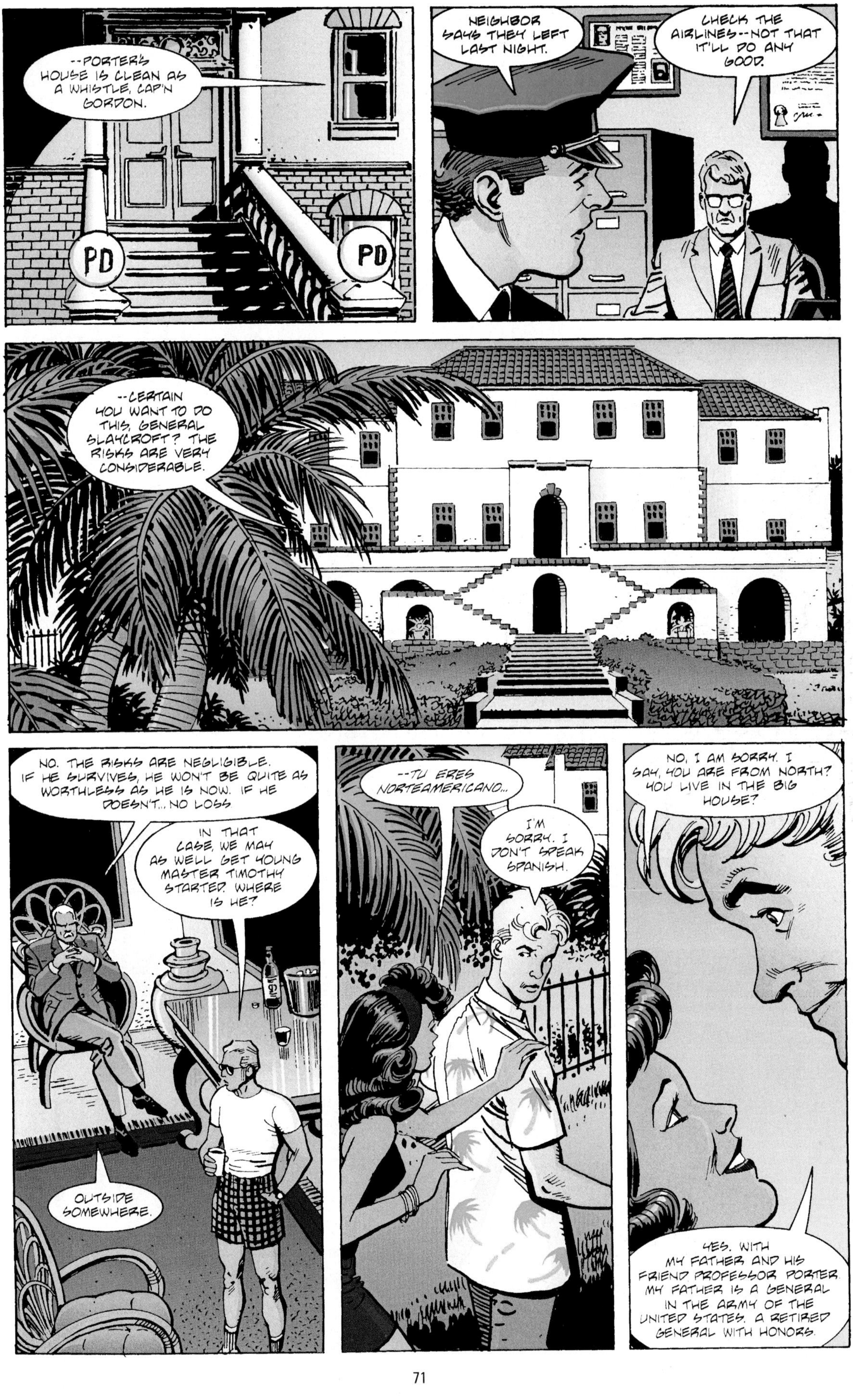
--PORTER'S HOUSE IS CLEAN AS A WHISTLE, CAP'N GORDON.
PD
PD
NEIGHBOR SAYS THEY LEFT LAST NIGHT.
CHECK THE AIRLINES--NOT THAT IT'LL DO ANY GOOD.
--CERTAIN YOU WANT TO DO THIS, GENERAL SLAYCROFT? THE RISKS ARE VERY CONSIDERABLE.
NO. THE RISKS ARE NEGLIGIBLE. IF HE SURVIVES, HE WON'T BE QUITE AS WORTHLESS AS HE IS NOW. IF HE DOESN'T... NO LOSS
IN THAT CASE, WE MAY AS WELL GET YOUNG MASTER TIMOTHY STARTED. WHERE IS HE?
OUTSIDE SOMEWHERE.
--TU ERES NORTEAMERICANO...
I'M SORRY. I DON'T SPEAK SPANISH.
NO, I AM SORRY. I SAY, YOU ARE FROM NORTH? YOU LIVE IN THE BIG HOUSE?
YES. WITH MY FATHER AND HIS FRIEND PROFESSOR PORTER. MY FATHER IS A GENERAL IN THE ARMY OF THE UNITED STATES. A RETIRED GENERAL WITH HONORS.

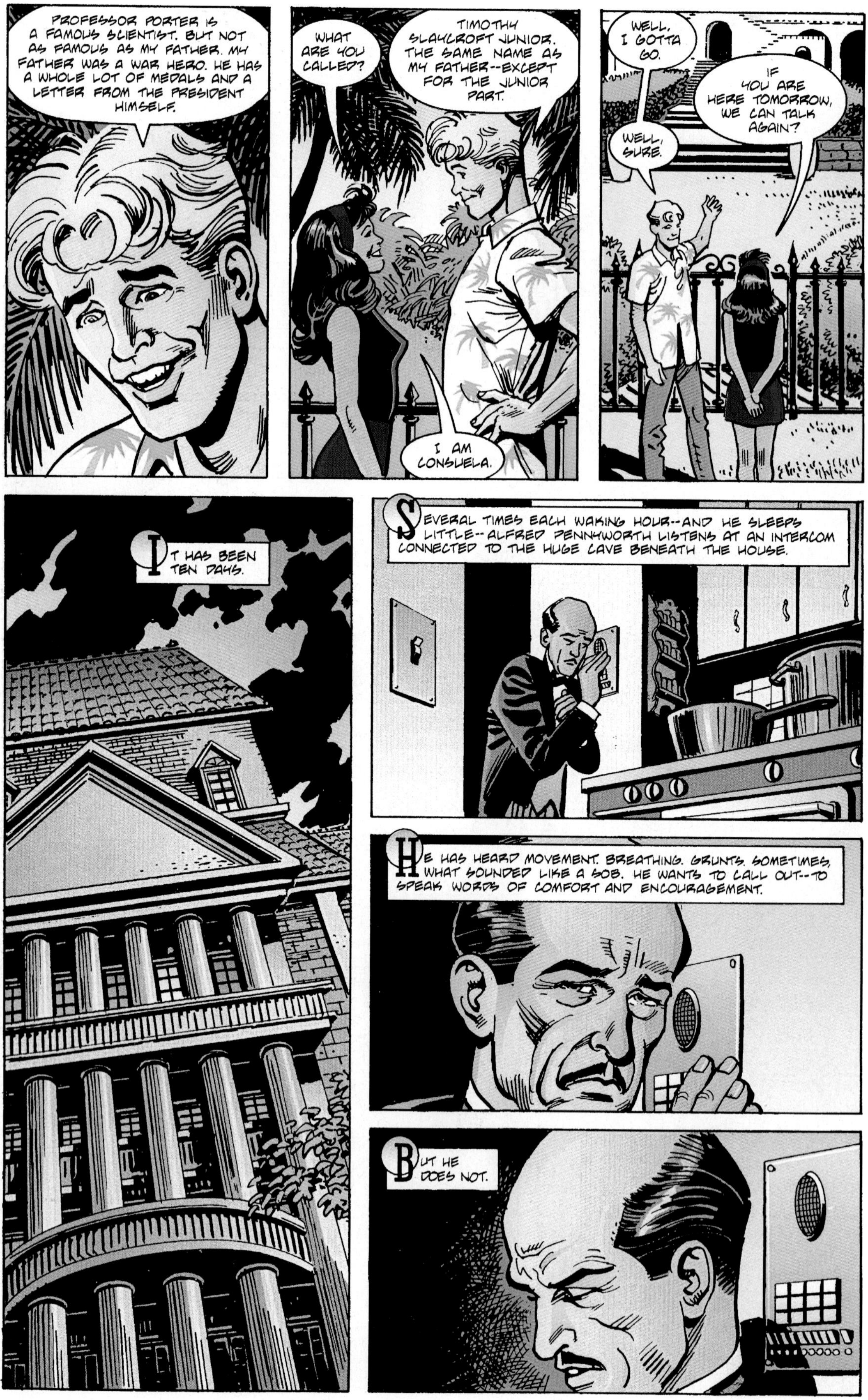
PROFESSOR PORTER IS A FAMOUS SCIENTIST. BUT NOT AS FAMOUS AS MY FATHER. MY FATHER WAS A WAR HERO. HE HAS A WHOLE LOT OF MEDALS AND A LETTER FROM THE PRESIDENT HIMSELF.
WHAT ARE YOU CALLED?
TIMOTHY SLAYCROFT JUNIOR. THE SAME NAME AS MY FATHER--EXCEPT FOR THE JUNIOR PART.
I AM CONSUELA.
WELL, I GOTTA GO.
IF YOU ARE HERE TOMORROW, WE CAN TALK AGAIN?
WELL, SURE.
IT HAS BEEN TEN DAYS.
SEVERAL TIMES EACH WAKING HOUR--AND HE SLEEPS LITTLE--ALFRED PENNYWORTH LISTENS AT AN INTERCOM CONNECTED TO THE HUGE CAVE BENEATH THE HOUSE.
HE HAS HEARD MOVEMENT. BREATHING. GRUNTS. SOMETIMES, WHAT SOUNDED LIKE A SOB. HE WANTS TO CALL OUT--TO SPEAK WORDS OF COMFORT AND ENCOURAGEMENT.
BUT HE DOES NOT.

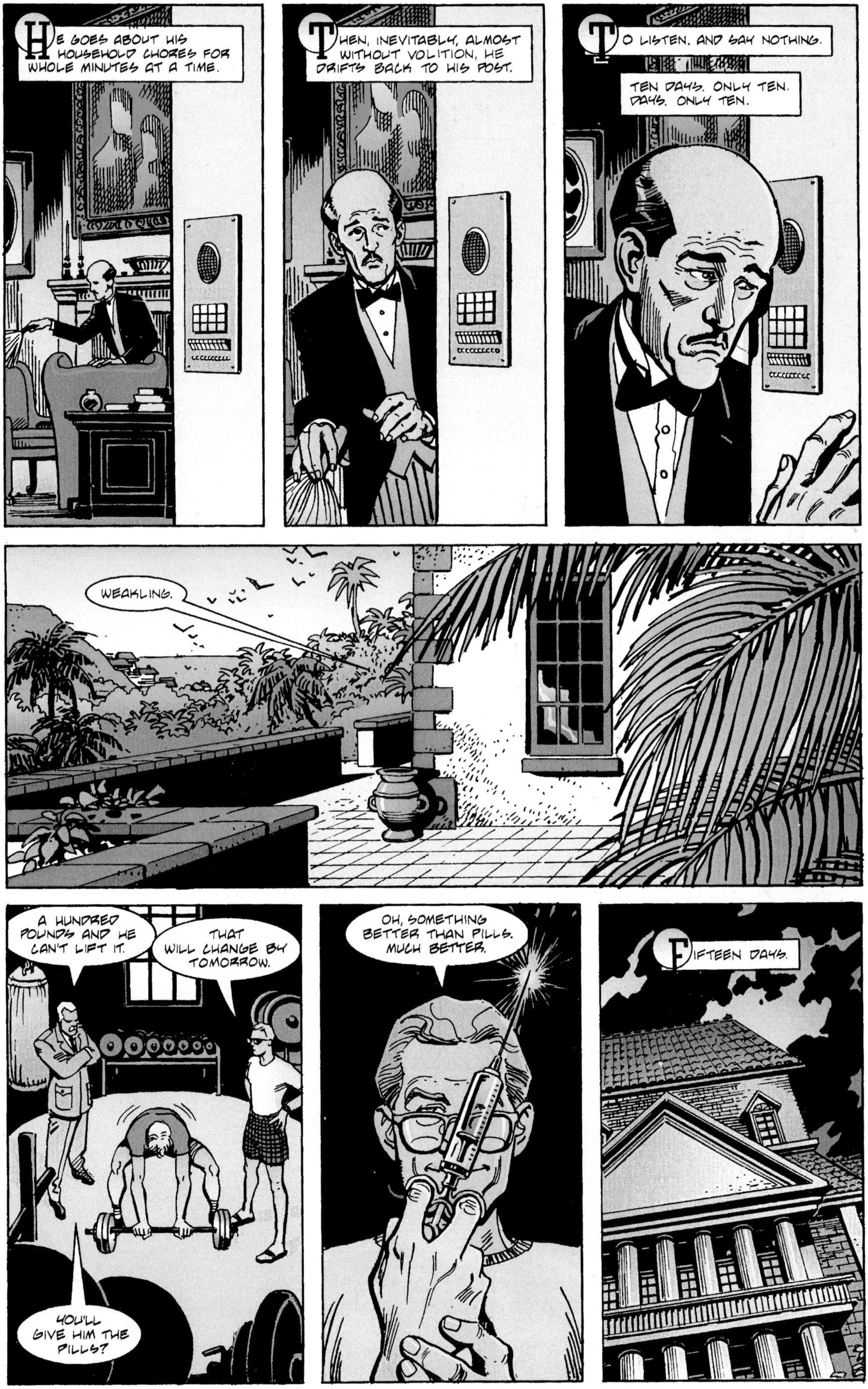
HE GOES ABOUT HIS HOUSEHOLD CHORES FOR WHOLE MINUTES AT A TIME.
THEN, INEVITABLY, ALMOST WITHOUT VOLITION, HE DRIFTS BACK TO HIS POST.
TO LISTEN. AND SAY NOTHING.
TEN DAYS. ONLY TEN. DAYS. ONLY TEN.
WEAKLING.
A HUNDRED POUNDS AND HE CAN'T LIFT IT.
THAT WILL CHANGE BY TOMORROW.
YOU'LL GIVE HIM THE PILLS?
OH, SOMETHING BETTER THAN PILLS. MUCH BETTER.
FIFTEEN DAYS.

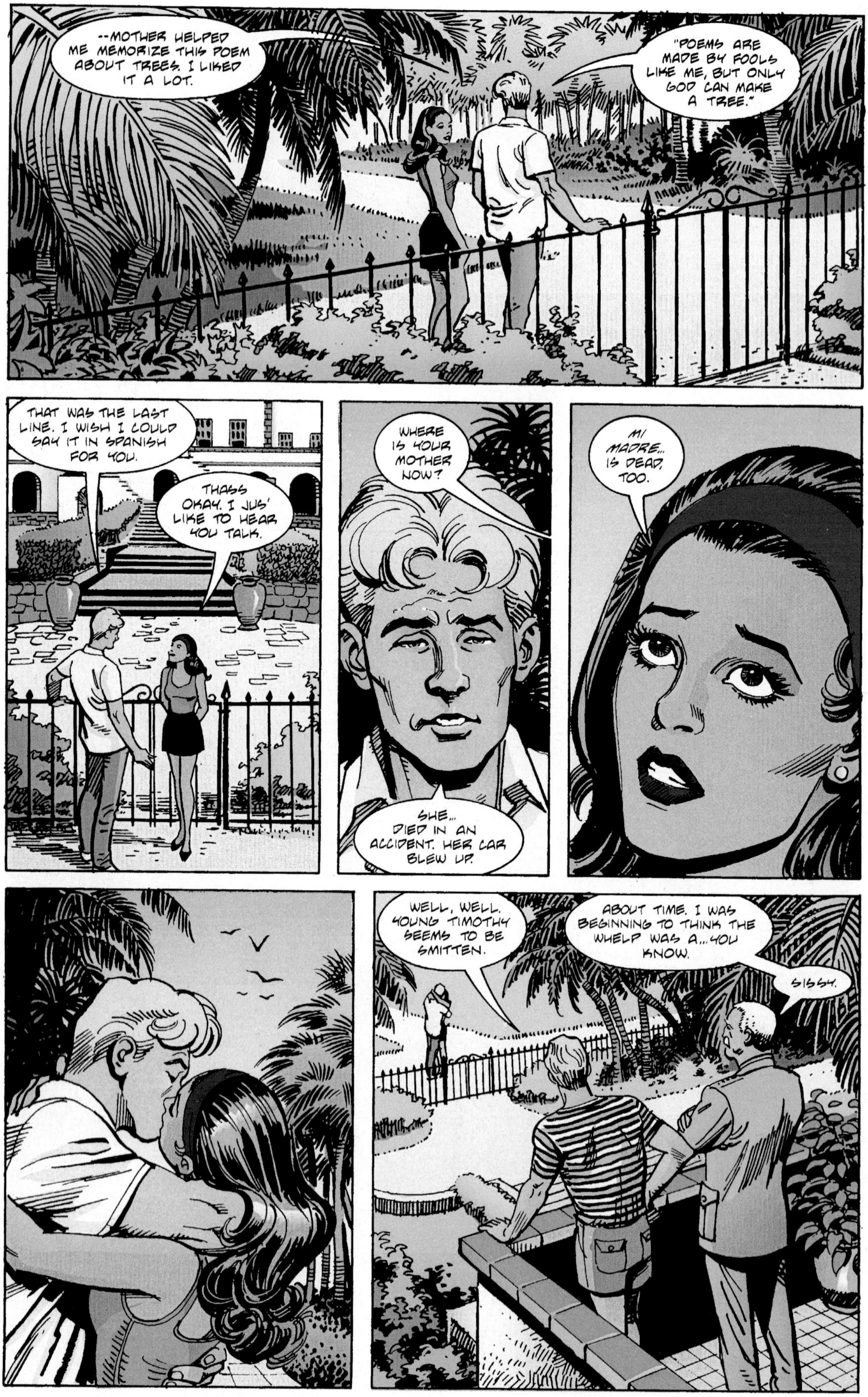
--MOTHER HELPED ME MEMORIZE THIS POEM ABOUT TREES. I LIKED IT A LOT.
"POEMS ARE MADE BY FOOLS LIKE ME, BUT ONLY GOD CAN MAKE A TREE."
THAT WAS THE LAST LINE. I WISH I COULD SAY IT IN SPANISH FOR YOU.
THASS OKAY. I JUS' LIKE TO HEAR YOU TALK.
WHERE IS YOUR MOTHER NOW?
SHE... DIED IN AN ACCIDENT. HER CAR BLEW UP.
MI MADRE... IS DEAD, TOO.
WELL, WELL. YOUNG TIMOTHY SEEMS TO BE SMITTEN.
ABOUT TIME. I WAS BEGINNING TO THINK THE WHELP WAS A... YOU KNOW.
SISSY.

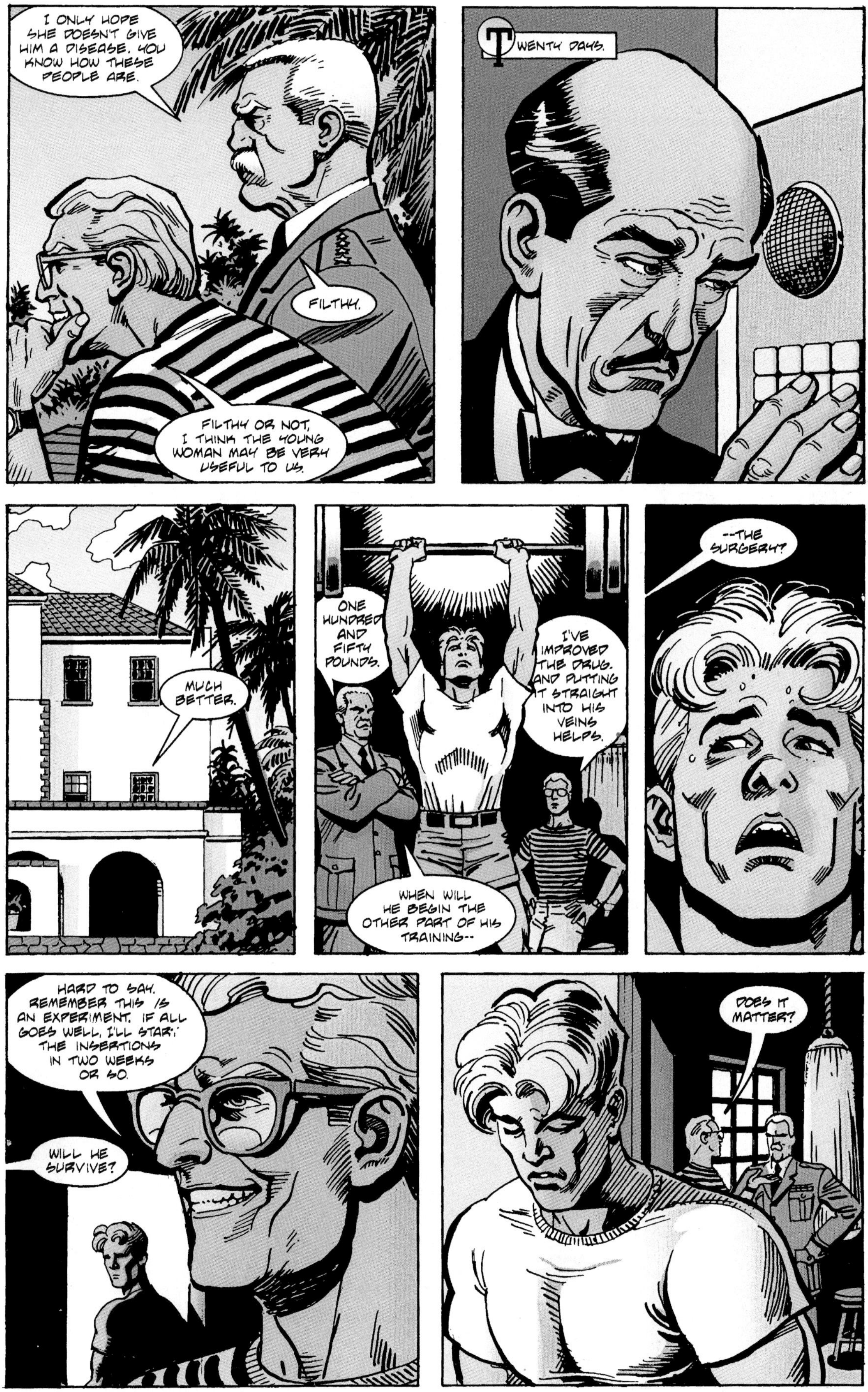
I ONLY HOPE SHE DOESN'T GIVE HIM A DISEASE. YOU KNOW HOW THESE PEOPLE ARE.
FILTHY.
FILTHY OR NOT, I THINK THE YOUNG WOMAN MAY BE VERY USEFUL TO US.
TWENTY DAYS.
MUCH BETTER.
ONE HUNDRED AND FIFTY POUNDS.
I'VE IMPROVED THE DRUG. AND PUTTING IT STRAIGHT INTO HIS VEINS HELPS.
WHEN WILL HE BEGIN THE OTHER PART OF HIS TRAINING--
--THE SURGERY?
HARD TO SAY. REMEMBER THIS IS AN EXPERIMENT. IF ALL GOES WELL, I'LL START THE INSERTIONS IN TWO WEEKS OR SO.
WILL HE SURVIVE?
DOES IT MATTER?

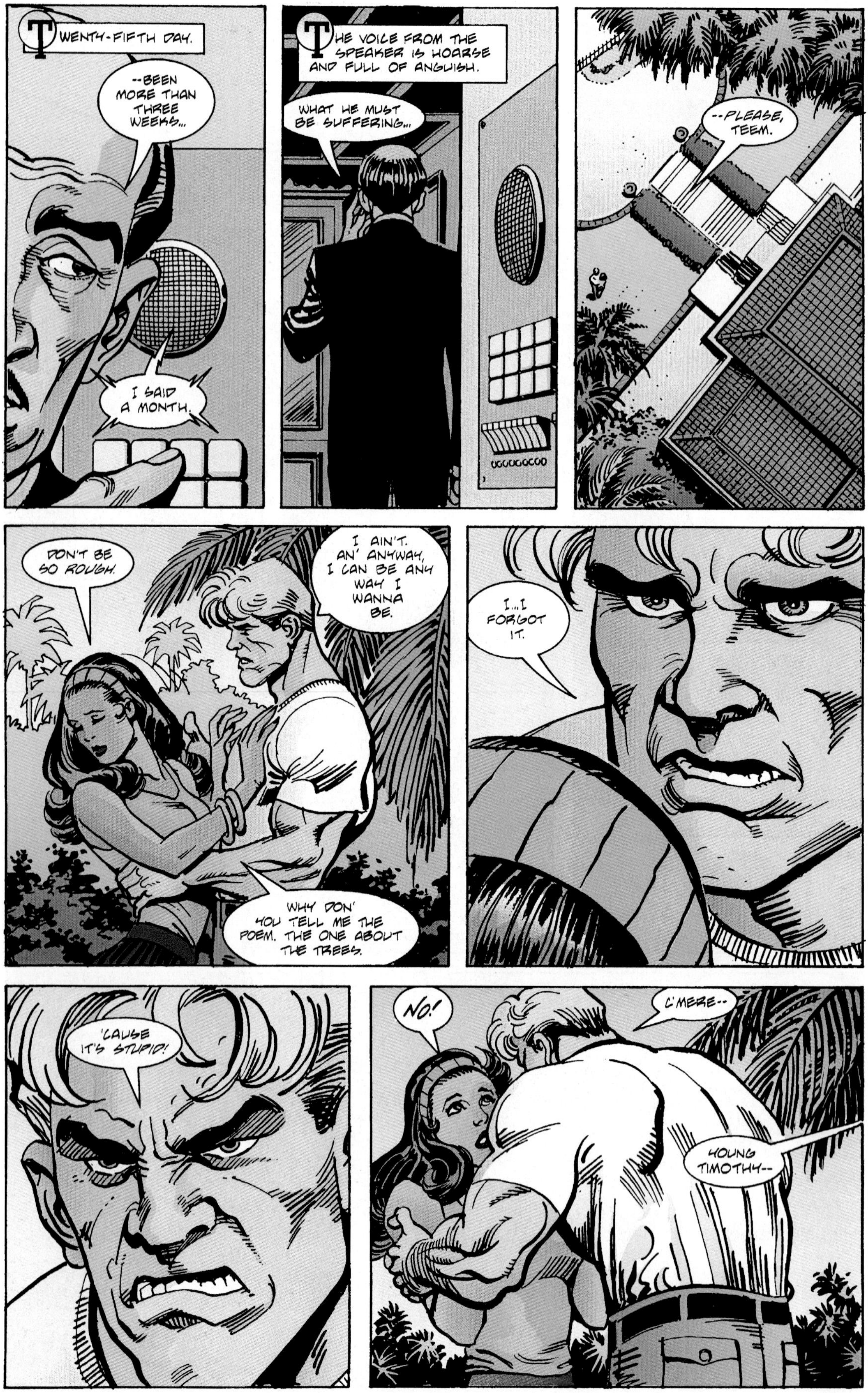
TWENTY-FIFTH DAY.
--BEEN MORE THAN THREE WEEKS...
I SAID A MONTH.
THE VOICE FROM THE SPEAKER IS HOARSE AND FULL OF ANGUISH.
WHAT HE MUST BE SUFFERING...
--PLEASE, TEEM.
DON'T BE SO ROUGH.
I AIN'T. AN' ANYWAY, I CAN BE ANY WAY I WANNA BE.
WHY DON' YOU TELL ME THE POEM. THE ONE ABOUT THE TREES.
I...I FORGOT IT.
'CAUSE IT'S STUPID!
NO!
C'MERE--
YOUNG TIMOTHY--

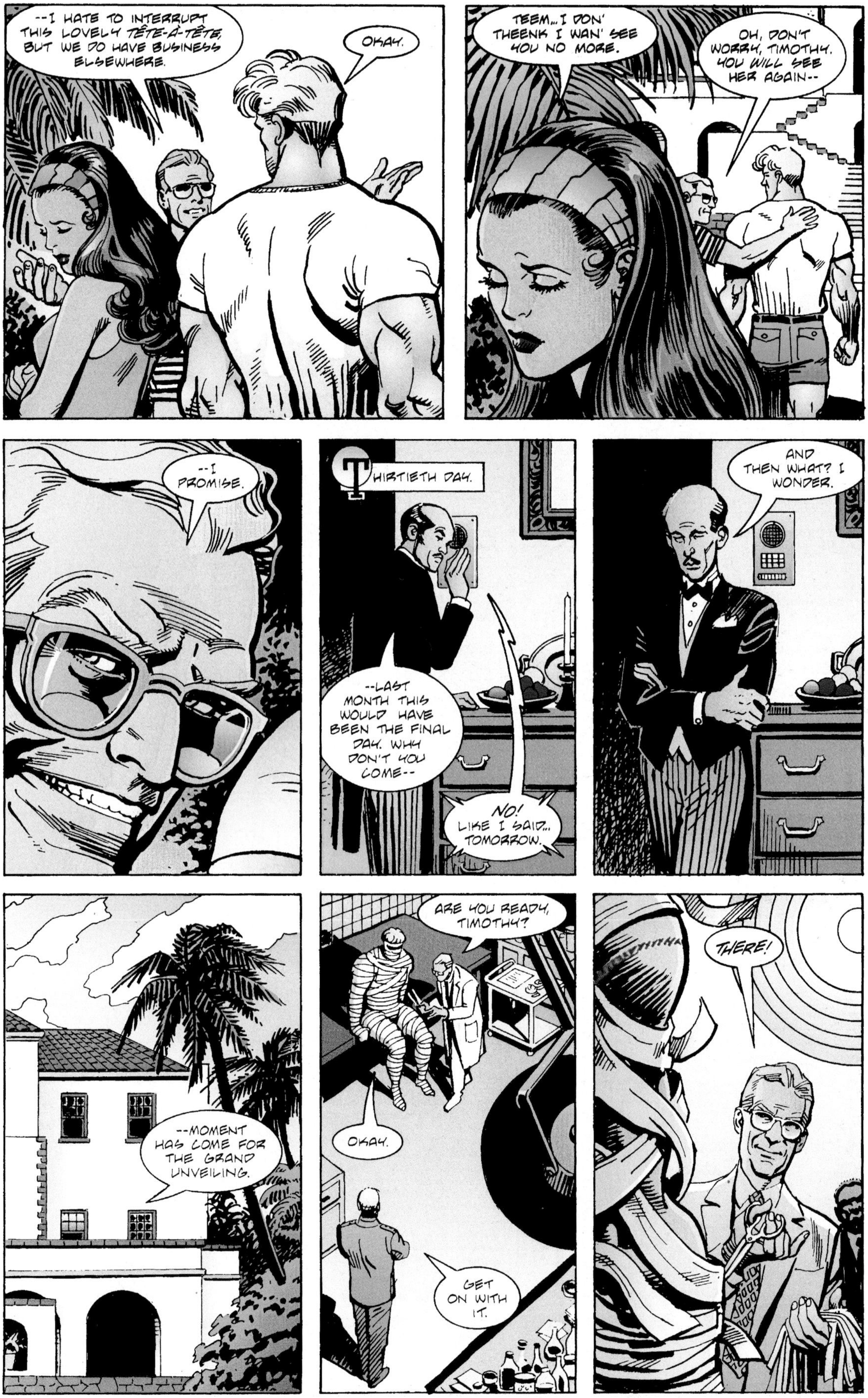
--I HATE TO INTERRUPT THIS LOVELY TÊTE-À-TÊTE, BUT WE DO HAVE BUSINESS ELSEWHERE.
OKAY.
TEEM... I DON' THEENK I WAN' SEE YOU NO MORE.
OH, DON'T WORRY, TIMOTHY. YOU WILL SEE HER AGAIN--
--I PROMISE.
THIRTIETH DAY.
--LAST MONTH THIS WOULD HAVE BEEN THE FINAL DAY. WHY DON'T YOU COME--
NO! LIKE I SAID... TOMORROW.
AND THEN WHAT? I WONDER.
--MOMENT HAS COME FOR THE GRAND UNVEILING.
ARE YOU READY, TIMOTHY?
OKAY.
GET ON WITH IT.
THERE!

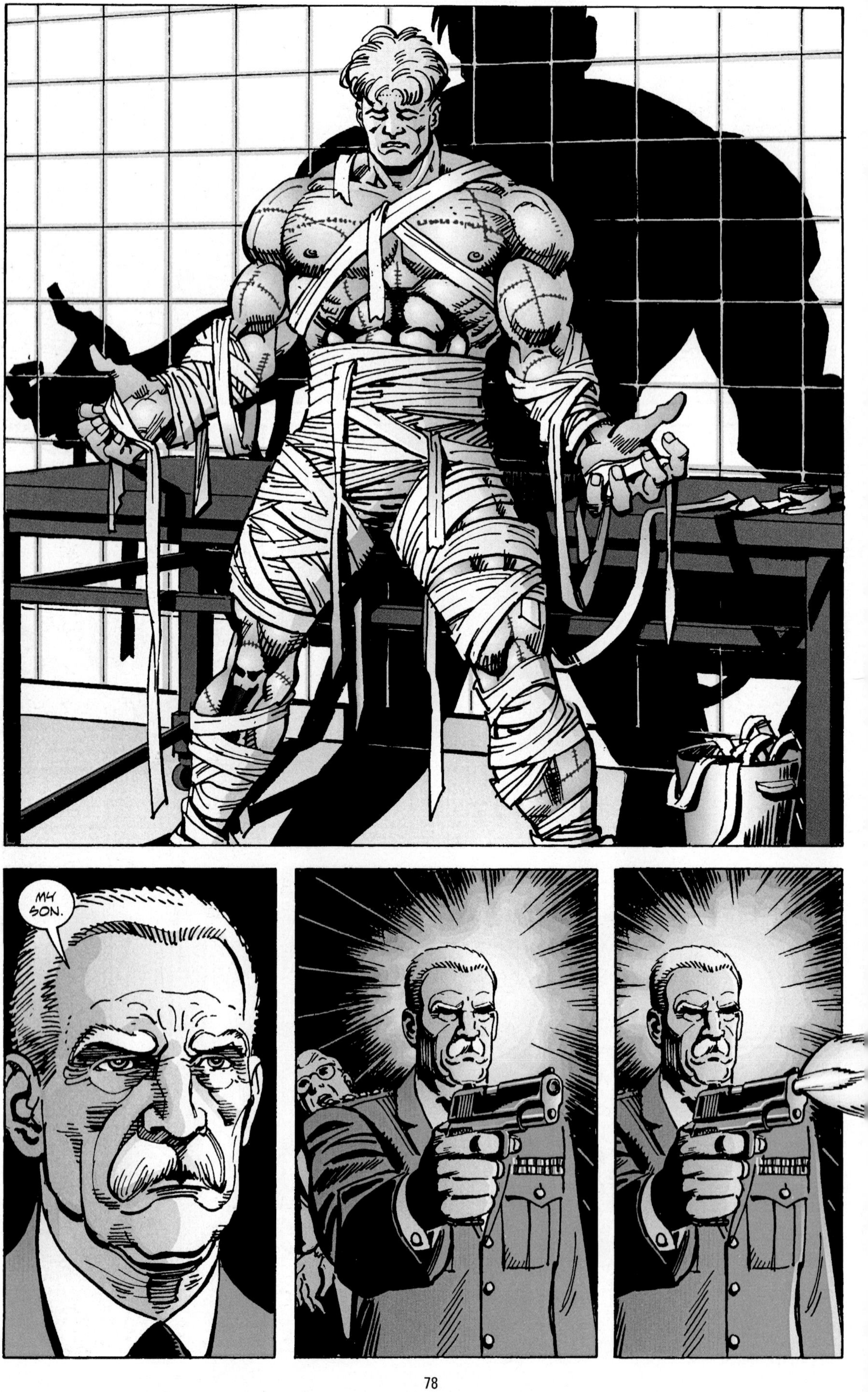
MY SON.

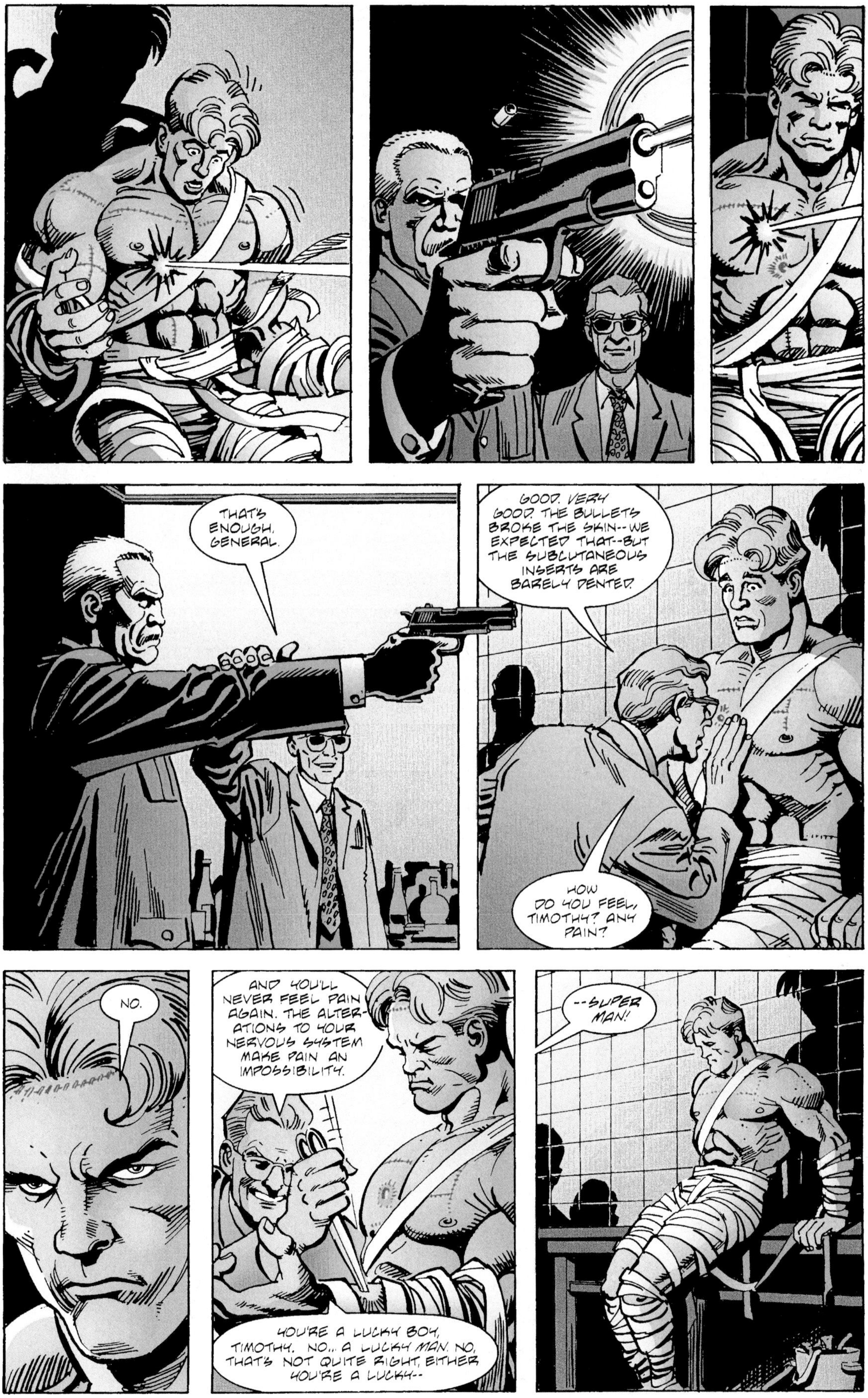
THAT'S ENOUGH, GENERAL.
GOOD. VERY GOOD. THE BULLETS BROKE THE SKIN--WE EXPECTED THAT--BUT THE SUBCUTANEOUS INSERTS ARE BARELY DENTED.
HOW DO YOU FEEL, TIMOTHY? ANY PAIN?
NO.
AND YOU'LL NEVER FEEL PAIN AGAIN. THE ALTERATIONS TO YOUR NERVOUS SYSTEM MAKE PAIN AN IMPOSSIBILITY.
YOU'RE A LUCKY BOY, TIMOTHY. NO... A LUCKY MAN. NO, THAT'S NOT QUITE RIGHT, EITHER. YOU'RE A LUCKY--
--SUPER MAN!

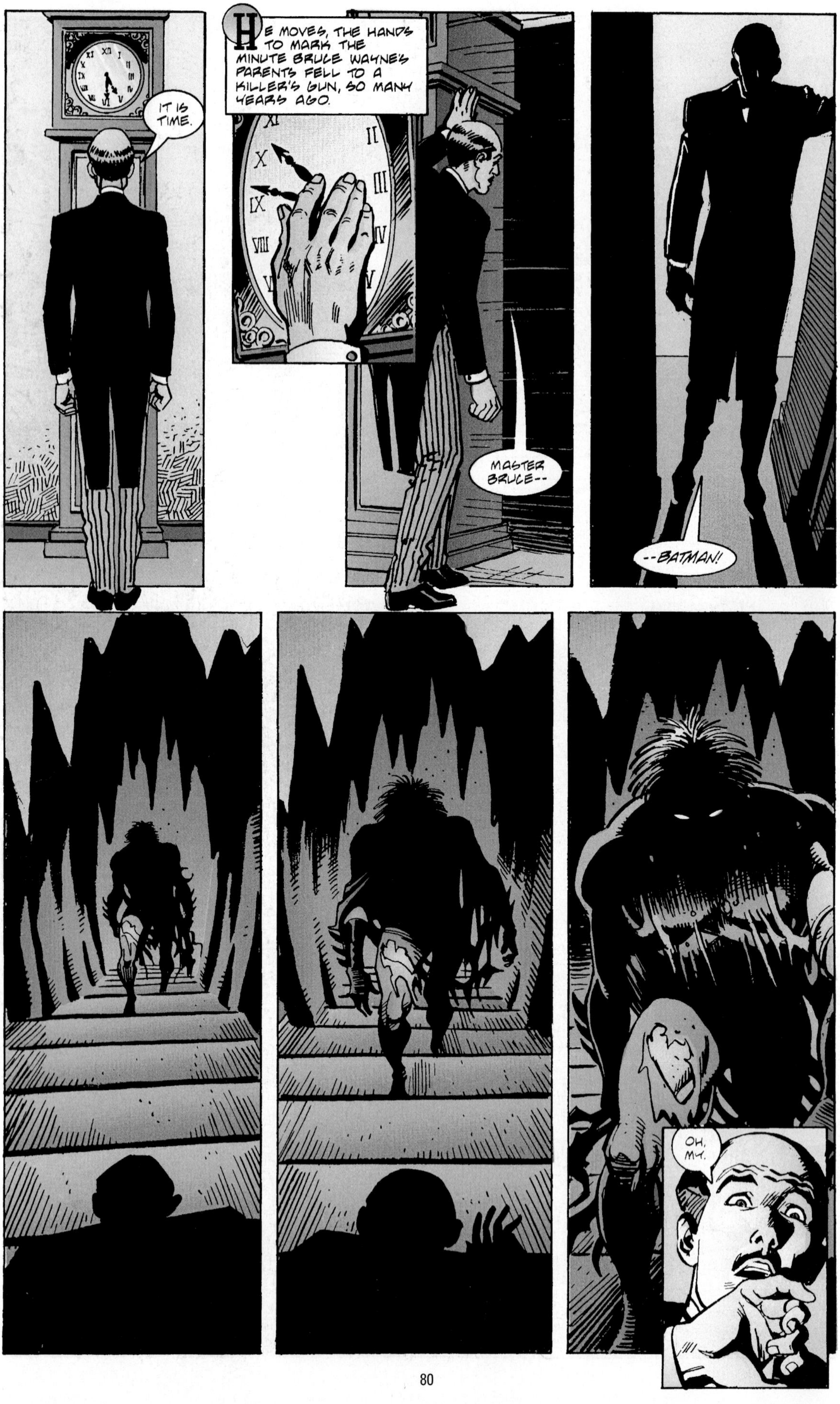
IT IS TIME.
HE MOVES, THE HANDS TO MARK THE MINUTE BRUCE WAYNE'S PARENTS FELL TO A KILLER'S GUN, SO MANY YEARS AGO.
MASTER BRUCE--
--BATMAN!
OH, MY.

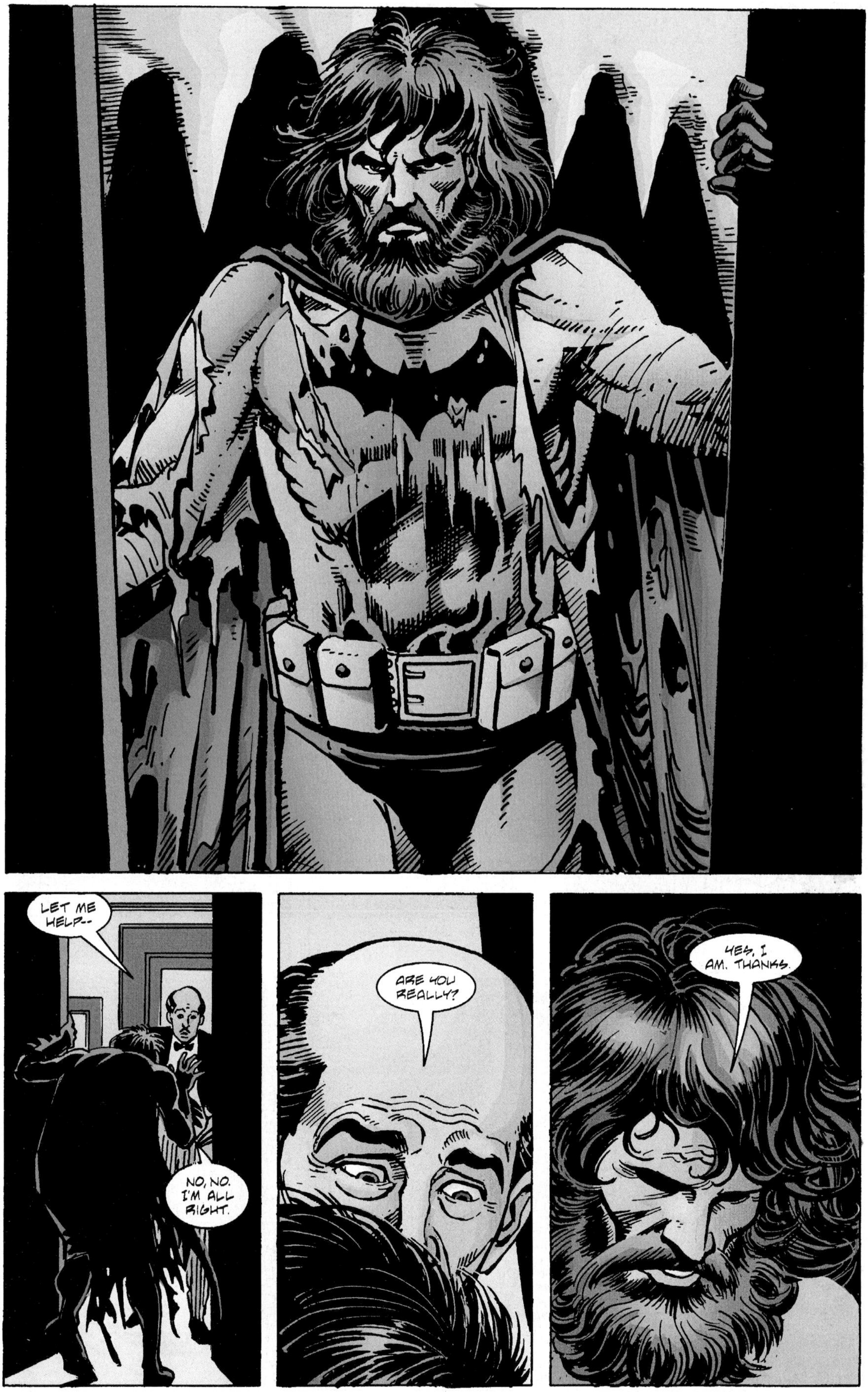
LET ME HELP--
NO, NO. I'M ALL RIGHT.
ARE YOU REALLY?
YES, I AM. THANKS.

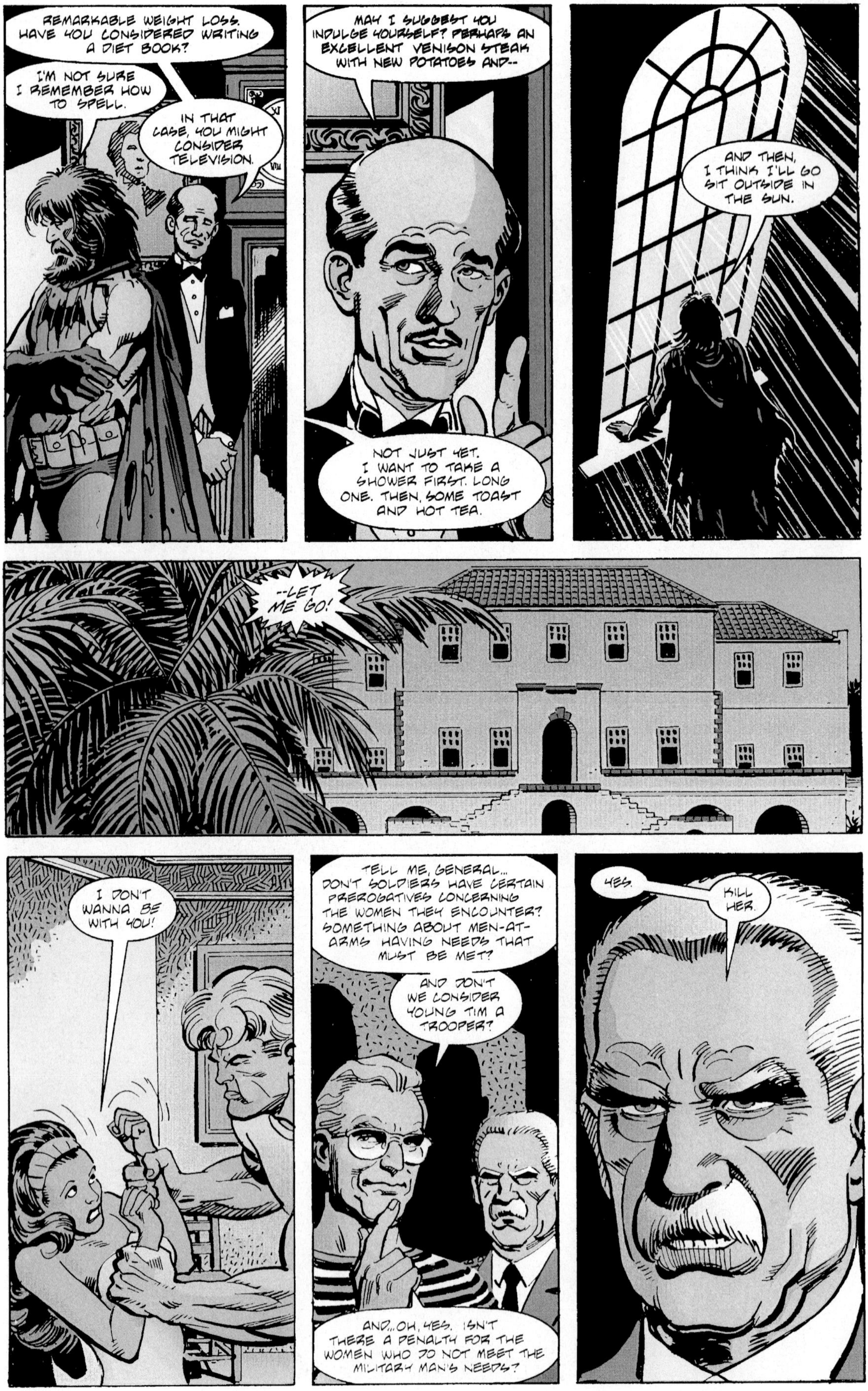
REMARKABLE WEIGHT LOSS. HAVE YOU CONSIDERED WRITING A DIET BOOK?
I'M NOT SURE I REMEMBER HOW TO SPELL.
IN THAT CASE, YOU MIGHT CONSIDER TELEVISION.
MAY I SUGGEST YOU INDULGE YOURSELF? PERHAPS AN EXCELLENT VENISON STEAK WITH NEW POTATOES AND--
NOT JUST YET. I WANT TO TAKE A SHOWER FIRST. LONG ONE. THEN, SOME TOAST AND HOT TEA.
AND THEN, I THINK I'LL GO SIT OUTSIDE IN THE SUN.
--LET ME GO!
I DON'T WANNA BE WITH YOU!
TELL ME, GENERAL... DON'T SOLDIERS HAVE CERTAIN PREROGATIVES CONCERNING THE WOMEN THEY ENCOUNTER? SOMETHING ABOUT MEN-AT-ARMS HAVING NEEDS THAT MUST BE MET?
AND DON'T WE CONSIDER YOUNG TIM A TROOPER?
AND...OH, YES. ISN'T THERE A PENALTY FOR THE WOMEN WHO DO NOT MEET THE MILITARY MAN'S NEEDS?
YES.
KILL HER.

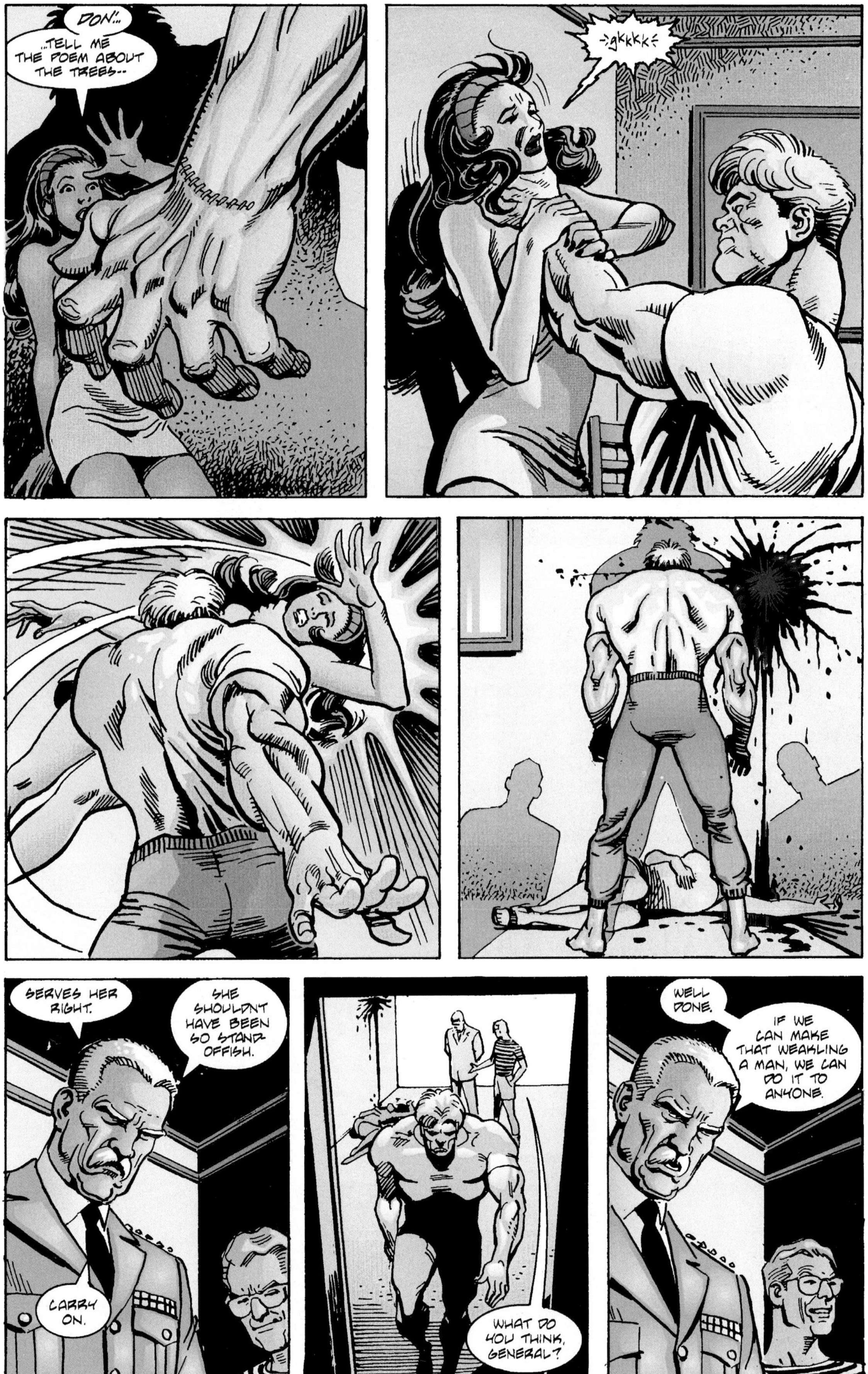
DON...
...TELL ME THE POEM ABOUT THE TREES...
-gkkkk-
SERVES HER RIGHT.
SHE SHOULDN'T HAVE BEEN SO STAND OFFISH.
CARRY ON.
WHAT DO YOU THINK, GENERAL?
WELL DONE.
IF WE CAN MAKE THAT WEAKLING A MAN, WE CAN DO IT TO ANYONE.

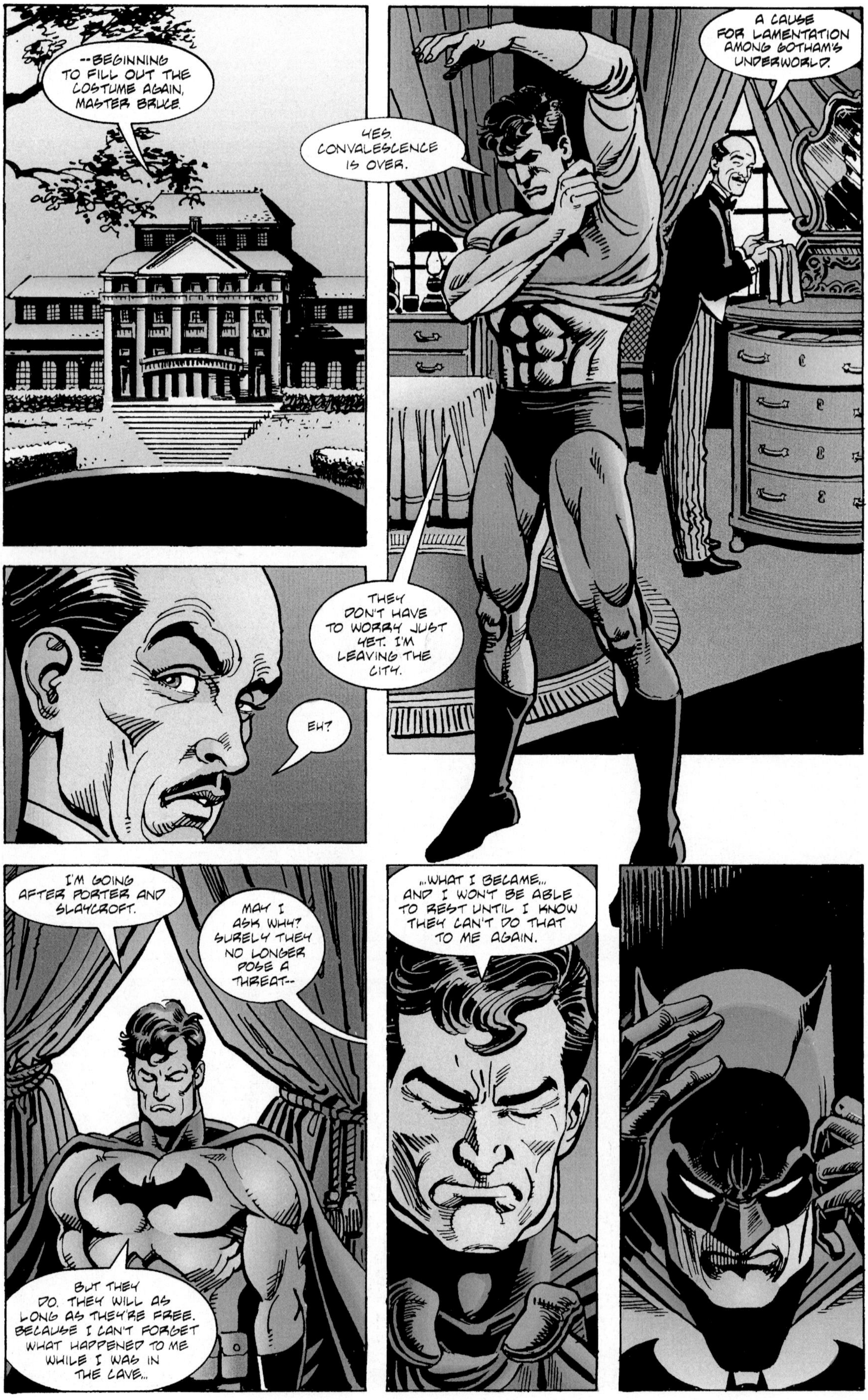
--BEGINNING TO FILL OUT THE COSTUME AGAIN, MASTER BRUCE.
YES. CONVALESCENCE IS OVER.
A CAUSE FOR LAMENTATION AMONG GOTHAM'S UNDERWORLD.
THEY DON'T HAVE TO WORRY JUST YET. I'M LEAVING THE CITY.
EH?
I'M GOING AFTER PORTER AND SLAYCROFT.
MAY I ASK WHY? SURELY THEY NO LONGER POSE A THREAT--
BUT THEY DO. THEY WILL AS LONG AS THEY'RE FREE. BECAUSE I CAN'T FORGET WHAT HAPPENED TO ME WHILE I WAS IN THE CAVE...
...WHAT I BECAME... AND I WON'T BE ABLE TO REST UNTIL I KNOW THEY CAN'T DO THAT TO ME AGAIN.

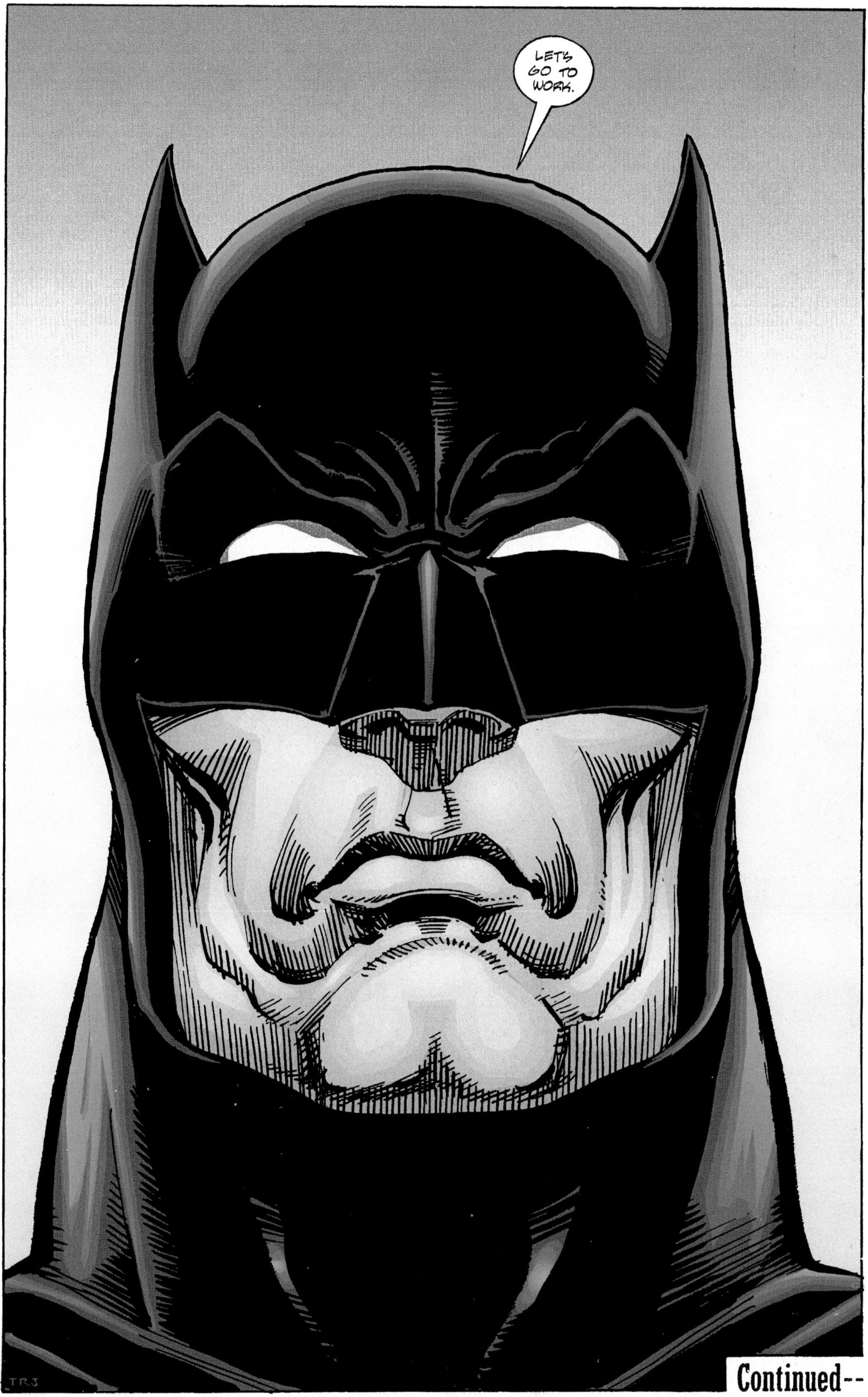
LET'S GO TO WORK.
TRJ
Continued--

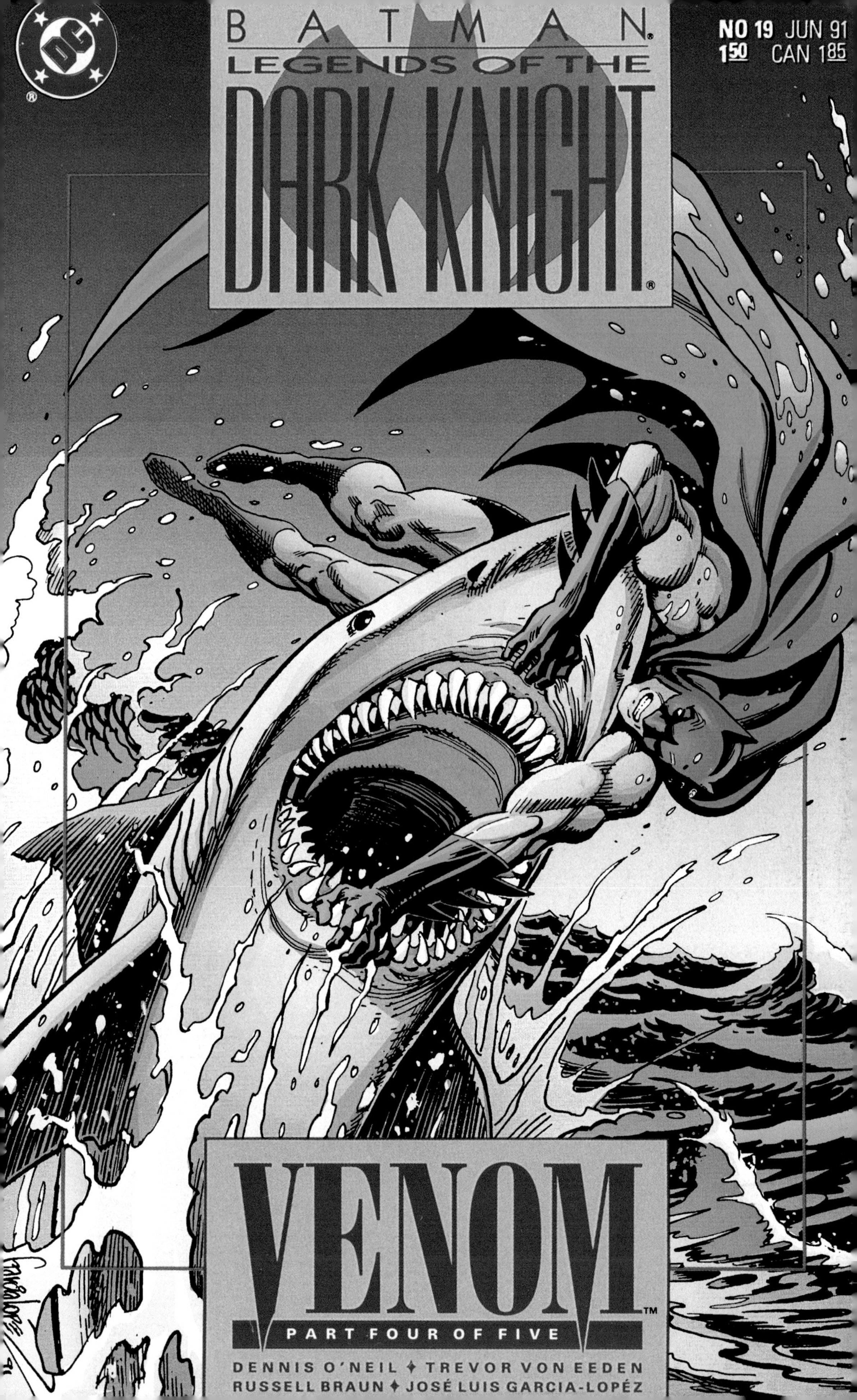
BATMAN
LEGENDS OF THE
DARK KNIGHT
NO 19 JUN 91
1.50 CAN 1.85
VENOM
PART FOUR OF FIVE
DENNIS O'NEIL ✦ TREVOR VON EEDEN
RUSSELL BRAUN ✦ JOSÉ LUIS GARCIA-LOPÉZ

VENOM: PART FOUR

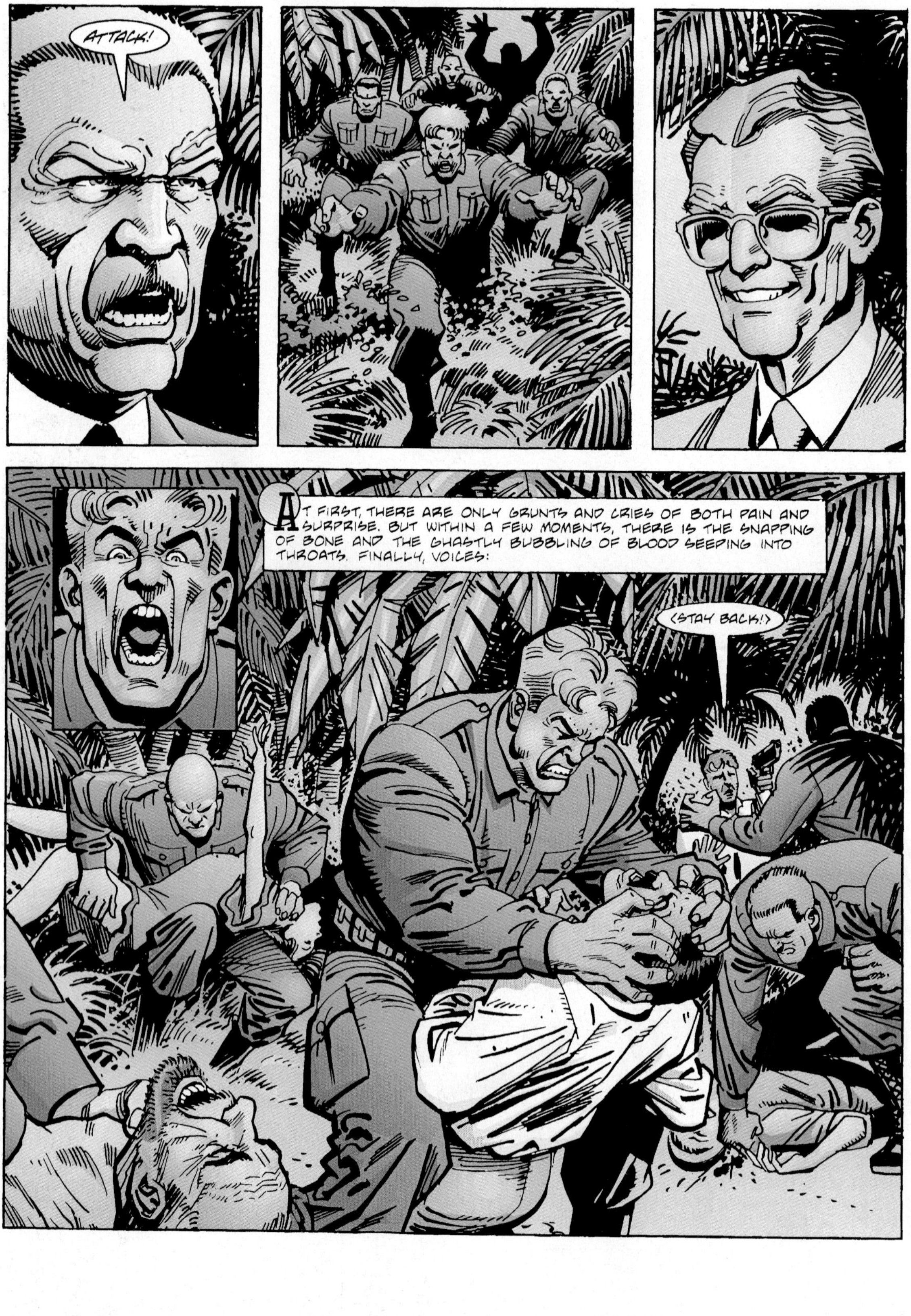
ATTACK!
AT FIRST, THERE ARE ONLY GRUNTS AND CRIES OF BOTH PAIN AND SURPRISE. BUT WITHIN A FEW MOMENTS, THERE IS THE SNAPPING OF BONE AND THE GHASTLY BUBBLING OF BLOOD SEEPING INTO THROATS. FINALLY, VOICES:
<STAY BACK!>

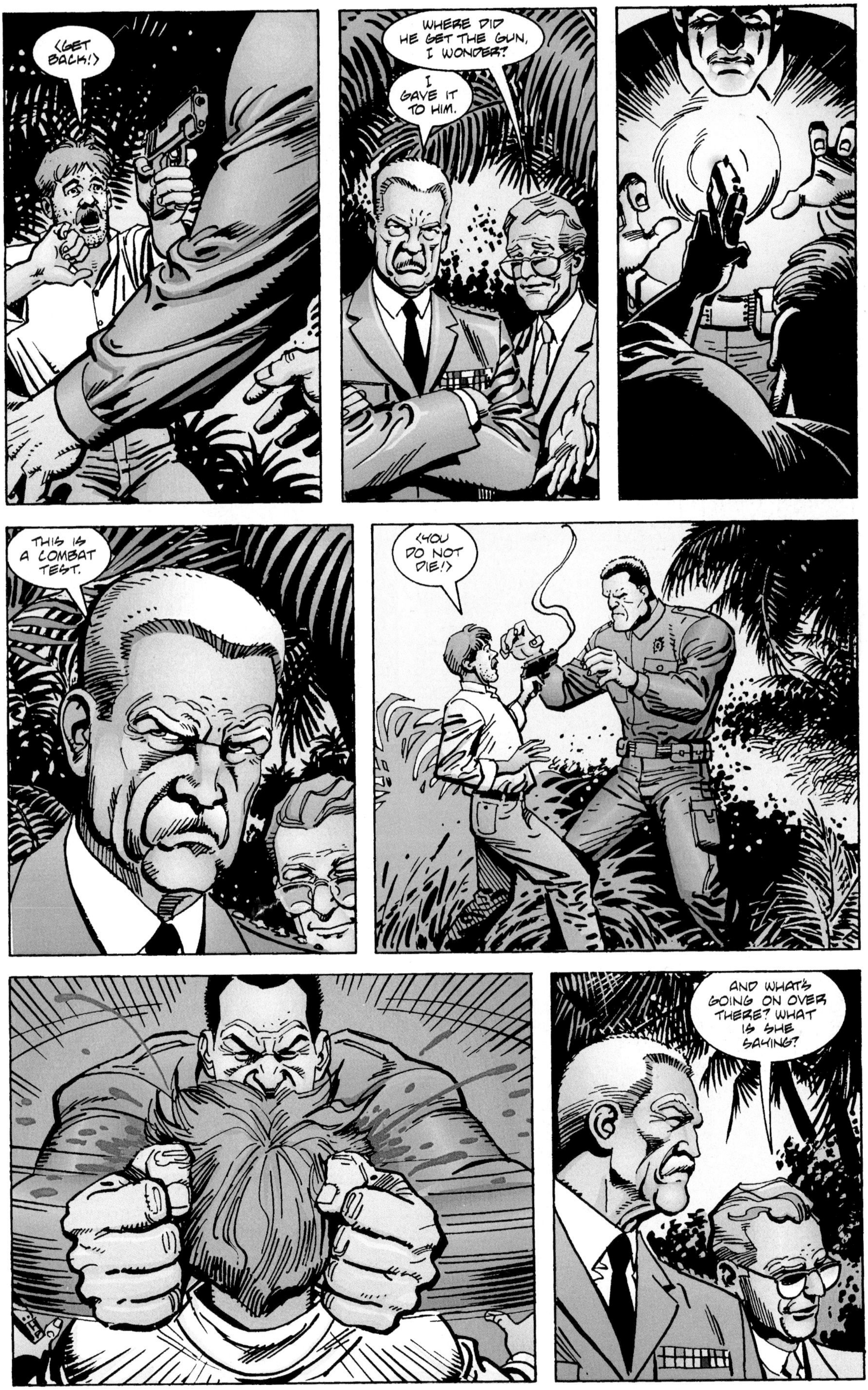

<GET BACK!>
WHERE DID HE GET THE GUN, I WONDER?
I GAVE IT TO HIM.
THIS IS A COMBAT TEST.
<YOU DO NOT DIE!>
AND WHAT'S GOING ON OVER THERE? WHAT IS SHE SAYING?

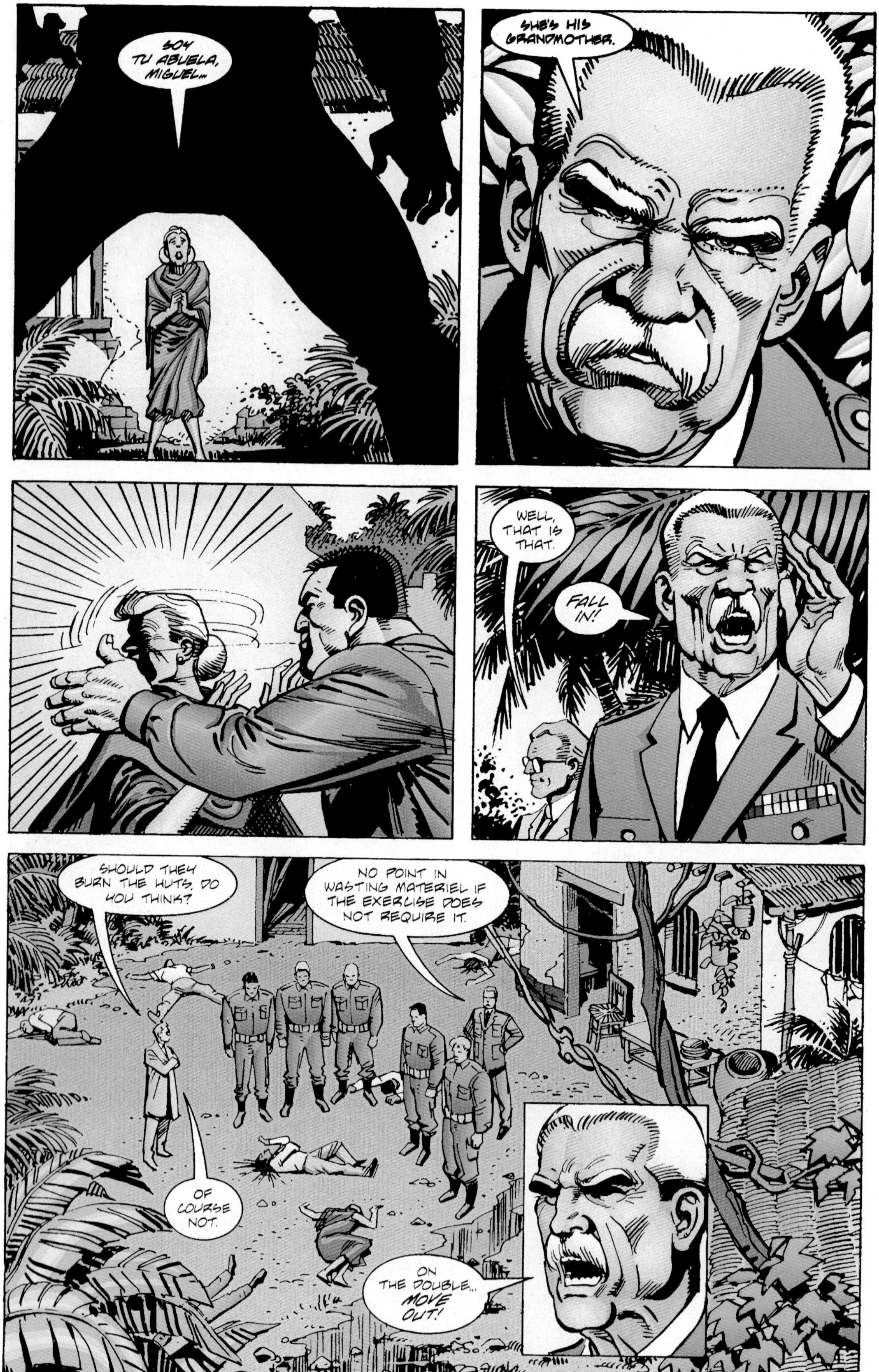
SOY TU ABUELA, MIGUEL...
SHE'S HIS GRANDMOTHER.
WELL, THAT IS THAT.
FALL IN!
SHOULD THEY BURN THE HUTS, DO YOU THINK?
NO POINT IN WASTING MATERIEL IF THE EXERCISE DOES NOT REQUIRE IT.
OF COURSE NOT.
ON THE DOUBLE... MOVE OUT!

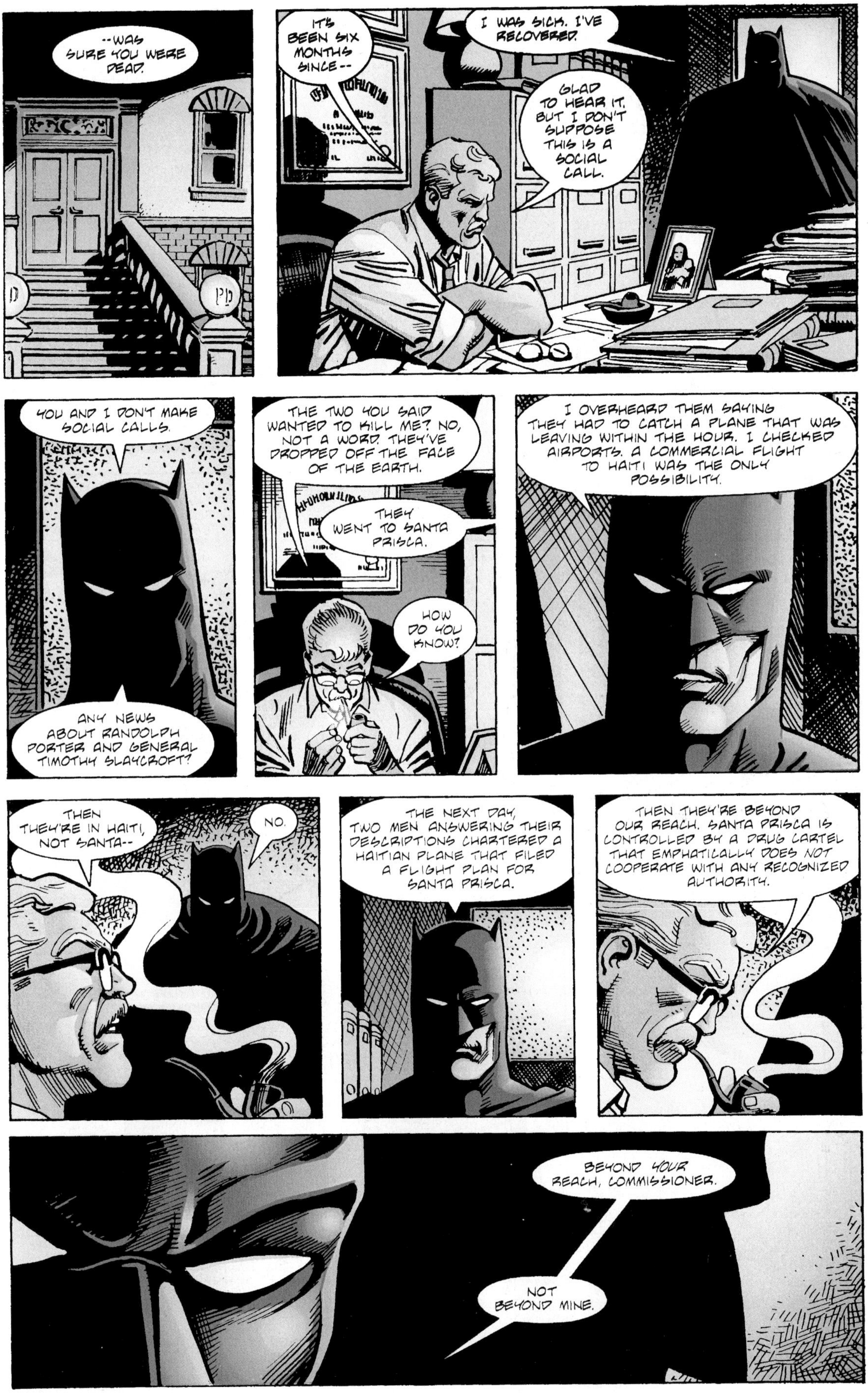

--WAS SURE YOU WERE DEAD.
IT'S BEEN SIX MONTHS SINCE--
I WAS SICK. I'VE RECOVERED.
GLAD TO HEAR IT, BUT I DON'T SUPPOSE THIS IS A SOCIAL CALL.
YOU AND I DON'T MAKE SOCIAL CALLS.
ANY NEWS ABOUT RANDOLPH PORTER AND GENERAL TIMOTHY SLAYCROFT?
THE TWO YOU SAID WANTED TO KILL ME? NO, NOT A WORD. THEY'VE DROPPED OFF THE FACE OF THE EARTH.
THEY WENT TO SANTA PRISCA.
HOW DO YOU KNOW?
I OVERHEARD THEM SAYING THEY HAD TO CATCH A PLANE THAT WAS LEAVING WITHIN THE HOUR. I CHECKED AIRPORTS. A COMMERCIAL FLIGHT TO HAITI WAS THE ONLY POSSIBILITY.
THEN THEY'RE IN HAITI, NOT SANTA--
NO.
THE NEXT DAY, TWO MEN ANSWERING THEIR DESCRIPTIONS CHARTERED A HAITIAN PLANE THAT FILED A FLIGHT PLAN FOR SANTA PRISCA.
THEN THEY'RE BEYOND OUR REACH. SANTA PRISCA IS CONTROLLED BY A DRUG CARTEL THAT EMPHATICALLY DOES NOT COOPERATE WITH ANY RECOGNIZED AUTHORITY.
BEYOND YOUR REACH, COMMISSIONER.
NOT BEYOND MINE.

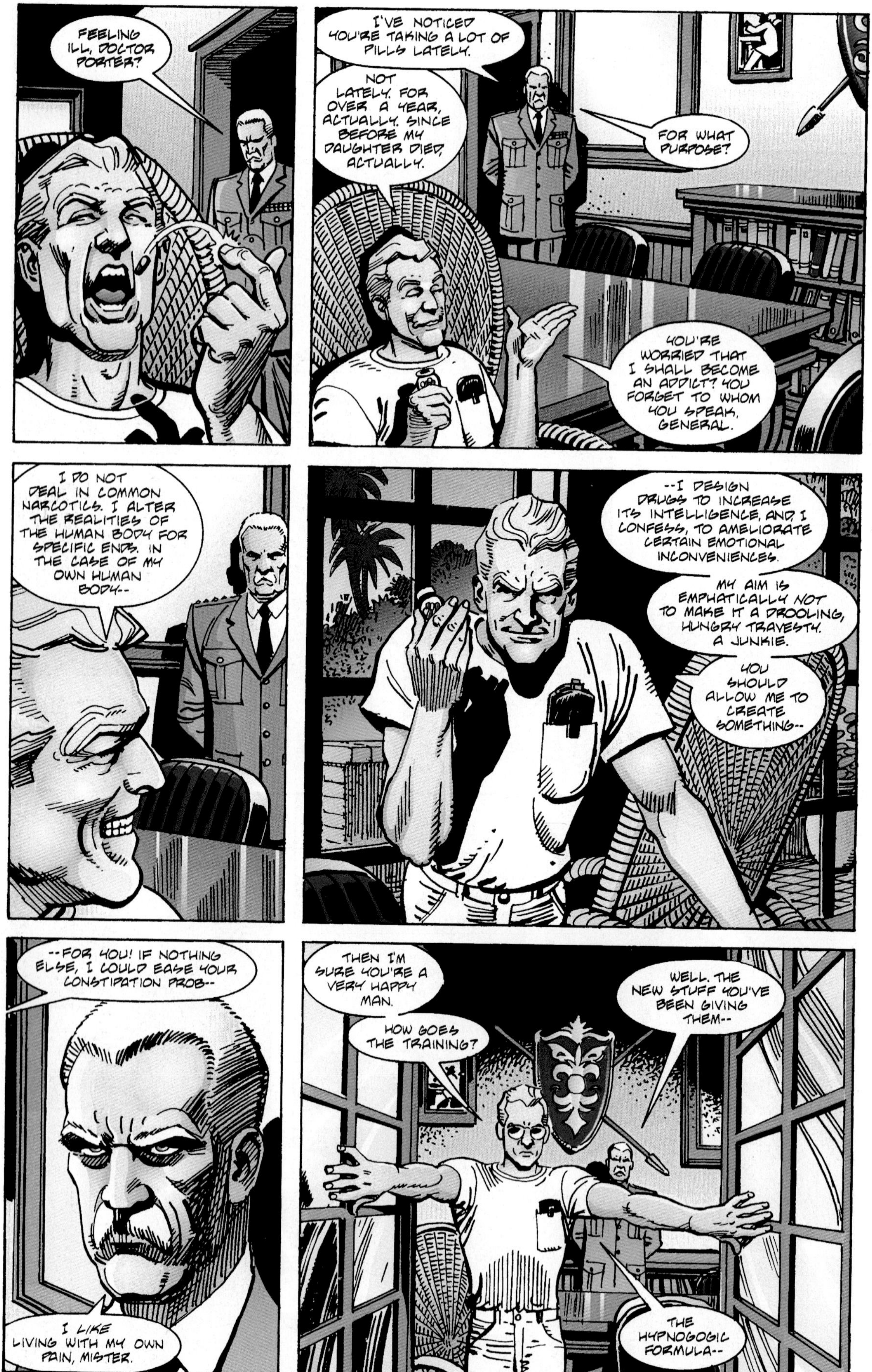
FEELING ILL, DOCTOR PORTER?
I'VE NOTICED YOU'RE TAKING A LOT OF PILLS LATELY.
NOT LATELY. FOR OVER A YEAR, ACTUALLY. SINCE BEFORE MY DAUGHTER DIED, ACTUALLY.
FOR WHAT PURPOSE?
YOU'RE WORRIED THAT I SHALL BECOME AN ADDICT? YOU FORGET TO WHOM YOU SPEAK, GENERAL.
I DO NOT DEAL IN COMMON NARCOTICS. I ALTER THE REALITIES OF THE HUMAN BODY FOR SPECIFIC ENDS. IN THE CASE OF MY OWN HUMAN BODY--
--I DESIGN DRUGS TO INCREASE ITS INTELLIGENCE, AND, I CONFESS, TO AMELIORATE CERTAIN EMOTIONAL INCONVENIENCES.
MY AIM IS EMPHATICALLY NOT TO MAKE IT A DROOLING, HUNGRY TRAVESTY. A JUNKIE.
YOU SHOULD ALLOW ME TO CREATE SOMETHING--
--FOR YOU! IF NOTHING ELSE, I COULD EASE YOUR CONSTIPATION PROB--
I LIKE LIVING WITH MY OWN PAIN, MISTER.
THEN I'M SURE YOU'RE A VERY HAPPY MAN.
HOW GOES THE TRAINING?
WELL. THE NEW STUFF YOU'VE BEEN GIVING THEM--
THE HYPNOGOGIC FORMULA--

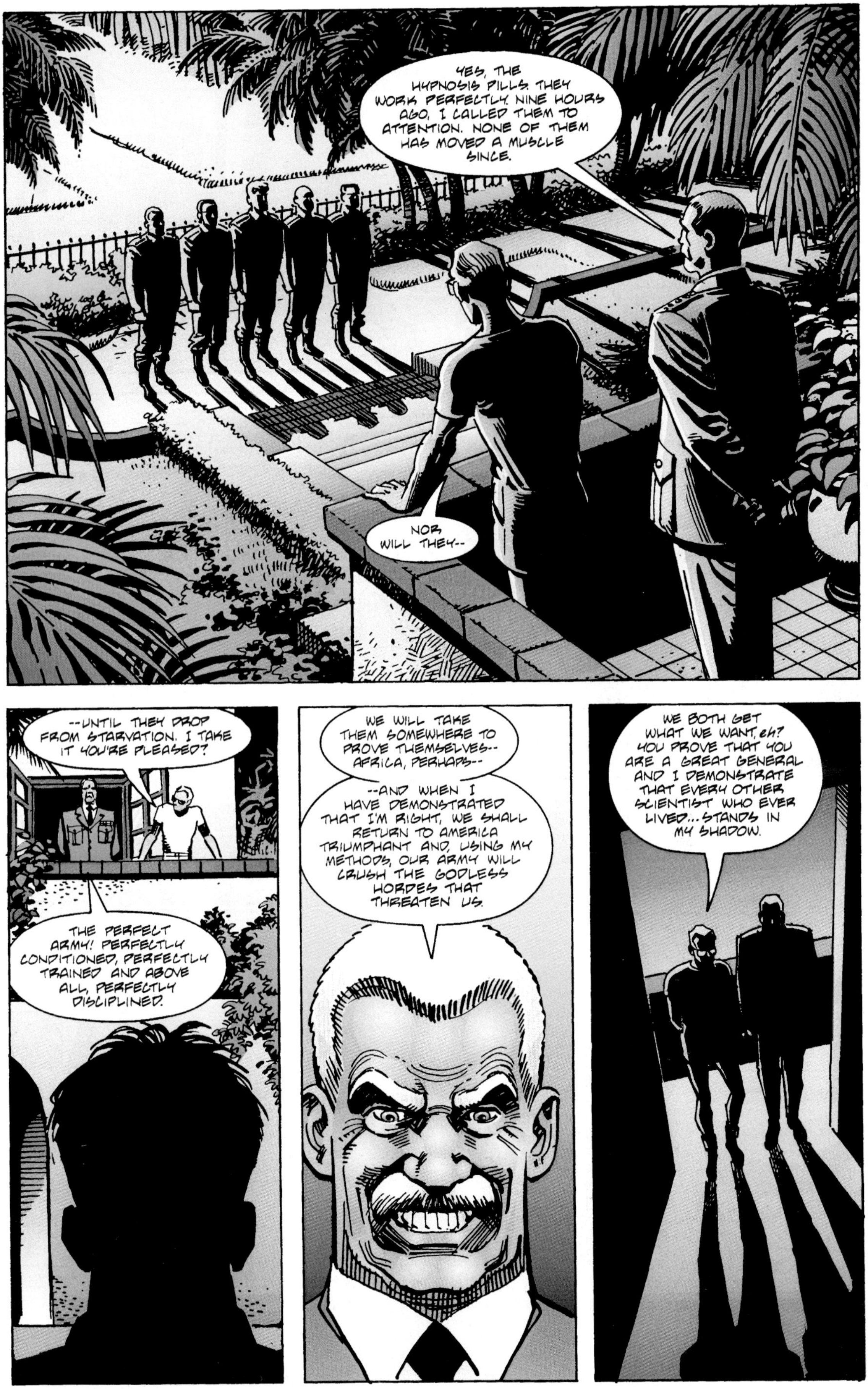
YES, THE HYPNOSIS PILLS. THEY WORK PERFECTLY. NINE HOURS AGO, I CALLED THEM TO ATTENTION. NONE OF THEM HAS MOVED A MUSCLE SINCE.
NOR WILL THEY--
--UNTIL THEY DROP FROM STARVATION. I TAKE IT YOU'RE PLEASED?
THE PERFECT ARMY! PERFECTLY CONDITIONED, PERFECTLY TRAINED AND ABOVE ALL, PERFECTLY DISCIPLINED.
WE WILL TAKE THEM SOMEWHERE TO PROVE THEMSELVES-- AFRICA, PERHAPS--
--AND WHEN I HAVE DEMONSTRATED THAT I'M RIGHT, WE SHALL RETURN TO AMERICA TRIUMPHANT AND, USING MY METHODS, OUR ARMY WILL CRUSH THE GODLESS HORDES THAT THREATEN US.
WE BOTH GET WHAT WE WANT, EH? YOU PROVE THAT YOU ARE A GREAT GENERAL AND I DEMONSTRATE THAT EVERY OTHER SCIENTIST WHO EVER LIVED... STANDS IN MY SHADOW.

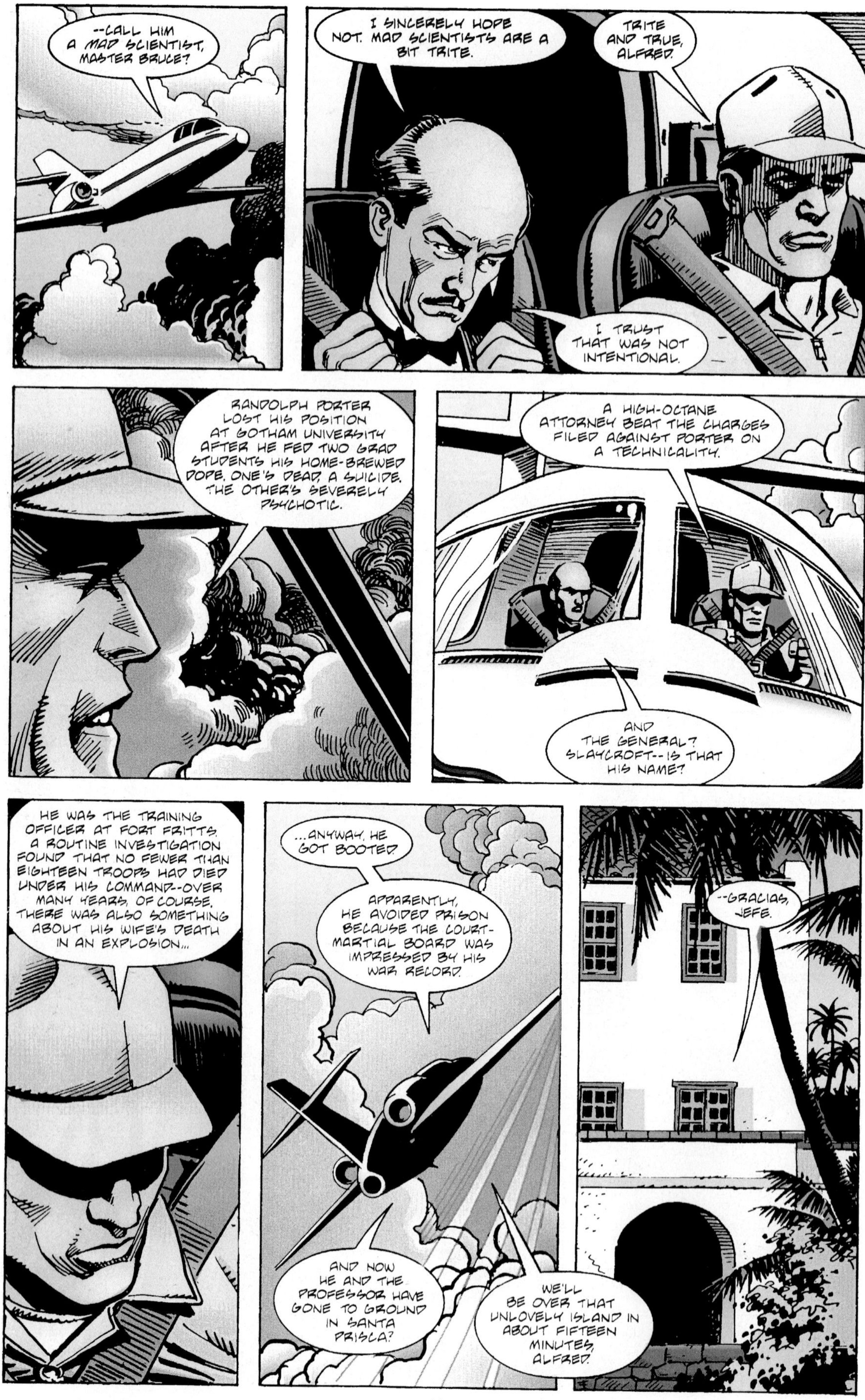
--CALL HIM A MAD SCIENTIST, MASTER BRUCE?
I SINCERELY HOPE NOT. MAD SCIENTISTS ARE A BIT TRITE.
TRITE AND TRUE, ALFRED.
I TRUST THAT WAS NOT INTENTIONAL.
RANDOLPH PORTER LOST HIS POSITION AT GOTHAM UNIVERSITY AFTER HE FED TWO GRAD STUDENTS HIS HOME-BREWED DOPE. ONE'S DEAD, A SUICIDE. THE OTHER'S SEVERELY PSYCHOTIC.
A HIGH-OCTANE ATTORNEY BEAT THE CHARGES FILED AGAINST PORTER ON A TECHNICALITY.
AND THE GENERAL? SLAYCROFT--IS THAT HIS NAME?
HE WAS THE TRAINING OFFICER AT FORT FRITTS. A ROUTINE INVESTIGATION FOUND THAT NO FEWER THAN EIGHTEEN TROOPS HAD DIED UNDER HIS COMMAND--OVER MANY YEARS, OF COURSE. THERE WAS ALSO SOMETHING ABOUT HIS WIFE'S DEATH IN AN EXPLOSION...
...ANYWAY, HE GOT BOOTED.
APPARENTLY, HE AVOIDED PRISON BECAUSE THE COURT-MARTIAL BOARD WAS IMPRESSED BY HIS WAR RECORD.
AND NOW HE AND THE PROFESSOR HAVE GONE TO GROUND IN SANTA PRISCA?
WE'LL BE OVER THAT UNLOVELY ISLAND IN ABOUT FIFTEEN MINUTES, ALFRED.
--GRACIAS, JEFE.

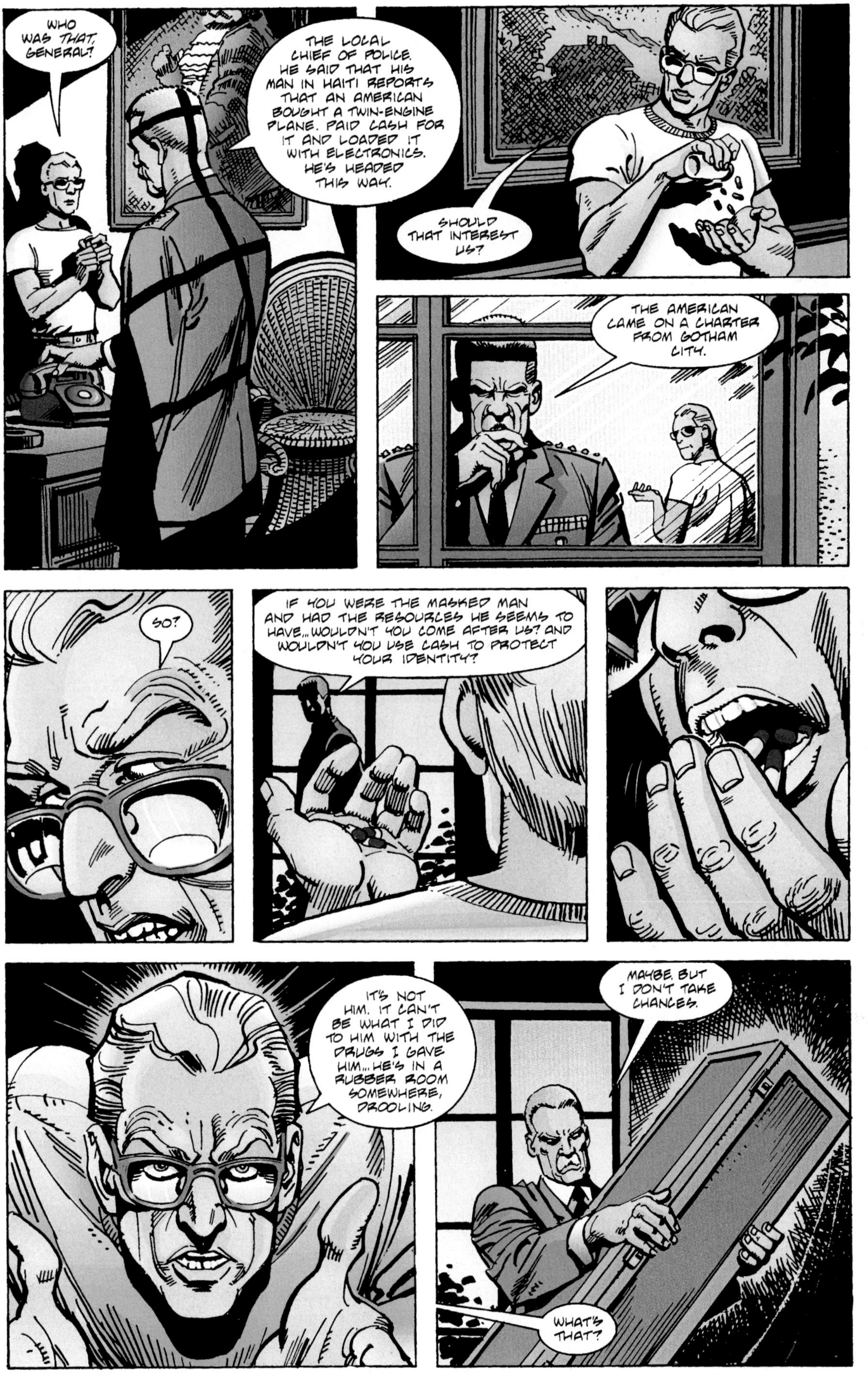
WHO WAS THAT, GENERAL?
THE LOCAL CHIEF OF POLICE. HE SAID THAT HIS MAN IN HAITI REPORTS THAT AN AMERICAN BOUGHT A TWIN-ENGINE PLANE. PAID CASH FOR IT AND LOADED IT WITH ELECTRONICS. HE'S HEADED THIS WAY.
SHOULD THAT INTEREST US?
THE AMERICAN CAME ON A CHARTER FROM GOTHAM CITY.
SO?
IF YOU WERE THE MASKED MAN AND HAD THE RESOURCES HE SEEMS TO HAVE...WOULDN'T YOU COME AFTER US? AND WOULDN'T YOU USE CASH TO PROTECT YOUR IDENTITY?
IT'S NOT HIM. IT CAN'T BE WHAT I DID TO HIM WITH THE DRUGS I GAVE HIM... HE'S IN A RUBBER ROOM SOMEWHERE, DROOLING.
MAYBE. BUT I DON'T TAKE CHANCES.
WHAT'S THAT?

A SOVIET-MADE S.A.-SEVEN ROCKET LAUNCHER.

IT WILL BRING DOWN ANYTHING IN THE SKY.

IT IS ESPECIALLY EFFECTIVE AGAINST SMALL TWIN-ENGINE AIRCRAFT.

--SURE ABOUT THIS, MASTER BRUCE?

JUST HOLD IT STEADY, ALFRED. I WANT TO SNAP A FEW PICTURES.

WOULDN'T IT BE EASIER TO BUY POSTCARDS?

I'M NOT GOING TO JUMP INTO ENEMY TERRITORY WITHOUT A FEW RECON PHOTOS. I MAKE IT A POLICY ALWAYS TO KNOW WHAT I'M GETTING INTO--

EXCEPT WHEN YOU DO NOT.

RIGHT. EXCEPT WHEN I DON'T.

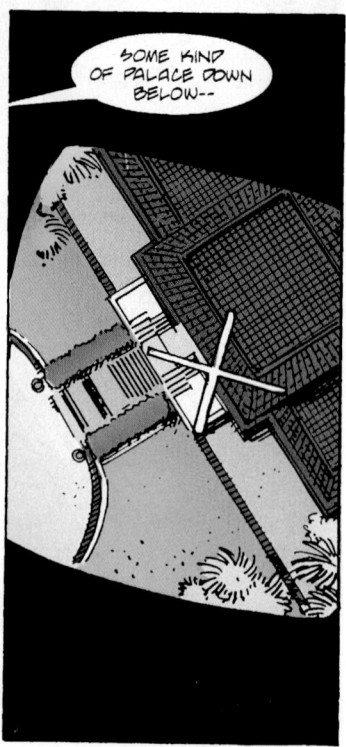

SOME KIND OF PALACE DOWN BELOW--

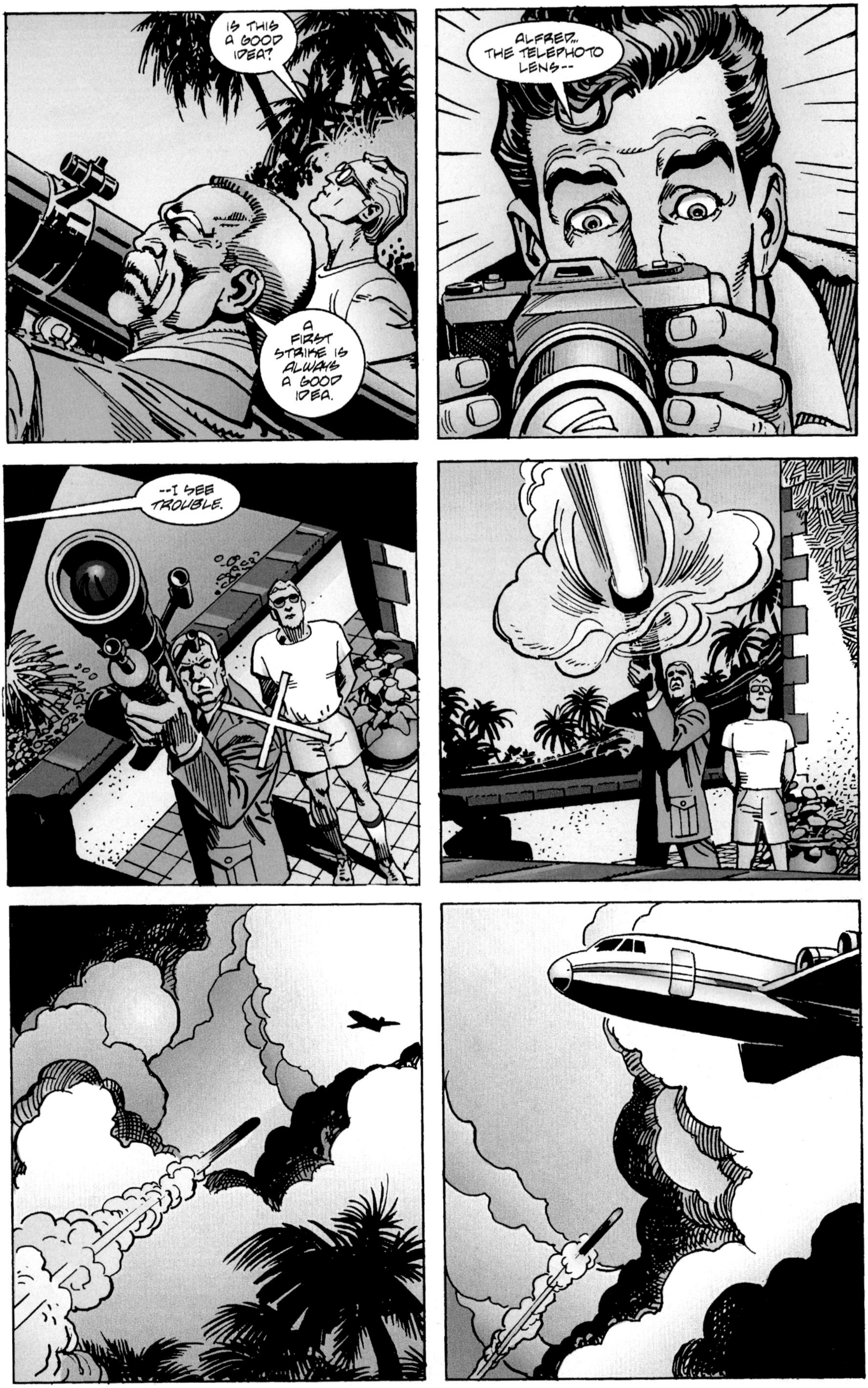
IS THIS A GOOD IDEA?
A FIRST STRIKE IS ALWAYS A GOOD IDEA.
ALFRED... THE TELEPHOTO LENS--
--I SEE TROUBLE.

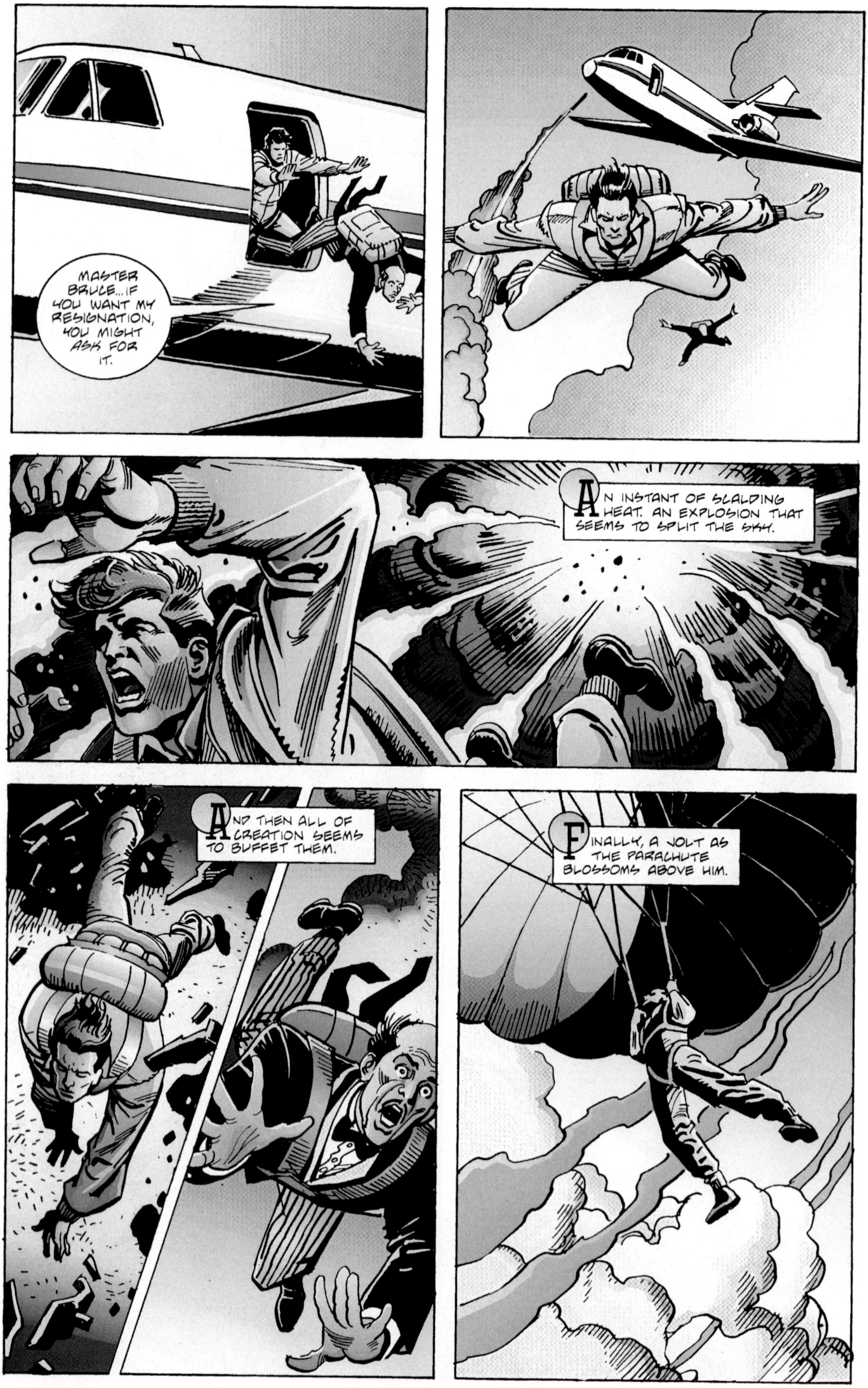
MASTER BRUCE...IF YOU WANT MY RESIGNATION, YOU MIGHT ASK FOR IT.
AN INSTANT OF SCALDING HEAT. AN EXPLOSION THAT SEEMS TO SPLIT THE SKY.
AND THEN ALL OF CREATION SEEMS TO BUFFET THEM.
FINALLY, A JOLT AS THE PARACHUTE BLOSSOMS ABOVE HIM.

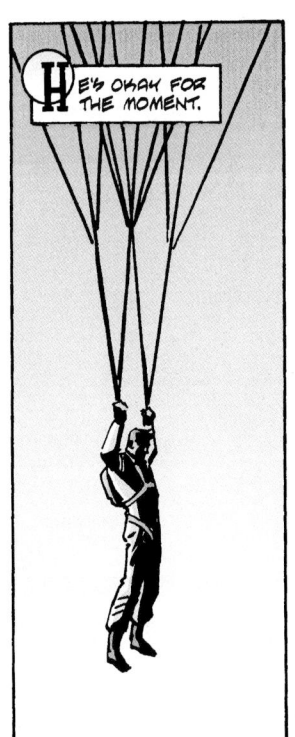

HE'S OKAY FOR THE MOMENT.

--AND SO IS ALFRED. HIS DESCENT WILL CARRY HIM TO THE NORTH END OF THE ISLAND--

--SO BRUCE ANGLES SOUTH AND HOPES THAT WHOEVER DOESN'T LIKE THEM DECIDES TO FOLLOW.

HE PROBABLY WOULDN'T BE RECOGNIZED--BRUCE WAYNE ISN'T *THAT* FAMOUS-- BUT HE'D PREFER TO OPERATE AS BATMAN ANYWAY.

WHEN HE'S BATMAN, THINGS LIKE INVADING AN ISLAND FULL OF HOSTILE RENEGADES DOESN'T SEEM INSANE.

EXACTLY.

ANDALE.

HE'S BEEN SPOTTED.

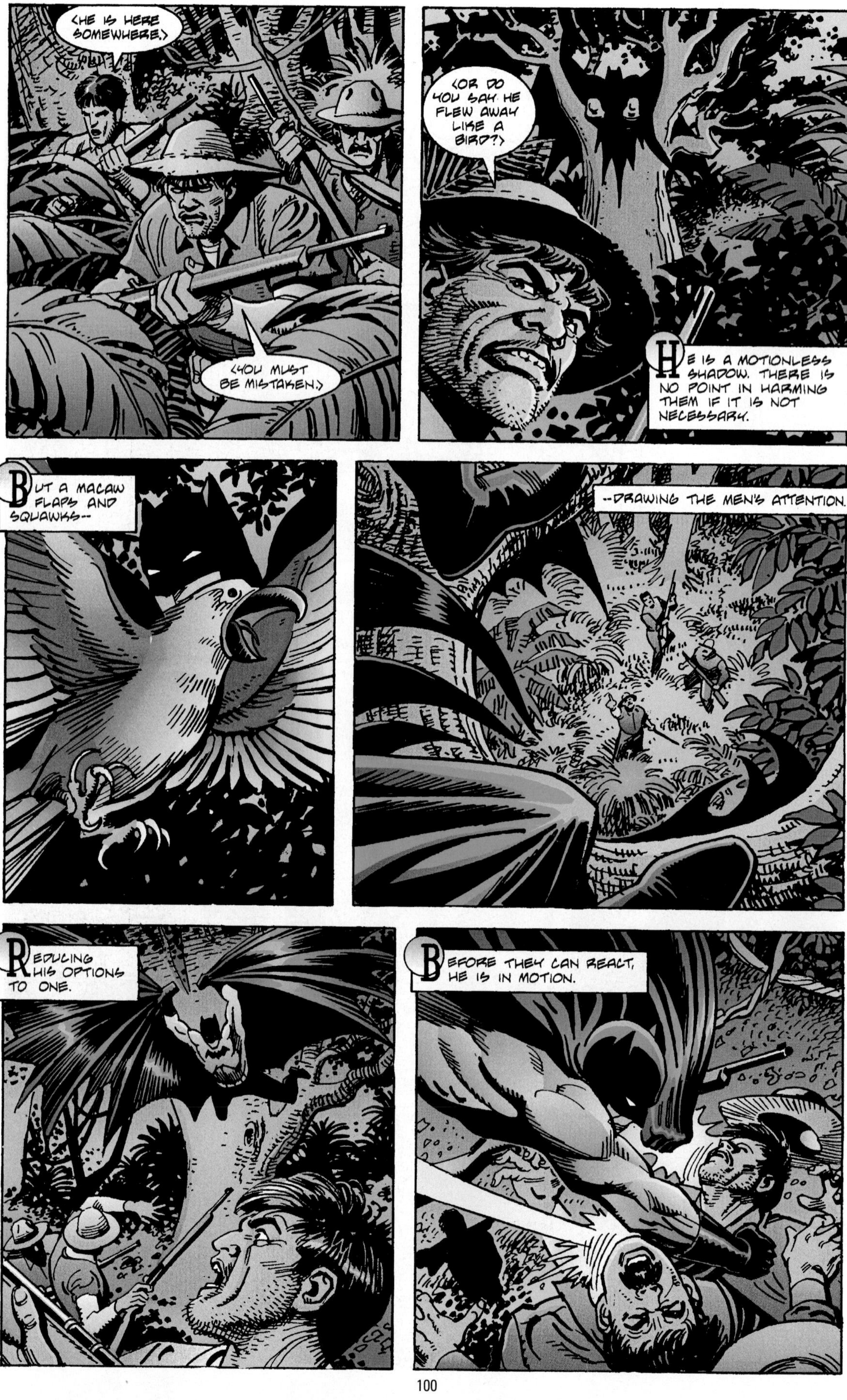
<HE IS HERE SOMEWHERE.>
<YOU MUST BE MISTAKEN.>
<OR DO YOU SAY HE FLEW AWAY LIKE A BIRD?>
HE IS A MOTIONLESS SHADOW. THERE IS NO POINT IN HARMING THEM IF IT IS NOT NECESSARY.
BUT A MACAW FLAPS AND SQUAWKS--
--DRAWING THE MEN'S ATTENTION.
REDUCING HIS OPTIONS TO ONE.
BEFORE THEY CAN REACT, HE IS IN MOTION.

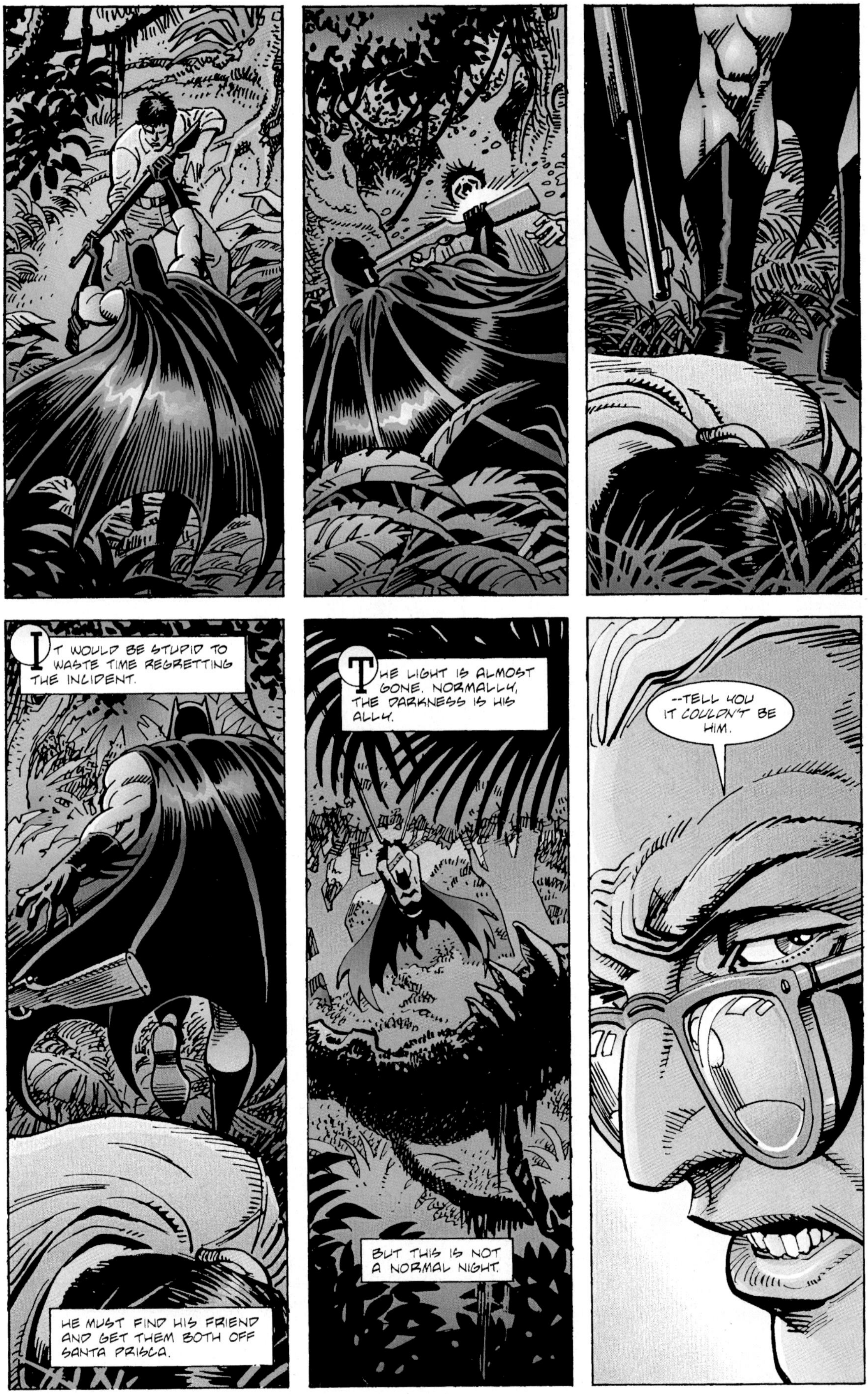
IT WOULD BE STUPID TO WASTE TIME REGRETTING THE INCIDENT.
HE MUST FIND HIS FRIEND AND GET THEM BOTH OFF SANTA PRISCA.
THE LIGHT IS ALMOST GONE. NORMALLY, THE DARKNESS IS HIS ALLY.
BUT THIS IS NOT A NORMAL NIGHT.
--TELL YOU IT COULDN'T BE HIM.

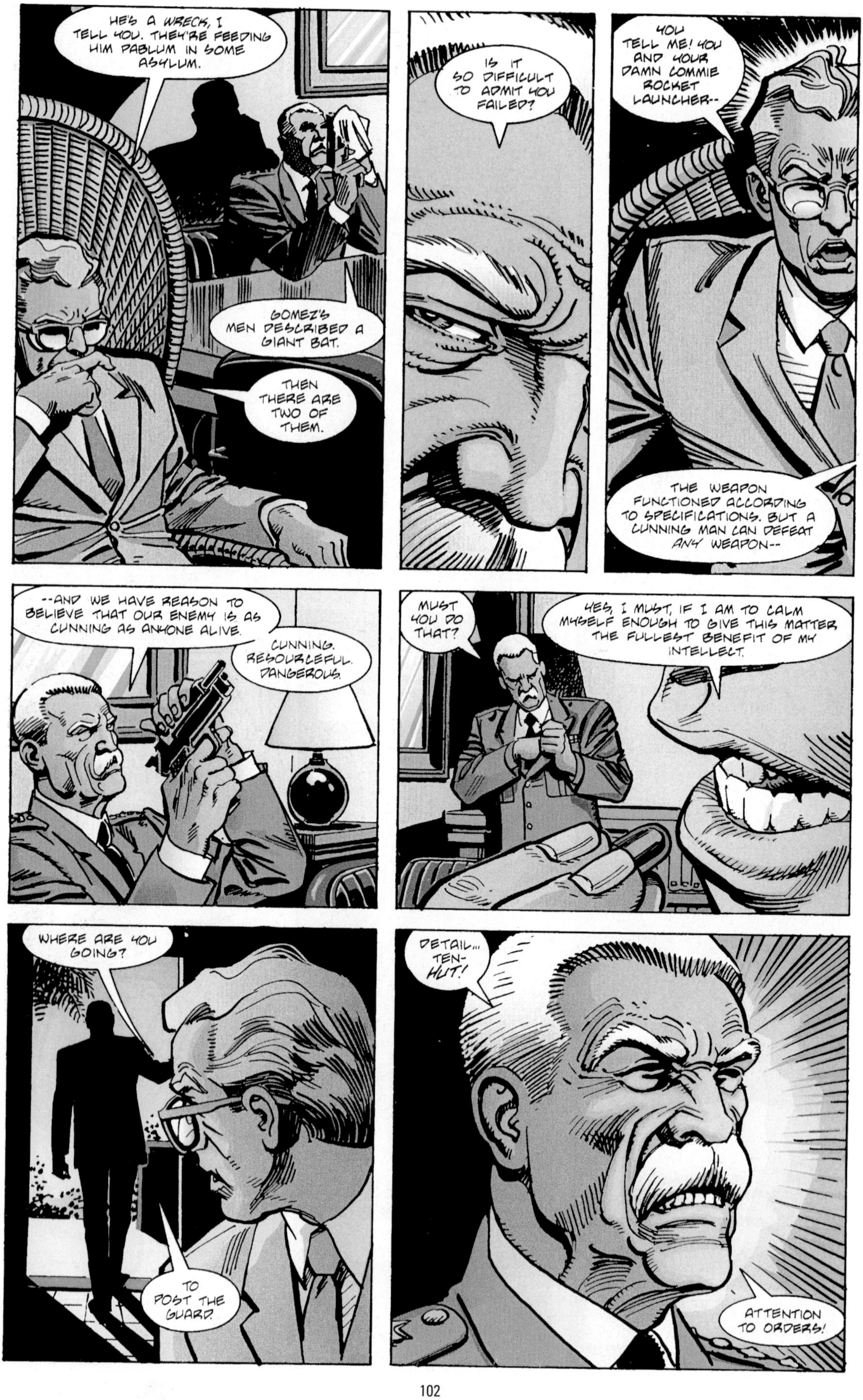
HE'S A WRECK, I TELL YOU. THEY'RE FEEDING HIM PABLUM IN SOME ASYLUM.
GOMEZ'S MEN DESCRIBED A GIANT BAT.
THEN THERE ARE TWO OF THEM.
IS IT SO DIFFICULT TO ADMIT YOU FAILED?
YOU TELL ME! YOU AND YOUR DAMN COMMIE ROCKET LAUNCHER--
THE WEAPON FUNCTIONED ACCORDING TO SPECIFICATIONS. BUT A CUNNING MAN CAN DEFEAT ANY WEAPON--
--AND WE HAVE REASON TO BELIEVE THAT OUR ENEMY IS AS CUNNING AS ANYONE ALIVE.
CUNNING. RESOURCEFUL. DANGEROUS.
MUST YOU DO THAT?
YES, I MUST, IF I AM TO CALM MYSELF ENOUGH TO GIVE THIS MATTER THE FULLEST BENEFIT OF MY INTELLECT.
WHERE ARE YOU GOING?
TO POST THE GUARD.
DETAIL... TEN-HUT!
ATTENTION TO ORDERS!

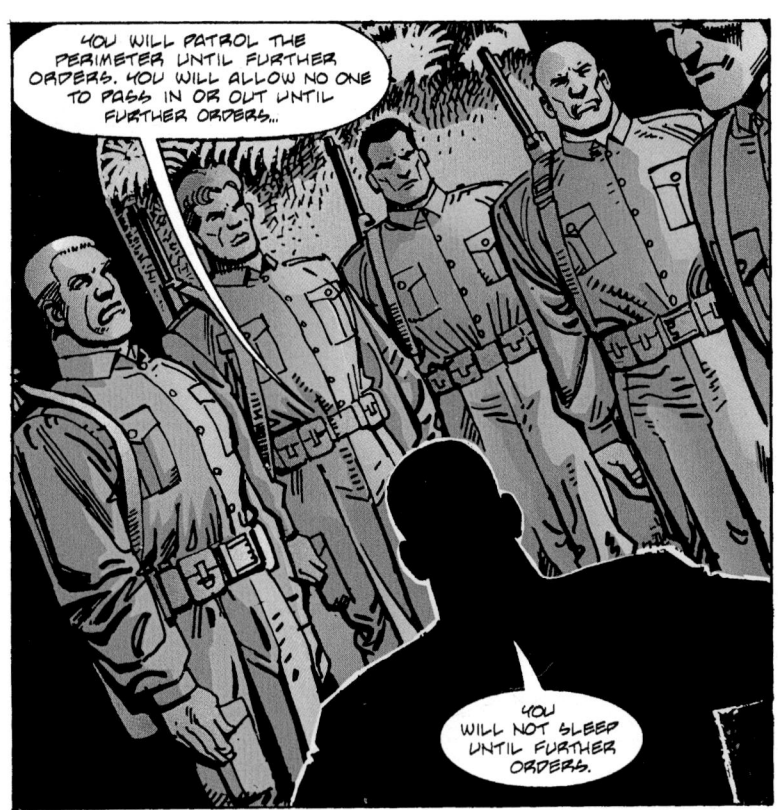

YOU WILL PATROL THE PERIMETER UNTIL FURTHER ORDERS. YOU WILL ALLOW NO ONE TO PASS IN OR OUT UNTIL FURTHER ORDERS...

YOU WILL NOT SLEEP UNTIL FURTHER ORDERS.

DISMISSED!

WE SHOULD BE SAFE.

BETWEEN YOUR ZOMBIE SQUAD AND GOMEZ'S MEN, I SHOULD HOPE SO.

I DON'T TRUST GOMEZ.

YOU SHOULD. HE'S VERY GRATEFUL TO ME, YOU KNOW.

WHY?

I SHOWED HIM A SIMPLE TRICK USING COCAINE. HIS AGENTS WILL PASS IT ON TO THEIR CUSTOMERS IN THE STATES--

--AND THAT WILL CREATE A HUGE DEMAND FOR THE PRODUCT.

I STILL DON'T TRUST HIM.

THE PHONE. GET IT, WILL YOU? MY SPANISH IS STILL LIMITED TO "BUENOS DIAS."

SI?

103

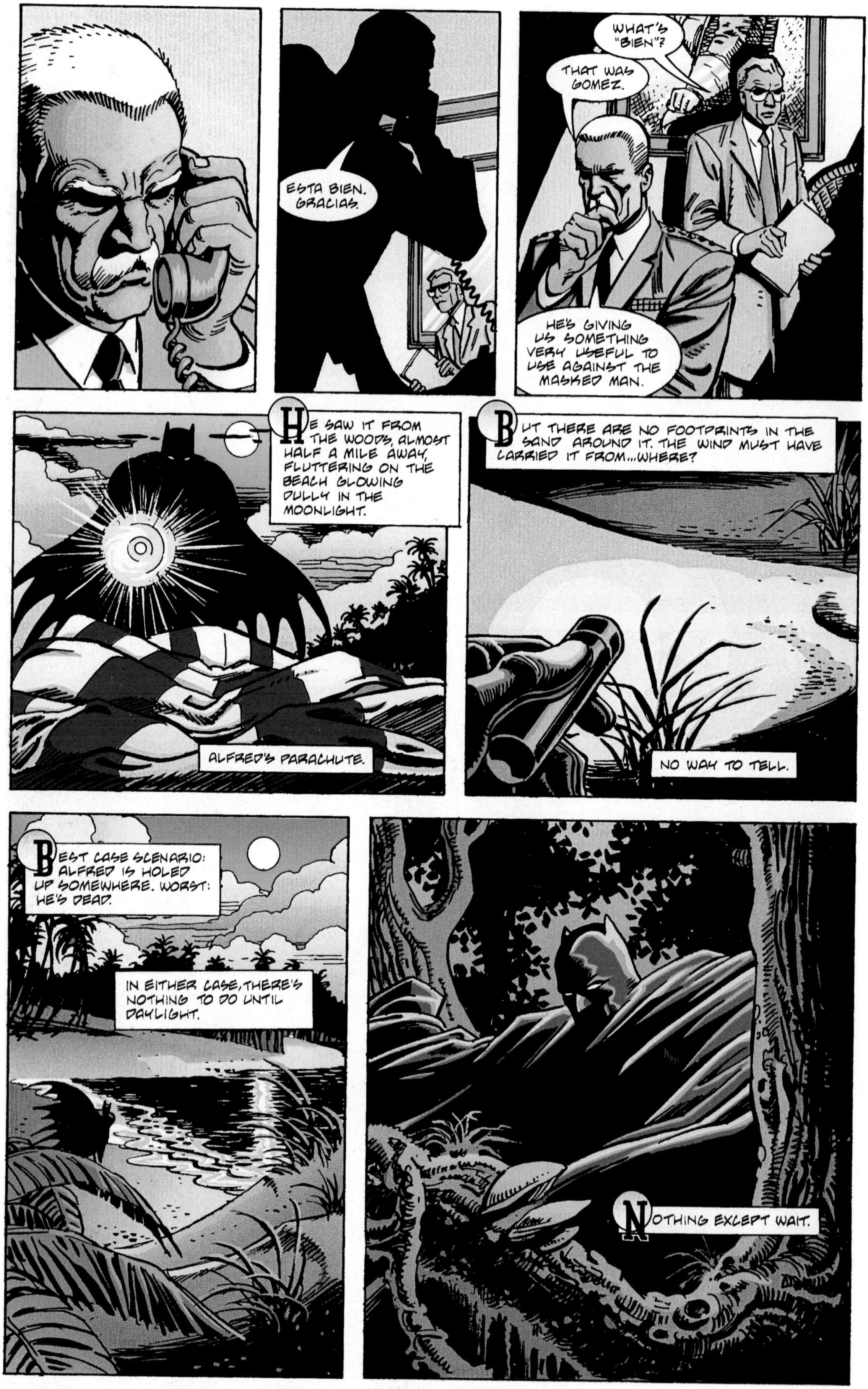
ESTA BIEN. GRACIAS.
WHAT'S "BIEN"?
THAT WAS GOMEZ.
HE'S GIVING US SOMETHING VERY USEFUL TO USE AGAINST THE MASKED MAN.
HE SAW IT FROM THE WOODS, ALMOST HALF A MILE AWAY, FLUTTERING ON THE BEACH GLOWING DULLY IN THE MOONLIGHT.
ALFRED'S PARACHUTE.
BUT THERE ARE NO FOOTPRINTS IN THE SAND AROUND IT. THE WIND MUST HAVE CARRIED IT FROM...WHERE?
NO WAY TO TELL.
BEST CASE SCENARIO: ALFRED IS HOLED UP SOMEWHERE. WORST: HE'S DEAD.
IN EITHER CASE, THERE'S NOTHING TO DO UNTIL DAYLIGHT.
NOTHING EXCEPT WAIT.

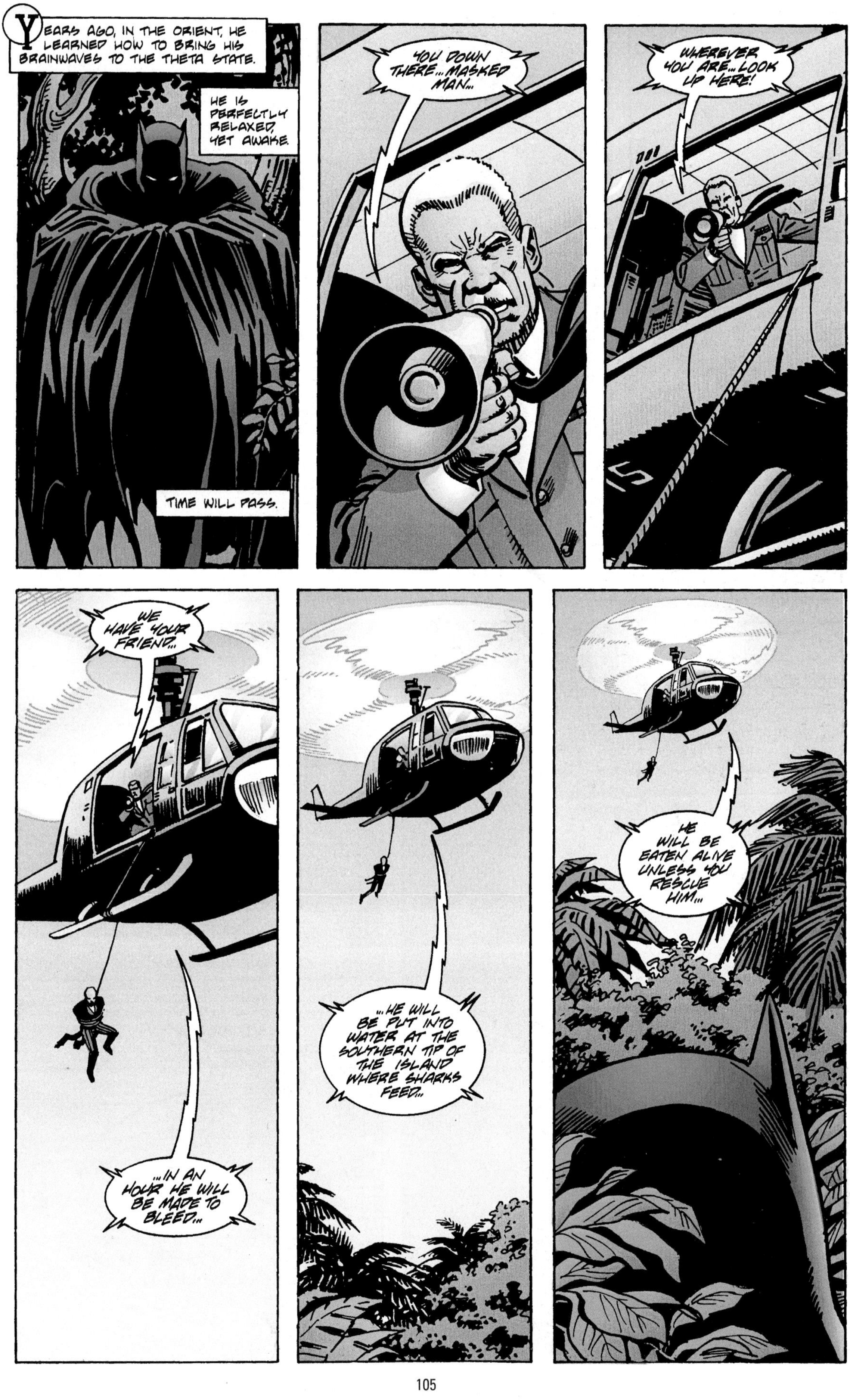
YEARS AGO, IN THE ORIENT, HE LEARNED HOW TO BRING HIS BRAINWAVES TO THE THETA STATE.
HE IS PERFECTLY RELAXED, YET AWAKE.
TIME WILL PASS.
YOU DOWN THERE...MASKED MAN...
WHEREVER YOU ARE...LOOK UP HERE!
WE HAVE YOUR FRIEND...
...IN AN HOUR HE WILL BE MADE TO BLEED...
...HE WILL BE PUT INTO WATER AT THE SOUTHERN TIP OF THE ISLAND WHERE SHARKS FEED...
HE WILL BE EATEN ALIVE UNLESS YOU RESCUE HIM...

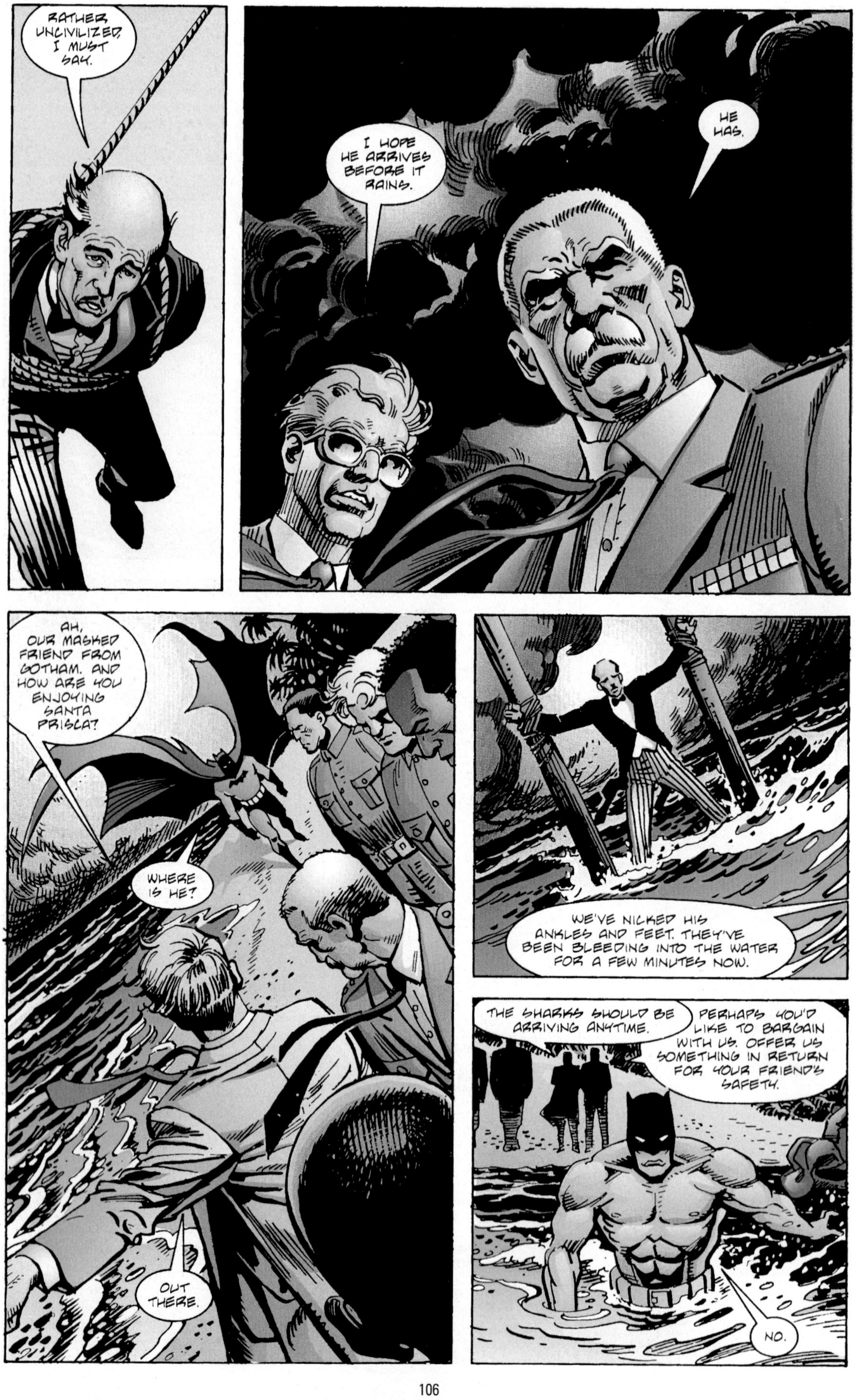
RATHER UNCIVILIZED, I MUST SAY.
I HOPE HE ARRIVES BEFORE IT RAINS.
HE HAS.
AH, OUR MASKED FRIEND FROM GOTHAM. AND HOW ARE YOU ENJOYING SANTA PRISCA?
WHERE IS HE?
OUT THERE.
WE'VE NICKED HIS ANKLES AND FEET. THEY'VE BEEN BLEEDING INTO THE WATER FOR A FEW MINUTES NOW.
THE SHARKS SHOULD BE ARRIVING ANYTIME.
PERHAPS YOU'D LIKE TO BARGAIN WITH US. OFFER US SOMETHING IN RETURN FOR YOUR FRIEND'S SAFETY.
NO.

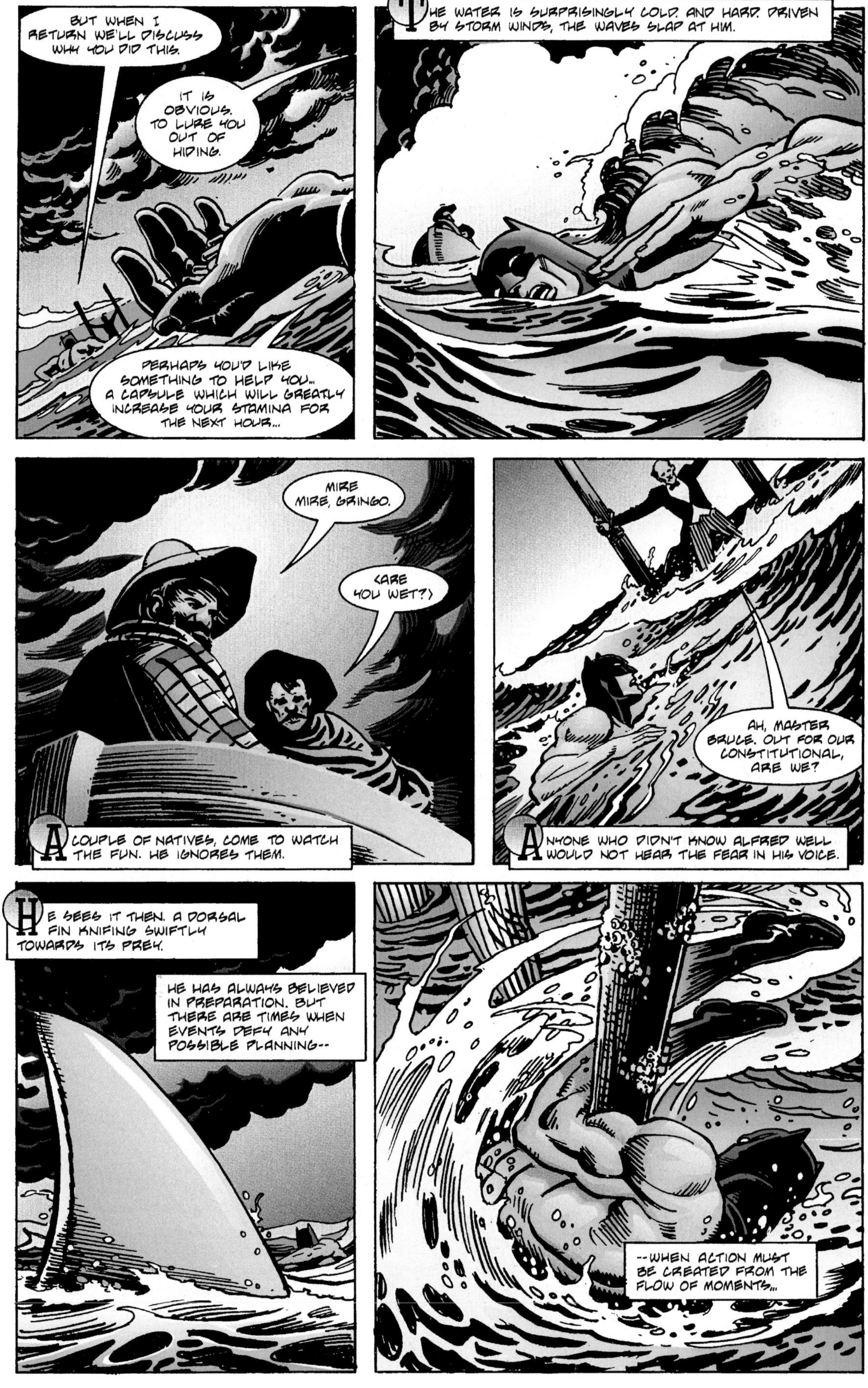
BUT WHEN I RETURN WE'LL DISCUSS WHY YOU DID THIS.
IT IS OBVIOUS. TO LURE YOU OUT OF HIDING.
PERHAPS YOU'D LIKE SOMETHING TO HELP YOU... A CAPSULE WHICH WILL GREATLY INCREASE YOUR STAMINA FOR THE NEXT HOUR...
THE WATER IS SURPRISINGLY COLD. AND HARD. DRIVEN BY STORM WINDS, THE WAVES SLAP AT HIM.
MIRE MIRE, GRINGO.
<ARE YOU WET?>
A COUPLE OF NATIVES, COME TO WATCH THE FUN. HE IGNORES THEM.
AH, MASTER BRUCE. OUT FOR OUR CONSTITUTIONAL, ARE WE?
ANYONE WHO DIDN'T KNOW ALFRED WELL WOULD NOT HEAR THE FEAR IN HIS VOICE.
HE SEES IT THEN. A DORSAL FIN KNIFING SWIFTLY TOWARDS ITS PREY.
HE HAS ALWAYS BELIEVED IN PREPARATION. BUT THERE ARE TIMES WHEN EVENTS DEFY ANY POSSIBLE PLANNING--
--WHEN ACTION MUST BE CREATED FROM THE FLOW OF MOMENTS...

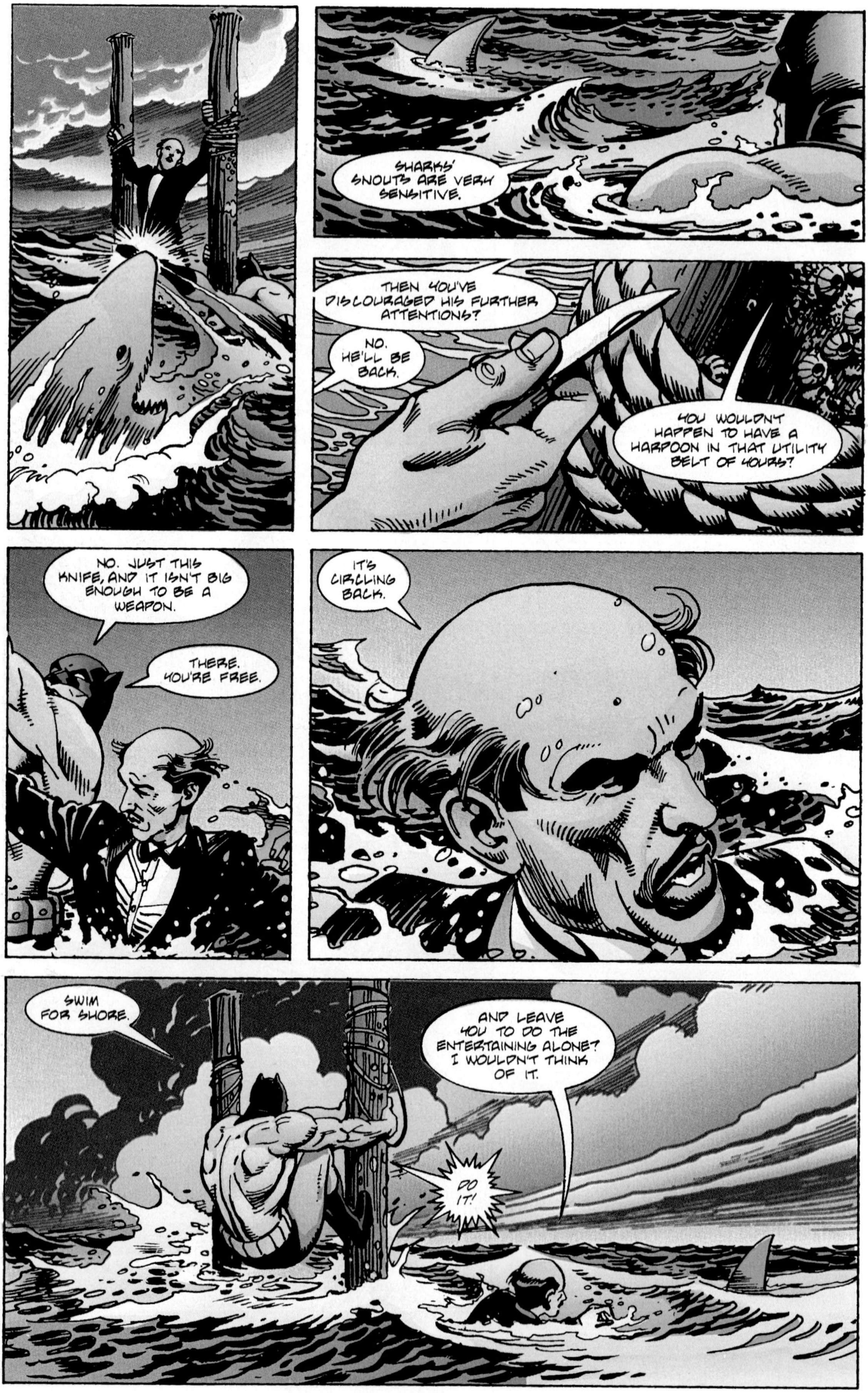
SHARKS' SNOUTS ARE VERY SENSITIVE.
THEN YOU'VE DISCOURAGED HIS FURTHER ATTENTIONS?
NO. HE'LL BE BACK.
YOU WOULDN'T HAPPEN TO HAVE A HARPOON IN THAT UTILITY BELT OF YOURS?
NO. JUST THIS KNIFE, AND IT ISN'T BIG ENOUGH TO BE A WEAPON.
THERE. YOU'RE FREE.
IT'S CIRCLING BACK.
SWIM FOR SHORE.
AND LEAVE YOU TO DO THE ENTERTAINING ALONE? I WOULDN'T THINK OF IT.
DO IT!

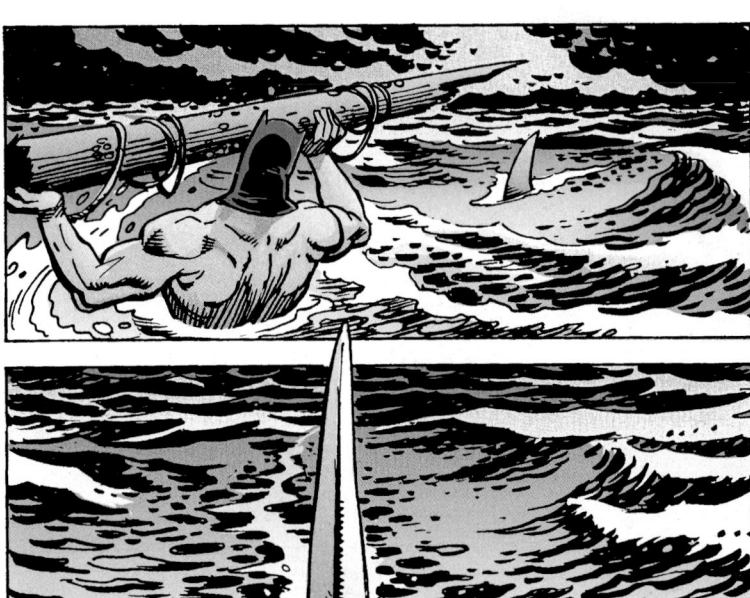
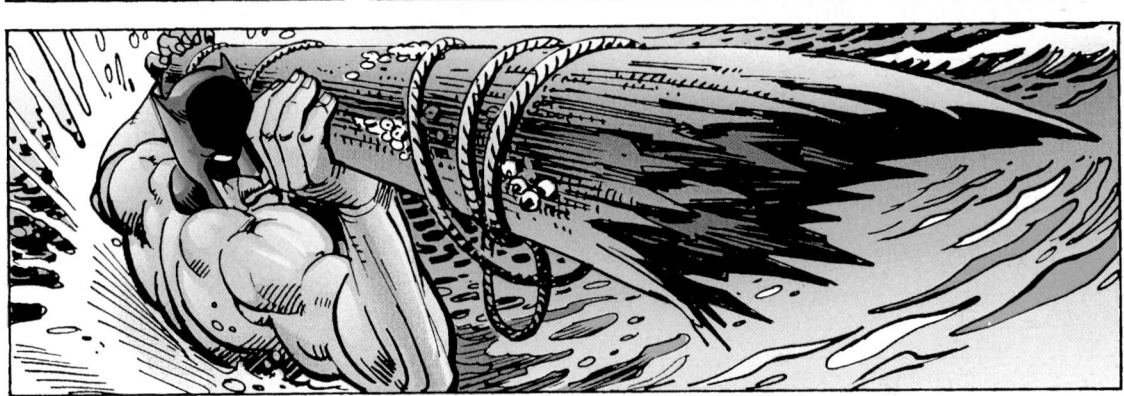

A FINAL REFLEX...A RAZORY FIN TEARS THROUGH FLESH.

-- AND THE SALT WATER SENDS A SHOCK OF AGONY THROUGH HIM...

MASTER BRUCE...

...THERE ARE MORE...

YES. TWO OF THEM ARE FEASTING ON THE ONE I KILLED, BUT THE THIRD HAS A YEN FOR US.

WE'LL NEVER BE ABLE TO OUTSWIM IT--

WE DON'T HAVE TO. HEAD FOR THE BOAT.

GRINGO... VAYA!

I DON'T SUPPOSE YOU CHAPS WOULD HAVE A BOTTLE OF SUNTAN LOTION I MIGHT BORROW?

PERO NO CON DIOS--

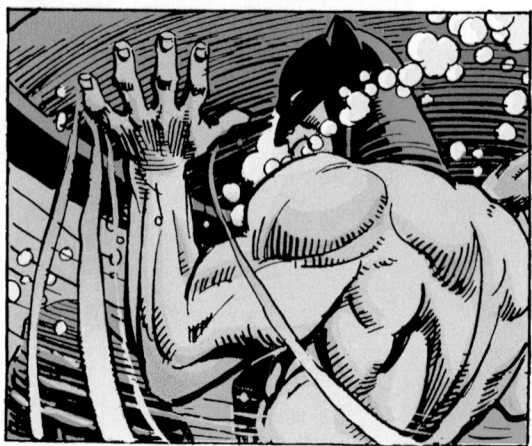

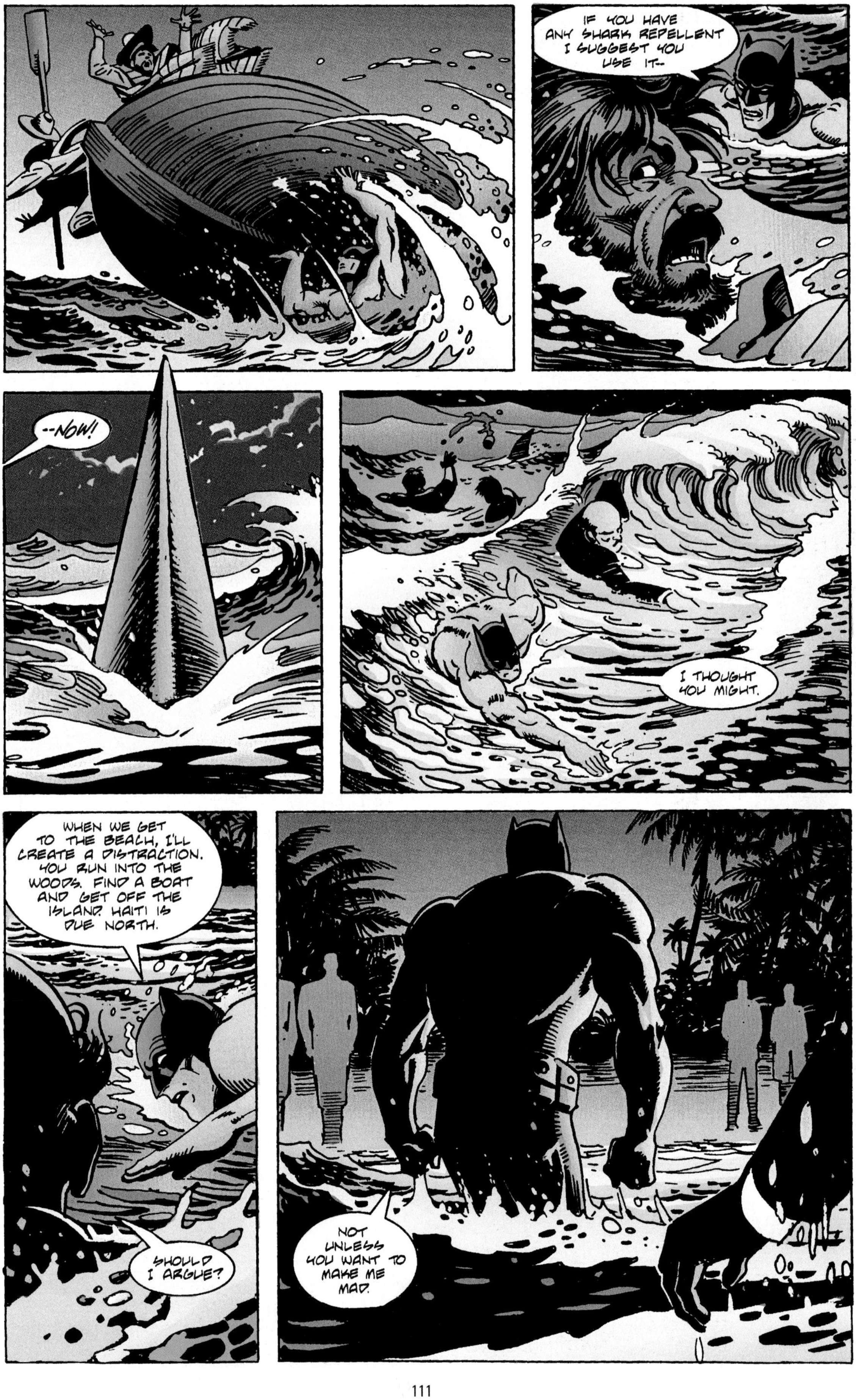
IF YOU HAVE ANY SHARK REPELLENT I SUGGEST YOU USE IT--
--NOW!
I THOUGHT YOU MIGHT.
WHEN WE GET TO THE BEACH, I'LL CREATE A DISTRACTION. YOU RUN INTO THE WOODS. FIND A BOAT AND GET OFF THE ISLAND. HAITI IS DUE NORTH.
SHOULD I ARGUE?
NOT UNLESS YOU WANT TO MAKE ME MAD.

AN IMPRESSIVE PERFORMANCE. BUT I SEE YOU'RE WOUNDED. I CAN OFFER YOU SOME EXCELLENT PAINKILLERS--

USE THEM YOURSELF.

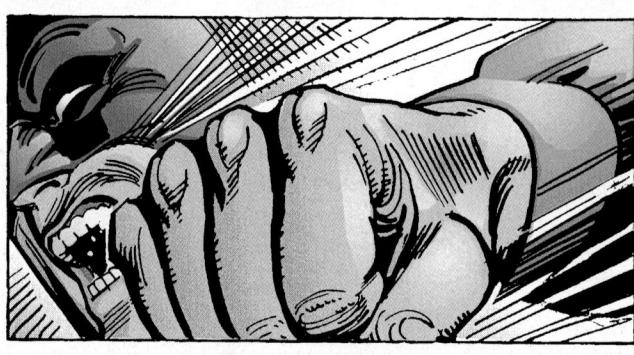

PRIVATE SLAYCROFT, ATTENTION TO ORDERS--

EXECUTE HIM.

To be concluded.

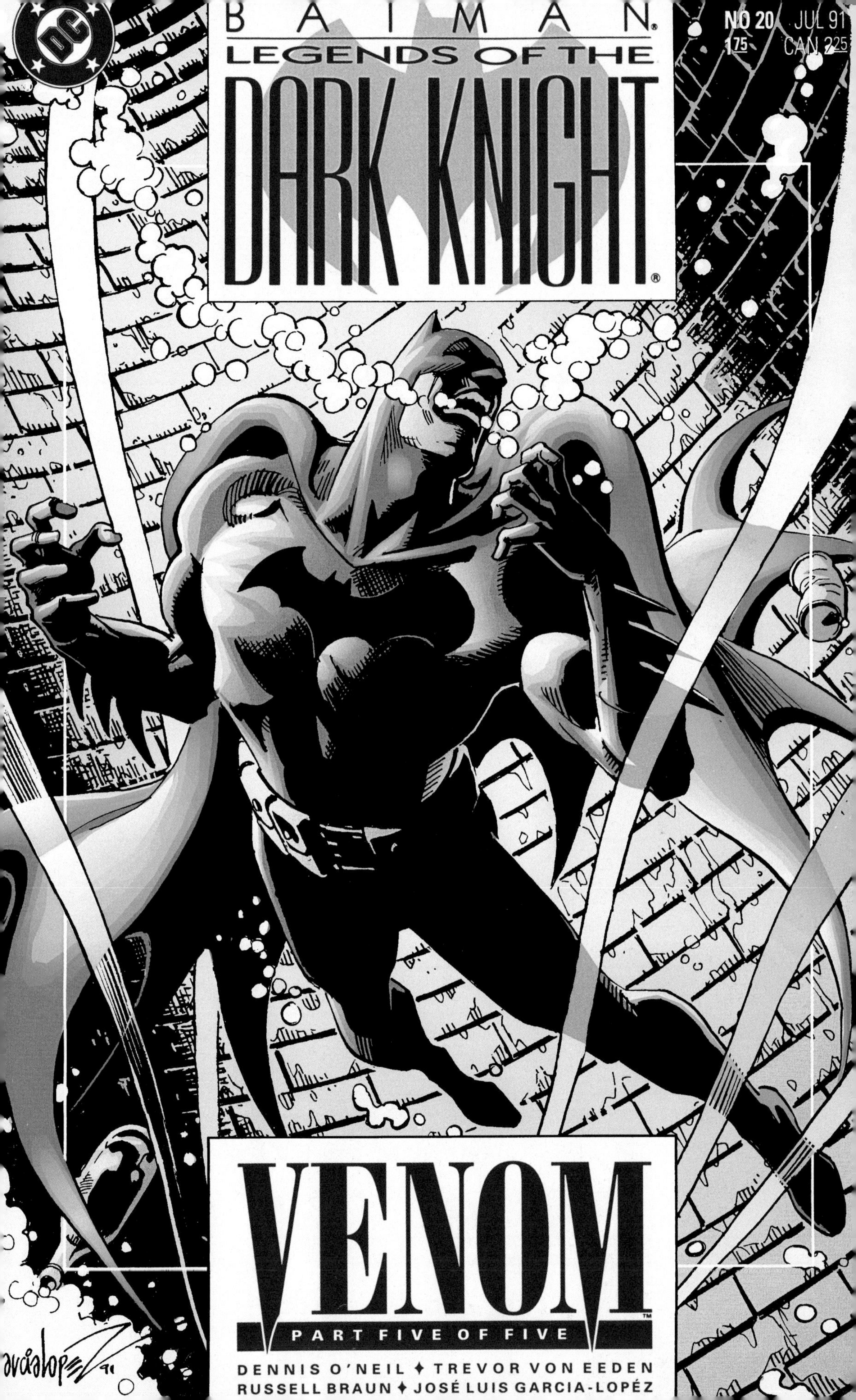

DC
BATMAN
LEGENDS OF THE
DARK KNIGHT
NO 20 JUL 91
1.75 CAN 2.25
VENOM
PART FIVE OF FIVE
DENNIS O'NEIL ✦ TREVOR VON EEDEN
RUSSELL BRAUN ✦ JOSÉ LUIS GARCIA-LOPÉZ

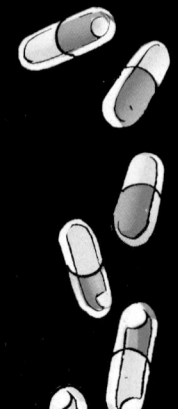

VENOM: PART FIVE

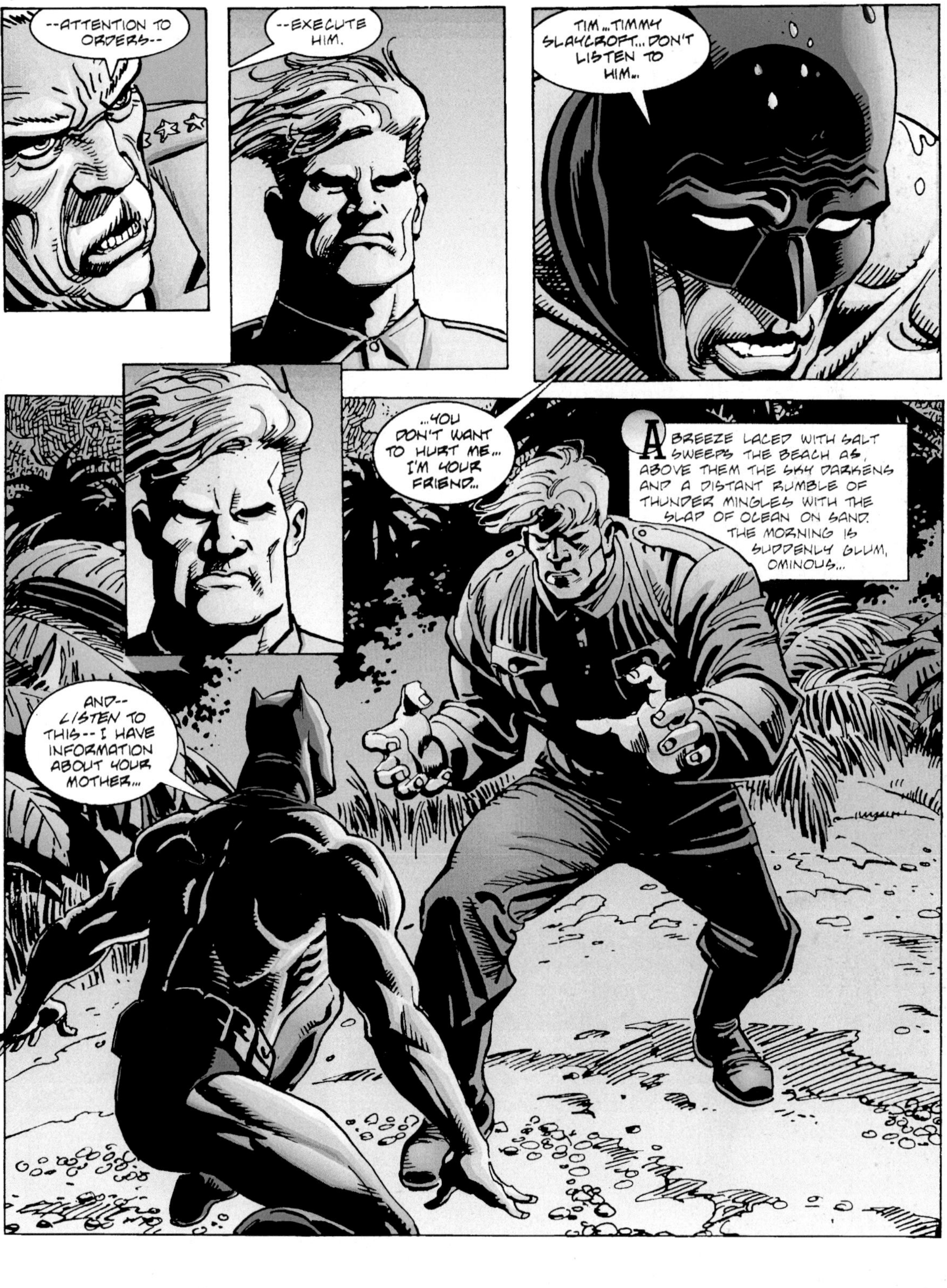
--ATTENTION TO ORDERS--
--EXECUTE HIM.
TIM...TIMMY SLAYCROFT...DON'T LISTEN TO HIM...
...YOU DON'T WANT TO HURT ME... I'M YOUR FRIEND...
A BREEZE LACED WITH SALT SWEEPS THE BEACH AS, ABOVE THEM THE SKY DARKENS AND A DISTANT RUMBLE OF THUNDER MINGLES WITH THE SLAP OF OCEAN ON SAND. THE MORNING IS SUDDENLY GLUM, OMINOUS...
AND-- LISTEN TO THIS-- I HAVE INFORMATION ABOUT YOUR MOTHER...

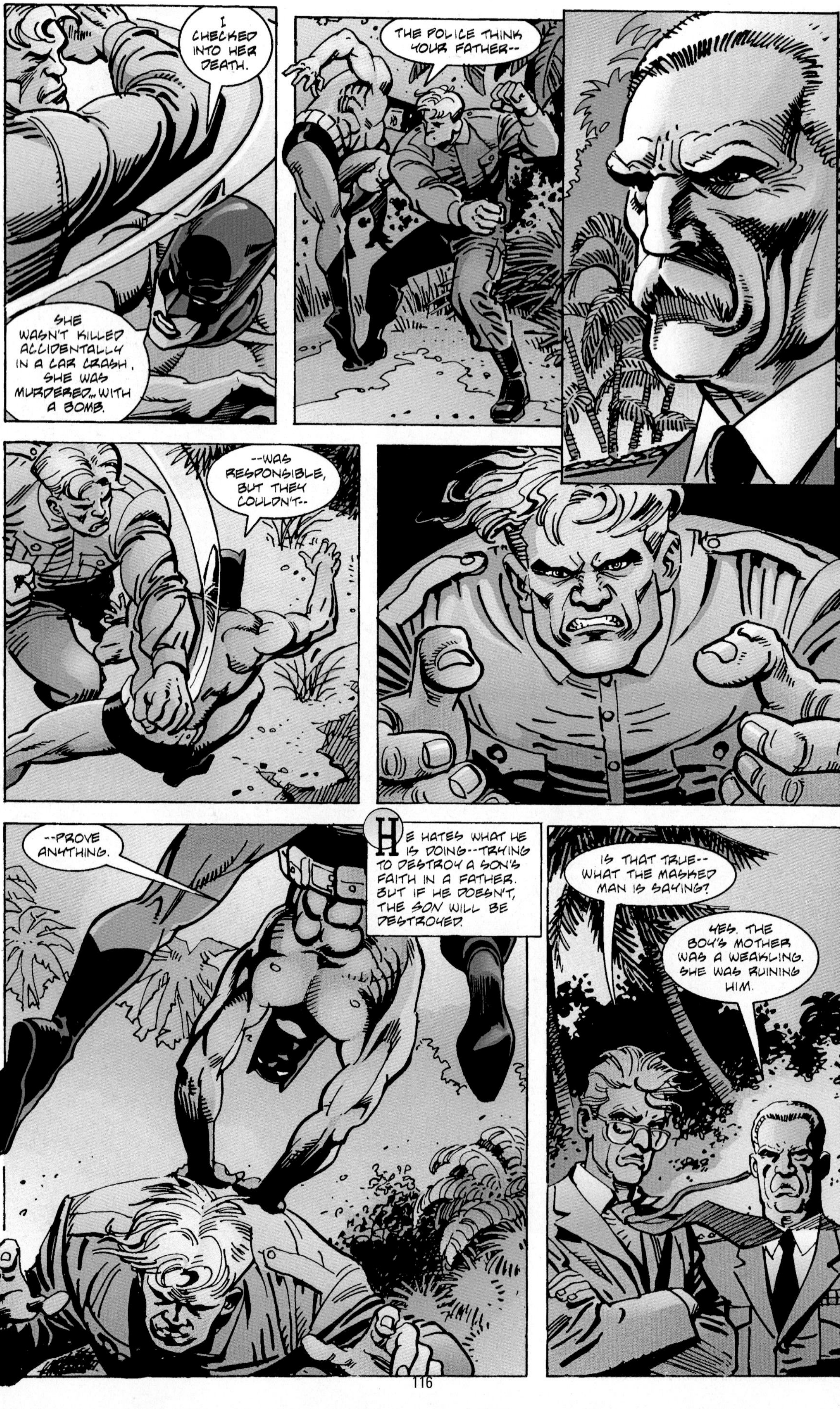
I CHECKED INTO HER DEATH.
SHE WASN'T KILLED ACCIDENTALLY IN A CAR CRASH. SHE WAS MURDERED... WITH A BOMB.
THE POLICE THINK YOUR FATHER--
--WAS RESPONSIBLE, BUT THEY COULDN'T-
--PROVE ANYTHING.
HE HATES WHAT HE IS DOING--TRYING TO DESTROY A SON'S FAITH IN A FATHER. BUT IF HE DOESN'T, THE SON WILL BE DESTROYED.
IS THAT TRUE-- WHAT THE MASKED MAN IS SAYING?
YES. THE BOY'S MOTHER WAS A WEAKLING. SHE WAS RUINING HIM.

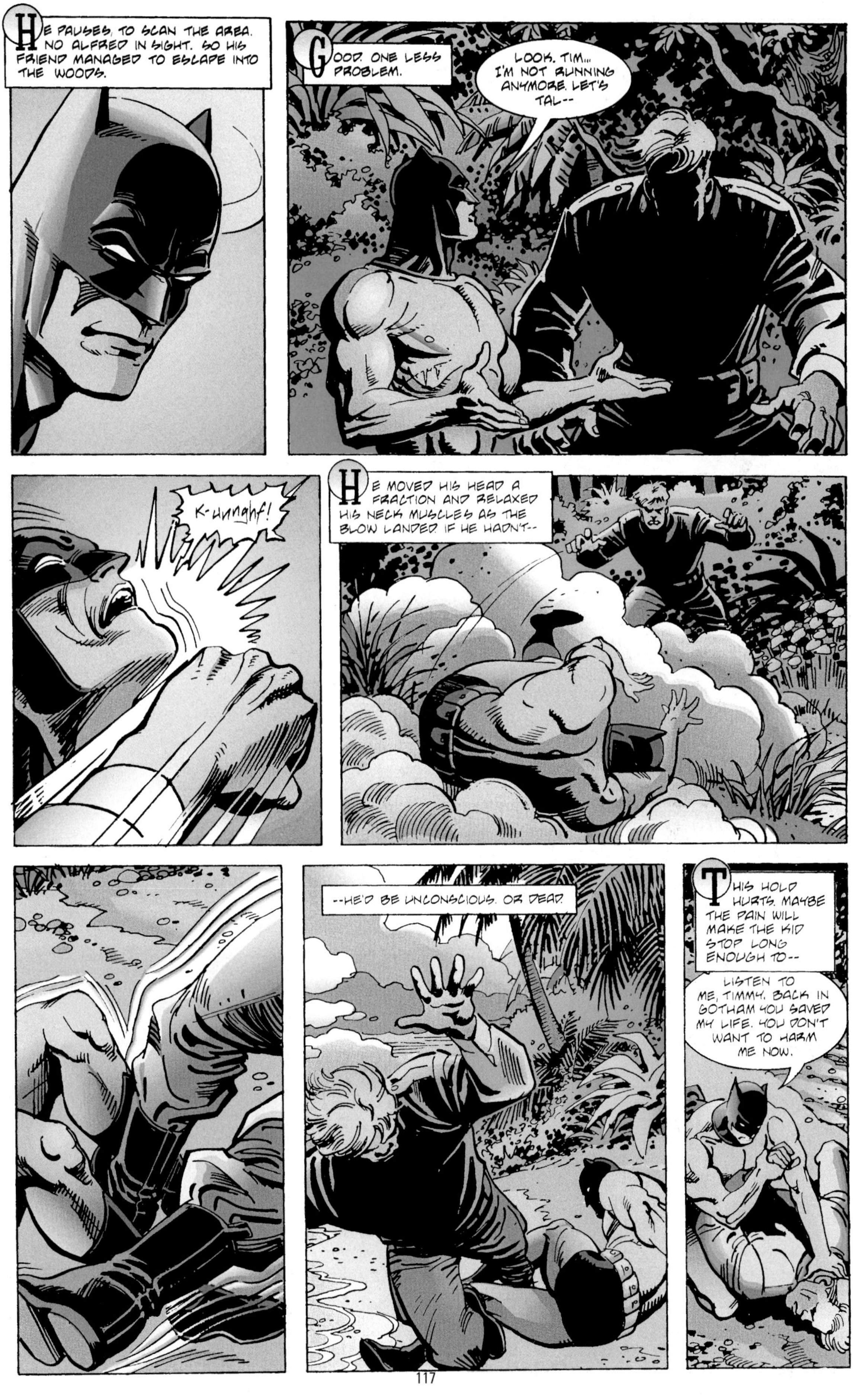
HE PAUSES, TO SCAN THE AREA. NO ALFRED IN SIGHT. SO HIS FRIEND MANAGED TO ESCAPE INTO THE WOODS.
GOOD. ONE LESS PROBLEM.
LOOK, TIM... I'M NOT RUNNING ANYMORE. LET'S TAL--
K-UNNGHF!
HE MOVED HIS HEAD A FRACTION AND RELAXED HIS NECK MUSCLES AS THE BLOW LANDED. IF HE HADN'T--
--HE'D BE UNCONSCIOUS. OR DEAD.
THIS HOLD HURTS. MAYBE THE PAIN WILL MAKE THE KID STOP LONG ENOUGH TO--
LISTEN TO ME, TIMMY. BACK IN GOTHAM YOU SAVED MY LIFE. YOU DON'T WANT TO HARM ME NOW.

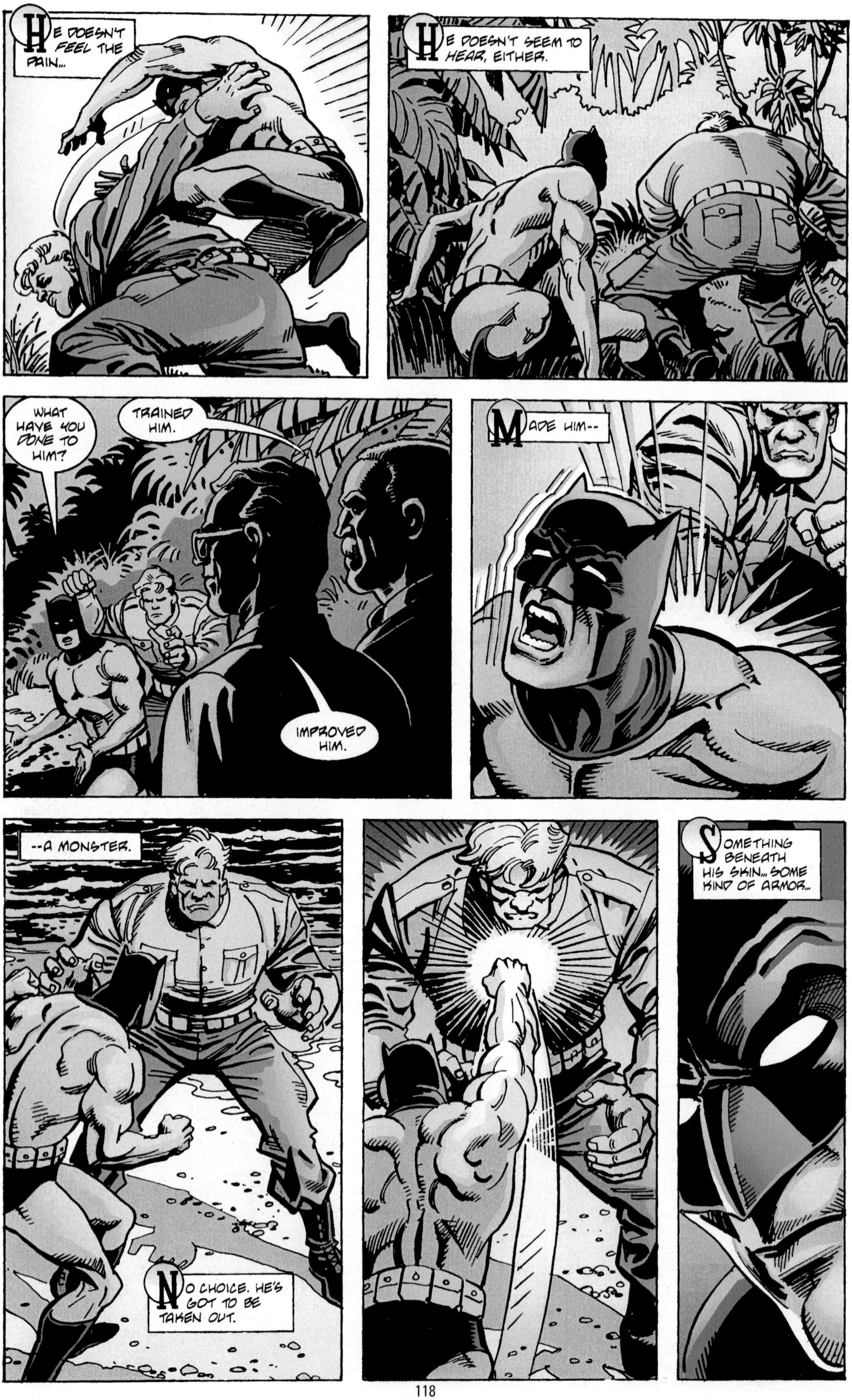
HE DOESN'T FEEL THE PAIN...
HE DOESN'T SEEM TO HEAR, EITHER.
WHAT HAVE YOU DONE TO HIM?
TRAINED HIM.
IMPROVED HIM.
MADE HIM--
--A MONSTER.
NO CHOICE. HE'S GOT TO BE TAKEN OUT.
SOMETHING BENEATH HIS SKIN... SOME KIND OF ARMOR...

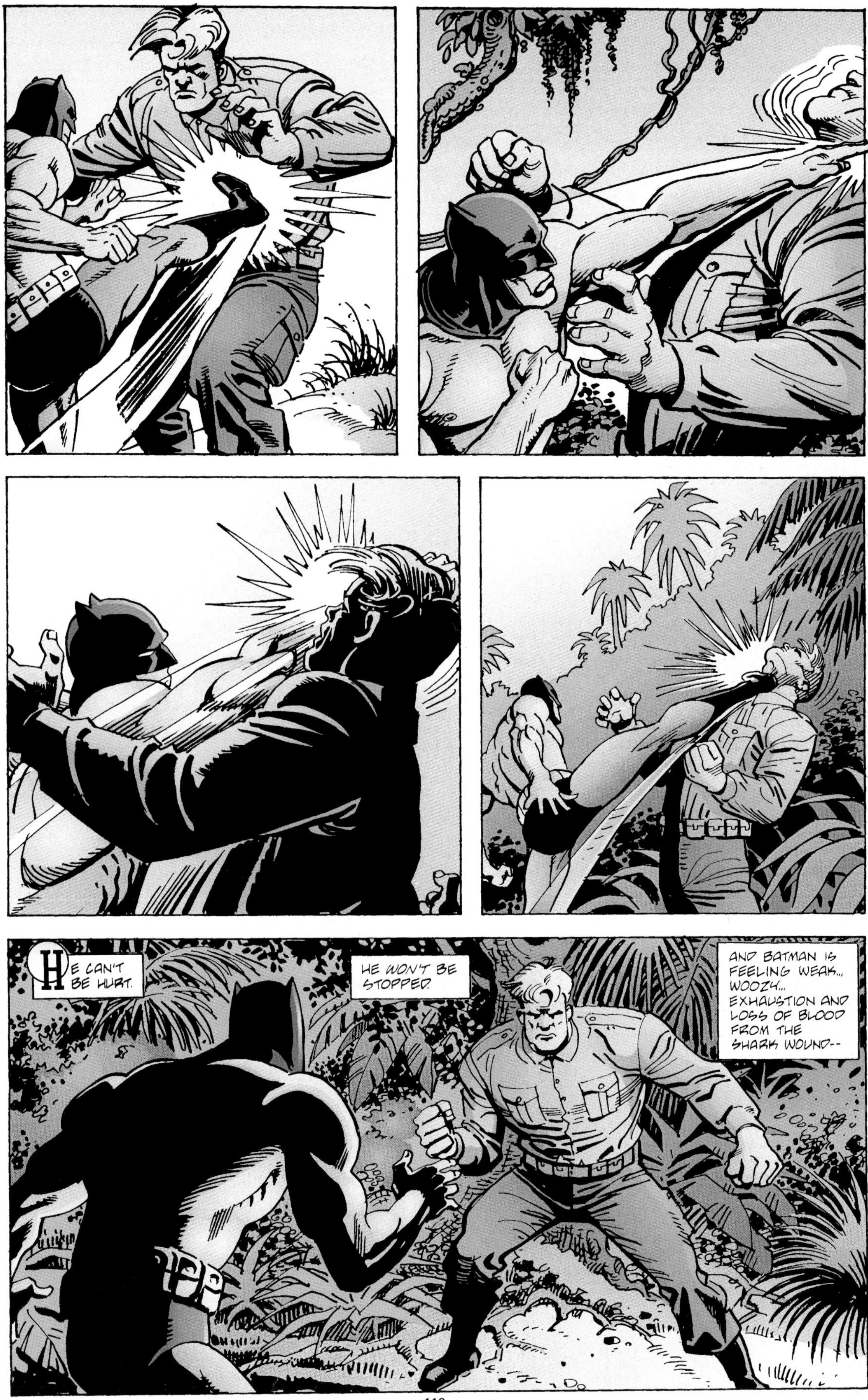
HE CAN'T BE HURT.
HE WON'T BE STOPPED.
AND BATMAN IS FEELING WEAK... WOOZY... EXHAUSTION AND LOSS OF BLOOD FROM THE SHARK WOUND--

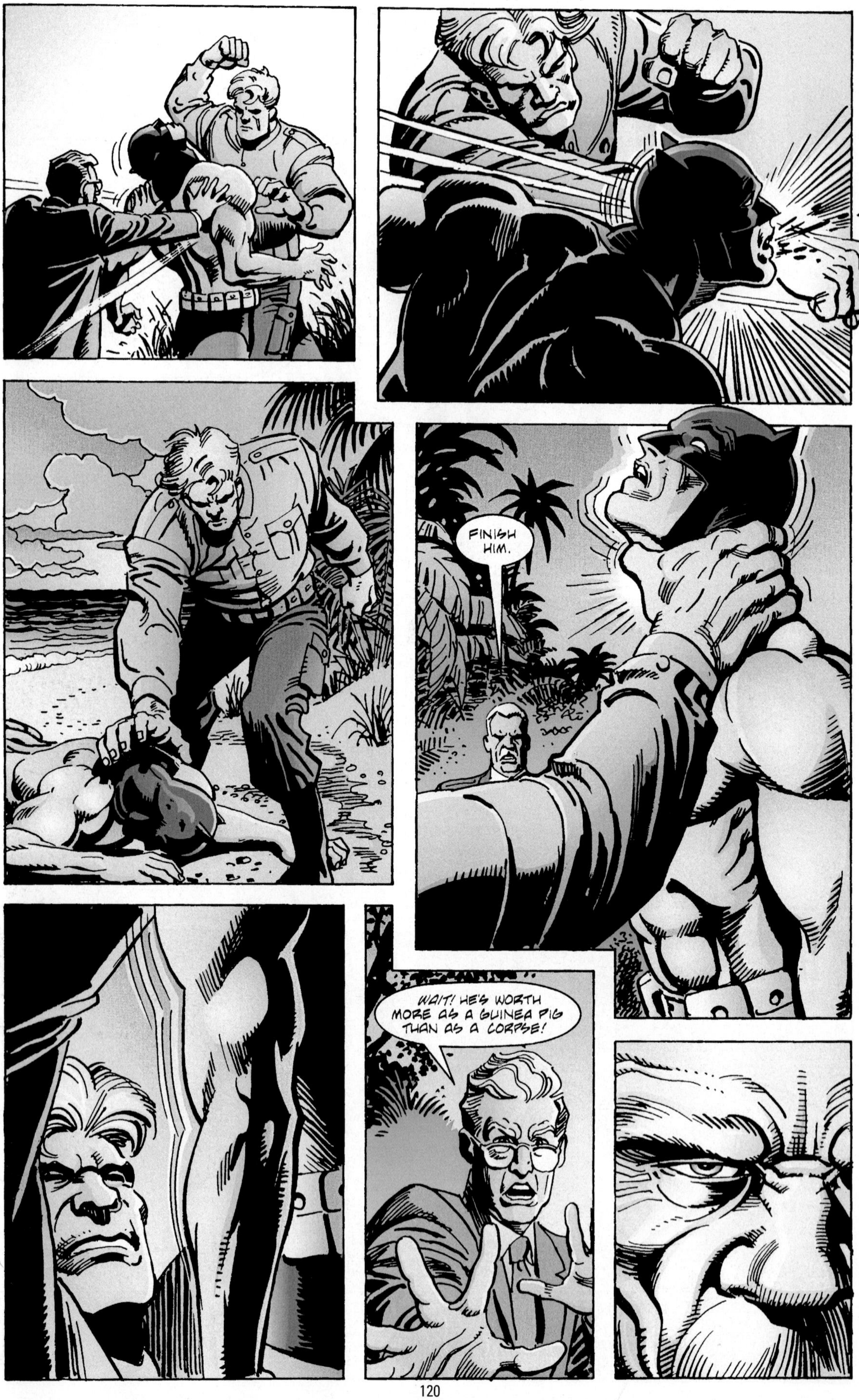
FINISH HIM.
WAIT! HE'S WORTH MORE AS A GUINEA PIG THAN AS A CORPSE!

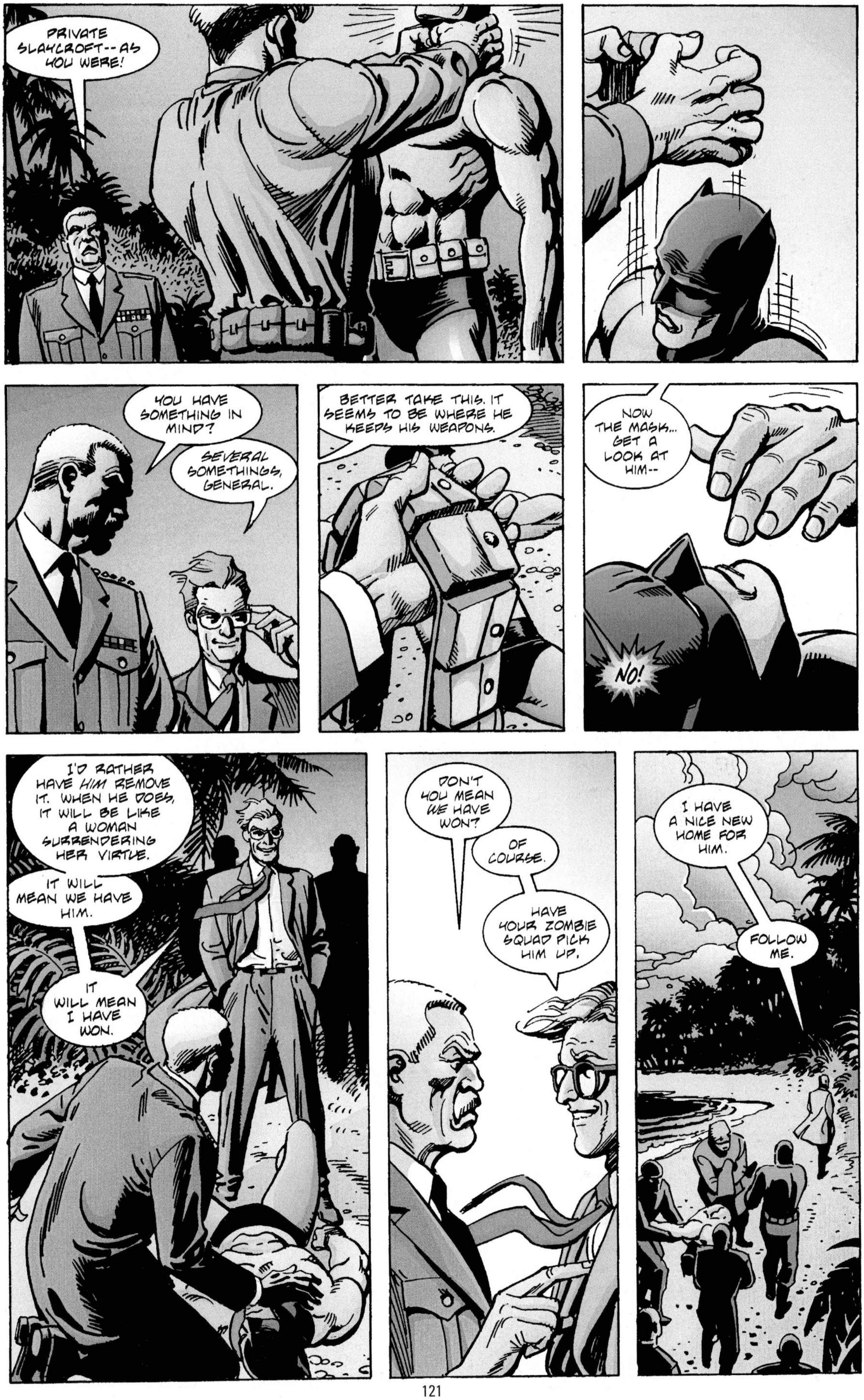
PRIVATE SLAYCROFT--AS YOU WERE!
YOU HAVE SOMETHING IN MIND?
SEVERAL SOMETHINGS, GENERAL.
BETTER TAKE THIS. IT SEEMS TO BE WHERE HE KEEPS HIS WEAPONS.
NOW THE MASK... GET A LOOK AT HIM--
NO!
I'D RATHER HAVE HIM REMOVE IT. WHEN HE DOES, IT WILL BE LIKE A WOMAN SURRENDERING HER VIRTUE.
IT WILL MEAN WE HAVE HIM.
IT WILL MEAN I HAVE WON.
DON'T YOU MEAN WE HAVE WON?
OF COURSE.
HAVE YOUR ZOMBIE SQUAD PICK HIM UP.
I HAVE A NICE NEW HOME FOR HIM.
FOLLOW ME.

--IN A SPANISH FORT BUILT IN THE SEVENTEENTH CENTURY... THE DUNGEON OF THE FORT, TO BE EXACT.

THE ISLAND'S LEADING CITIZEN, HECTOR LOPEZ--

--THE DRUG KINGPIN--

--THAT IS WHAT THEY SAY. ANYWAY, HE'S FOUND SEVERAL USES FOR IT AND HE'S BEEN KIND ENOUGH TO LEND IT FOR OUR EXPERIMENT.

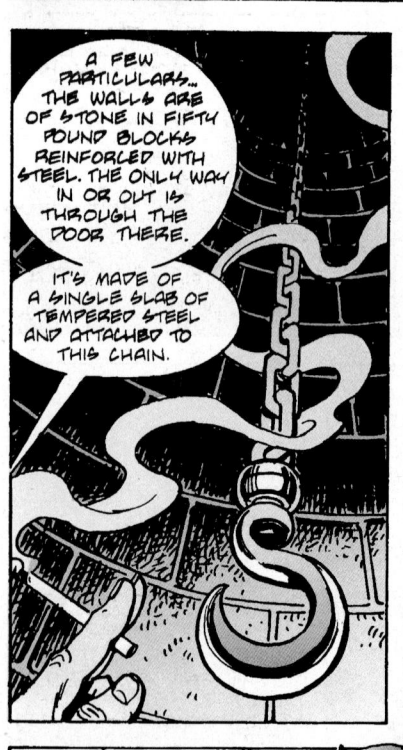

A FEW PARTICULARS... THE WALLS ARE OF STONE IN FIFTY POUND BLOCKS REINFORCED WITH STEEL. THE ONLY WAY IN OR OUT IS THROUGH THE DOOR THERE.

IT'S MADE OF A SINGLE SLAB OF TEMPERED STEEL AND ATTACHED TO THIS CHAIN.

AM I SUPPOSED TO BE IMPRESSED?

NOTICE THAT PIPE NEAR THE CEILING... SOON WATER WILL BEGIN TO TRICKLE THROUGH IT.

WITHIN 24 HOURS IT WILL FILL THE ENTIRE CHAMBER--

--AND YOU WILL DROWN. THAT IS, UNLESS YOU CAN OPEN THE DOOR BY PULLING ON THE CHAIN. DID I MENTION THAT THE DOOR WEIGHS EIGHT HUNDRED POUNDS?

NOT TOO MUCH FOR A VERY STRONG MAN TO LIFT--BUT PERHAPS TOO MUCH FOR YOU, EH?

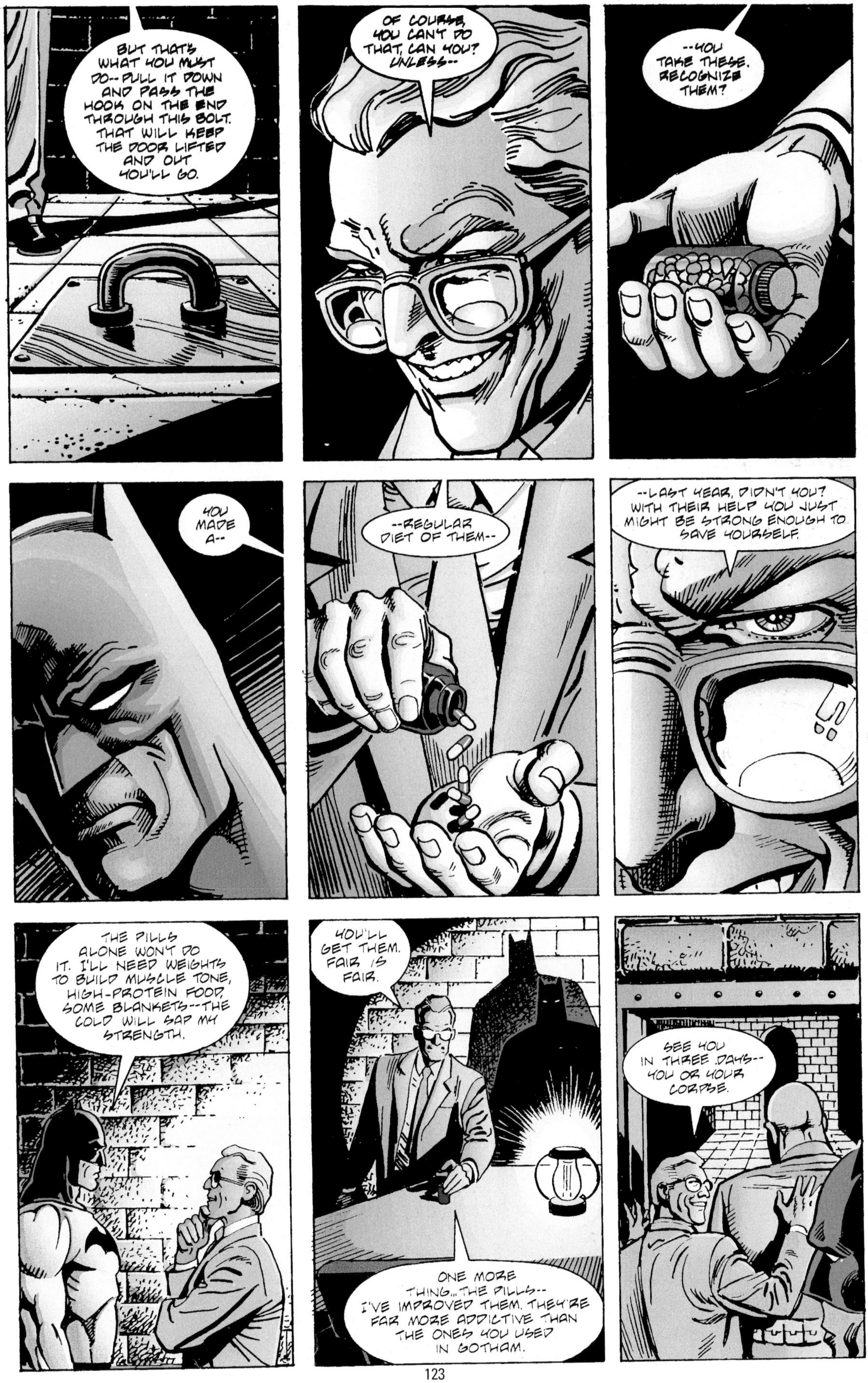
BUT THAT'S WHAT YOU MUST DO--PULL IT DOWN AND PASS THE HOOK ON THE END THROUGH THIS BOLT. THAT WILL KEEP THE DOOR LIFTED AND OUT YOU'LL GO.
OF COURSE, YOU CAN'T DO THAT, CAN YOU? UNLESS--
--YOU TAKE THESE. RECOGNIZE THEM?
YOU MADE A--
--REGULAR DIET OF THEM--
--LAST YEAR, DIDN'T YOU? WITH THEIR HELP YOU JUST MIGHT BE STRONG ENOUGH TO SAVE YOURSELF.
THE PILLS ALONE WON'T DO IT. I'LL NEED WEIGHTS TO BUILD MUSCLE TONE, HIGH-PROTEIN FOOD, SOME BLANKETS--THE COLD WILL SAP MY STRENGTH.
YOU'LL GET THEM. FAIR IS FAIR.
ONE MORE THING... THE PILLS-- I'VE IMPROVED THEM. THEY'RE FAR MORE ADDICTIVE THAN THE ONES YOU USED IN GOTHAM.
SEE YOU IN THREE DAYS-- YOU OR YOUR CORPSE.

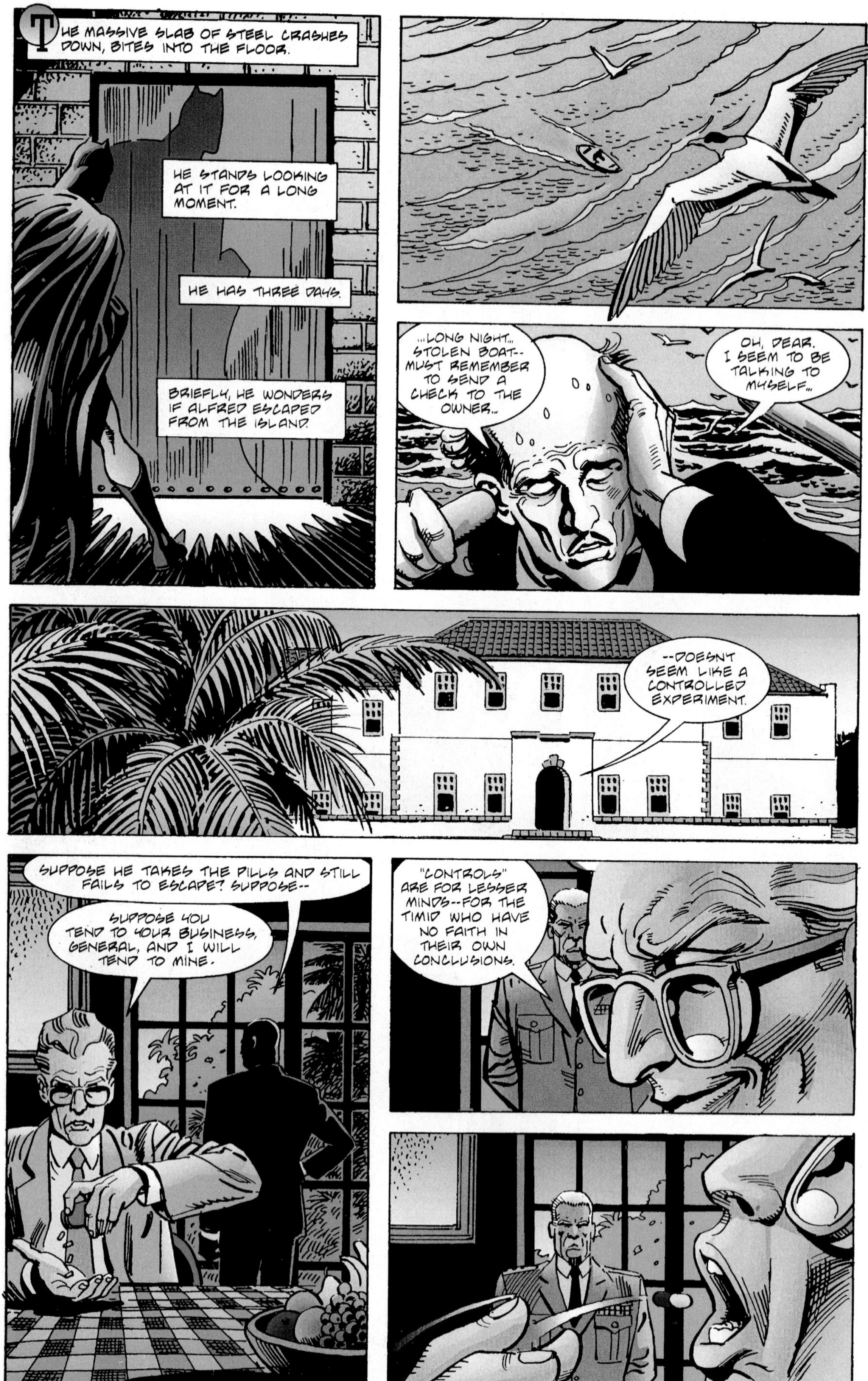
THE MASSIVE SLAB OF STEEL CRASHES DOWN, BITES INTO THE FLOOR.
HE STANDS LOOKING AT IT FOR A LONG MOMENT.
HE HAS THREE DAYS.
BRIEFLY, HE WONDERS IF ALFRED ESCAPED FROM THE ISLAND.
...LONG NIGHT... STOLEN BOAT-- MUST REMEMBER TO SEND A CHECK TO THE OWNER...
OH, DEAR. I SEEM TO BE TALKING TO MYSELF...
--DOESN'T SEEM LIKE A CONTROLLED EXPERIMENT.
SUPPOSE HE TAKES THE PILLS AND STILL FAILS TO ESCAPE? SUPPOSE--
SUPPOSE YOU TEND TO YOUR BUSINESS, GENERAL, AND I WILL TEND TO MINE.
"CONTROLS" ARE FOR LESSER MINDS--FOR THE TIMID WHO HAVE NO FAITH IN THEIR OWN CONCLUSIONS.

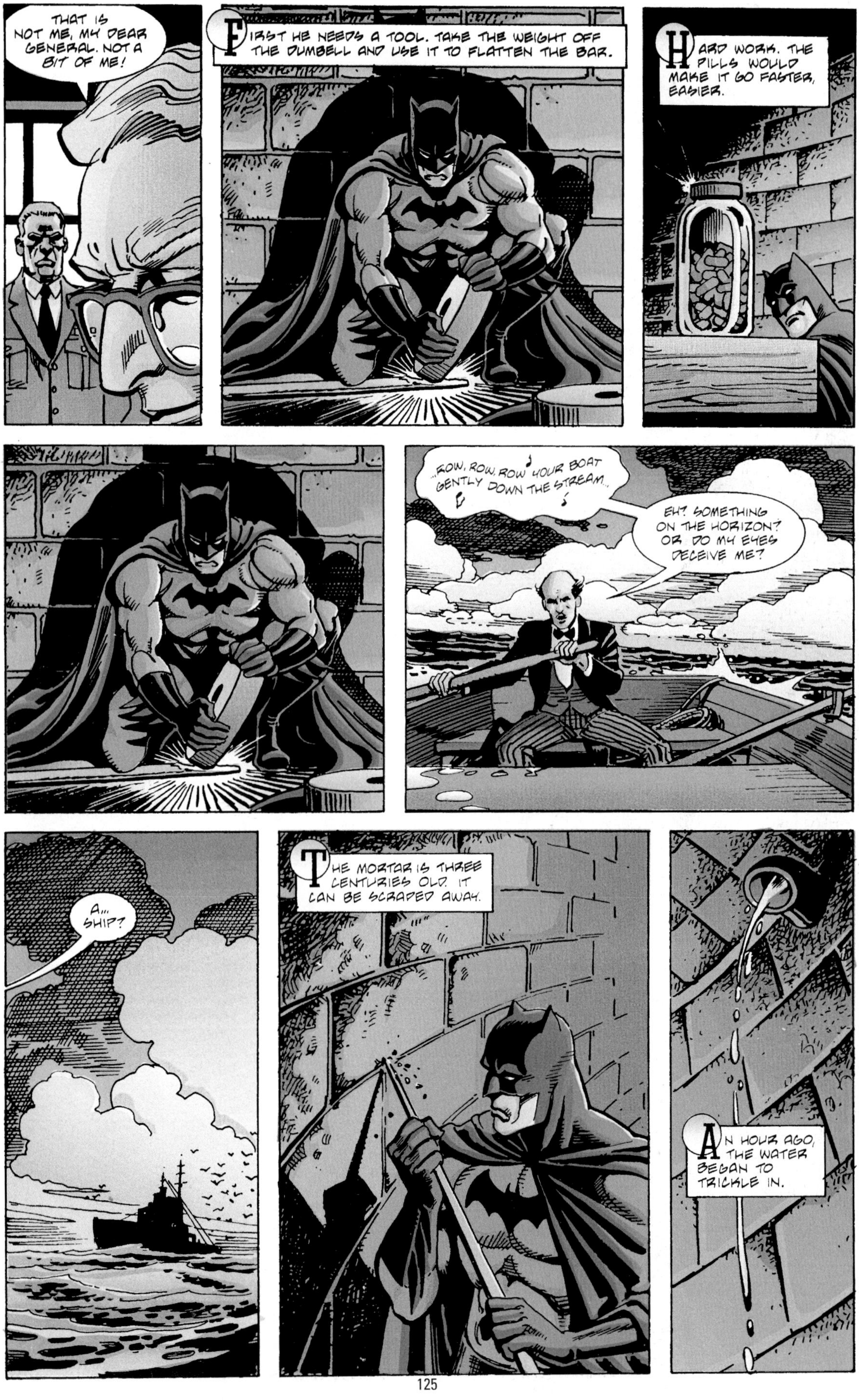
THAT IS NOT ME, MY DEAR GENERAL. NOT A BIT OF ME!
FIRST HE NEEDS A TOOL. TAKE THE WEIGHT OFF THE DUMBELL AND USE IT TO FLATTEN THE BAR.
HARD WORK. THE PILLS WOULD MAKE IT GO FASTER, EASIER.
...ROW, ROW, ROW YOUR BOAT GENTLY DOWN THE STREAM...
EH? SOMETHING ON THE HORIZON? OR DO MY EYES DECEIVE ME?
A... SHIP?
THE MORTAR IS THREE CENTURIES OLD. IT CAN BE SCRAPED AWAY.
AN HOUR AGO, THE WATER BEGAN TO TRICKLE IN.

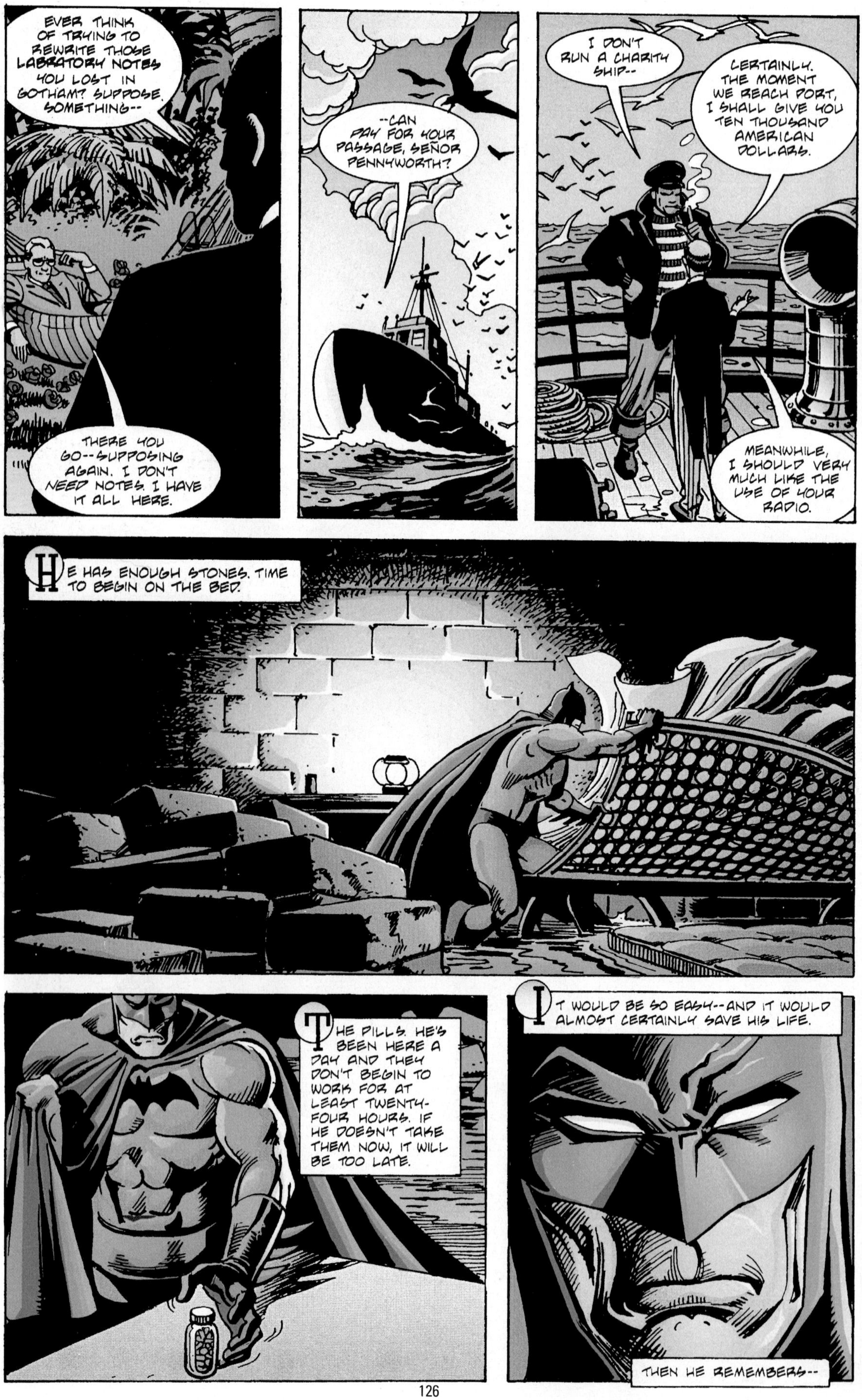

EVER THINK OF TRYING TO REWRITE THOSE LABRATORY NOTES YOU LOST IN GOTHAM? SUPPOSE SOMETHING--
THERE YOU GO--SUPPOSING AGAIN. I DON'T NEED NOTES. I HAVE IT ALL HERE.
--CAN PAY FOR YOUR PASSAGE, SEÑOR PENNYWORTH?
I DON'T RUN A CHARITY SHIP--
CERTAINLY. THE MOMENT WE REACH PORT, I SHALL GIVE YOU TEN THOUSAND AMERICAN DOLLARS.
MEANWHILE, I SHOULD VERY MUCH LIKE THE USE OF YOUR RADIO.
HE HAS ENOUGH STONES. TIME TO BEGIN ON THE BED.
THE PILLS. HE'S BEEN HERE A DAY AND THEY DON'T BEGIN TO WORK FOR AT LEAST TWENTY-FOUR HOURS. IF HE DOESN'T TAKE THEM NOW, IT WILL BE TOO LATE.
IT WOULD BE SO EASY--AND IT WOULD ALMOST CERTAINLY SAVE HIS LIFE.
THEN HE REMEMBERS--

--WHAT HE BECAME.

NOTHING IS WORTH THAT, NOT EVEN LIFE ITSELF.

BACK TO WORK.

CAPTAIN GORDON?

LONG AGO, ALFRED LEARNED TO IMITATE BRUCE WAYNE'S BATMAN VOICE PERFECTLY.

YOU! WHAT IS IT?

USE YOUR INFLUENCE. GET THE MILITARY TO SANTA PRISCA AND--

127

OUT OF THE QUESTION. THAT WOULD BE AN ACT OF WAR. I'M SORRY.

OH, BRUCE...

--MEANING OF THIS, GENERAL?

I WANT THOSE NOTES.

SO YOU CAN STEAL THE FRUITS OF MY GENIUS?

EXACTLY. YOU HAVE BECOME UNRELIABLE.

GO STUFF YOURSELF.

I LEARNED CERTAIN INTERROGATION TECHNIQUES IN SOUTH AMERICA.

YOU WILL GIVE ME WHAT I WANT.

IT'S TIME.

THE STRIPS OF BLANKET ARE WOUND AROUND WIRE FROM THE MATTRESS SUPPORT OF THE BED-- THEY SHOULD HOLD.

NOW TO BEGIN.

"NO MORE..." PLEASE, NO MORE.

TALK.

TWELVE BLOCKS-- BUT IT'S NOT ENOUGH-- AND HE CAN'T GET THE LEVERAGE UNDER WATER TO DIG OUT ANYMORE.

NO CHOICE BUT TO TRY TO ADD HIS OWN WEIGHT--PULL--

--AND PRAY HE CAN GET TO THE RISING DOOR BEFORE IT SLAMS SHUT AGAIN--

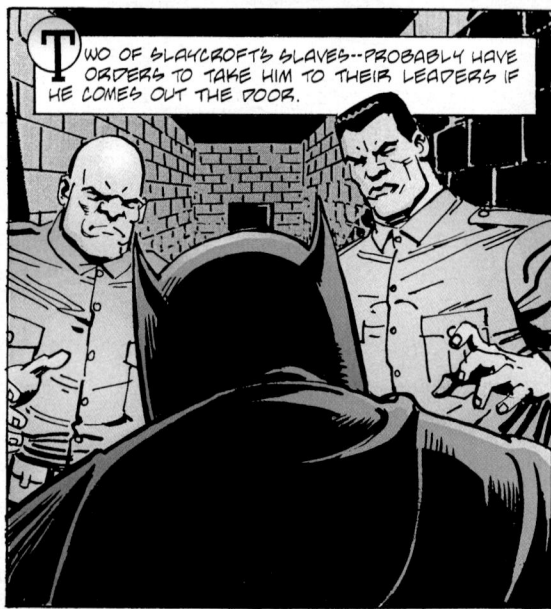

TWO OF SLAYCROFT'S SLAVES--PROBABLY HAVE ORDERS TO TAKE HIM TO THEIR LEADERS IF HE COMES OUT THE DOOR.

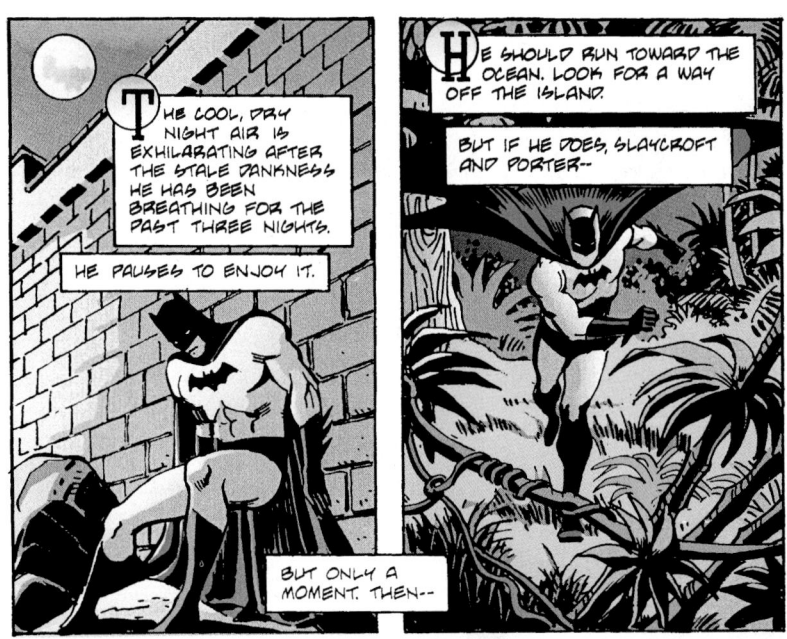

THE COOL, DRY NIGHT AIR IS EXHILARATING AFTER THE STALE DANKNESS HE HAS BEEN BREATHING FOR THE PAST THREE NIGHTS.

HE PAUSES TO ENJOY IT.

BUT ONLY A MOMENT. THEN--

HE SHOULD RUN TOWARD THE OCEAN. LOOK FOR A WAY OFF THE ISLAND.

BUT IF HE DOES, SLAYCROFT AND PORTER--

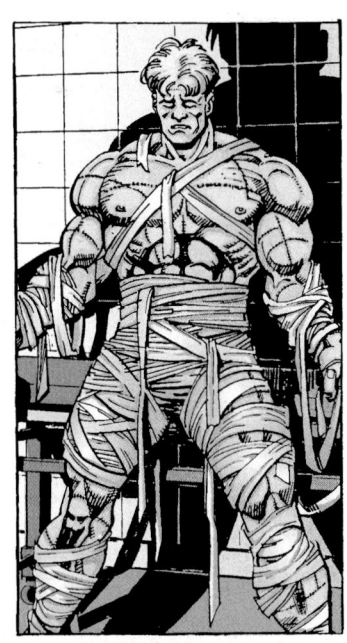

--MORE TIMMYS--

--WHAT THEY DID TO HIM.

NOT GOING TO HAPPEN.

GUARDS. CAN'T GO THROUGH THEM--

--BUT HE DOESN'T HAVE TO.

131

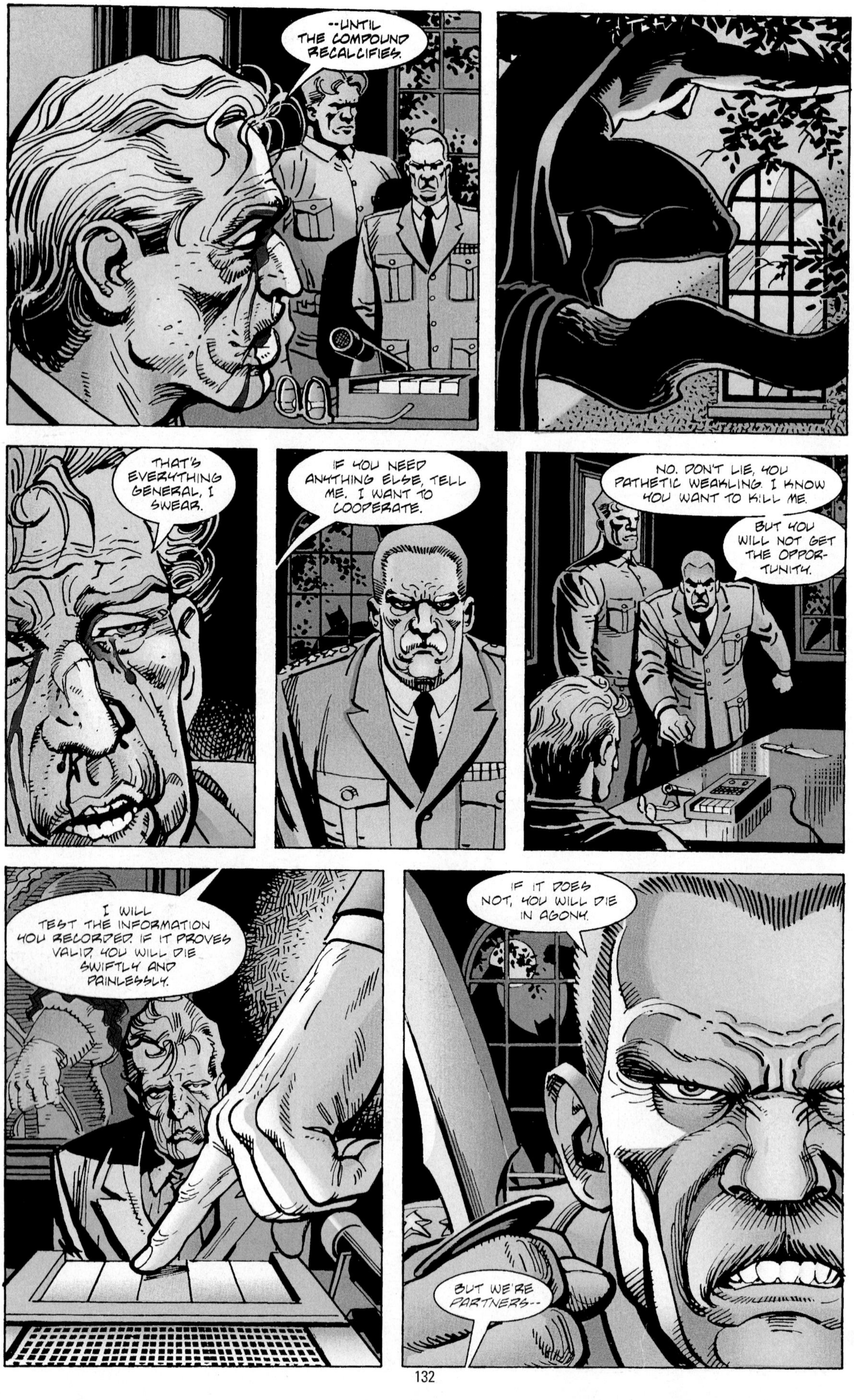
--UNTIL THE COMPOUND RECALCIFIES.
THAT'S EVERYTHING GENERAL, I SWEAR.
IF YOU NEED ANYTHING ELSE, TELL ME. I WANT TO COOPERATE.
NO. DON'T LIE, YOU PATHETIC WEAKLING. I KNOW YOU WANT TO KILL ME.
BUT YOU WILL NOT GET THE OPPOR-TUNITY.
I WILL TEST THE INFORMATION YOU RECORDED. IF IT PROVES VALID, YOU WILL DIE SWIFTLY AND PAINLESSLY.
IF IT DOES NOT, YOU WILL DIE IN AGONY.
BUT WE'RE PARTNERS--

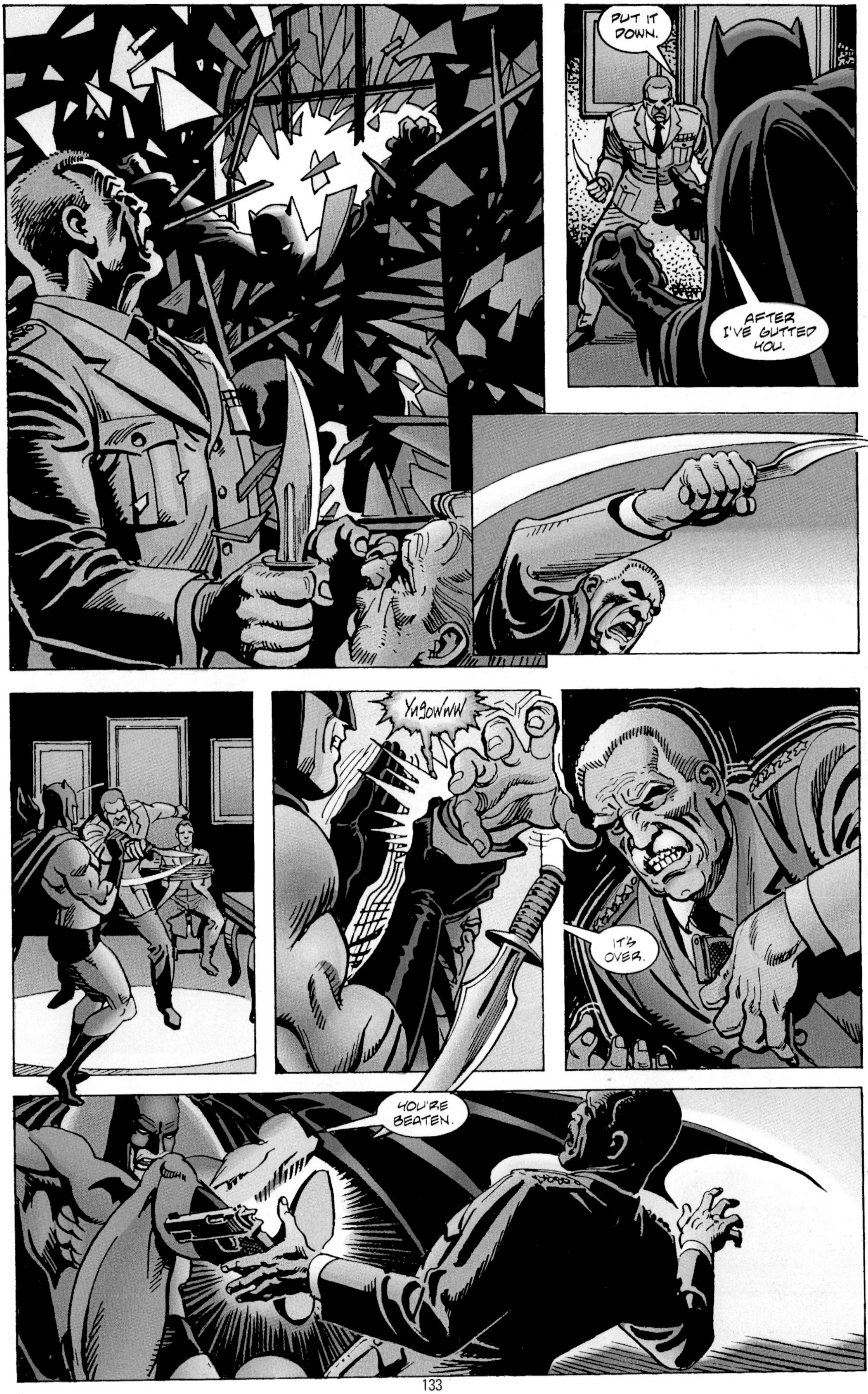
PUT IT DOWN.
AFTER I'VE GUTTED YOU.
YNGOWWW
IT'S OVER.
YOU'RE BEATEN.

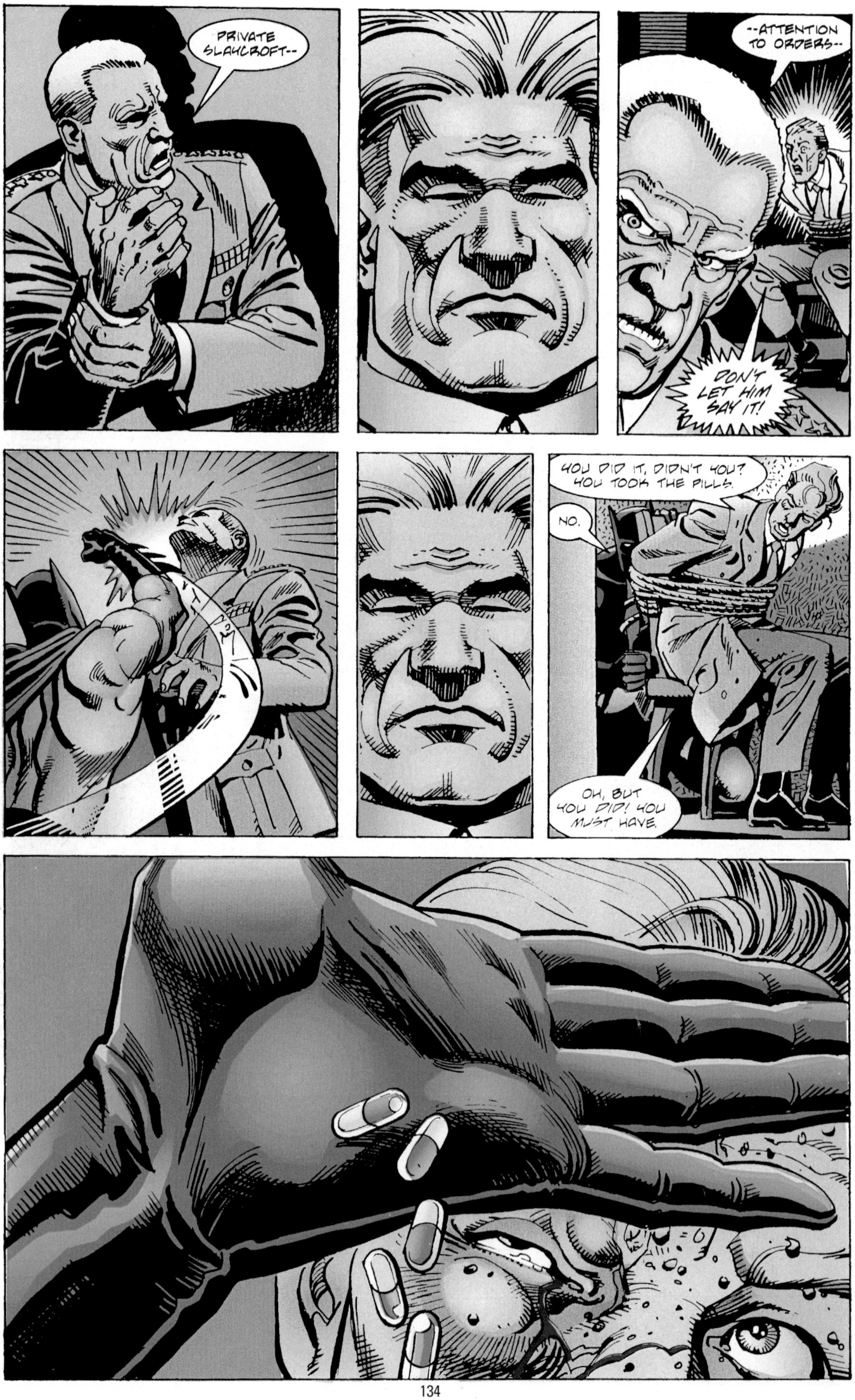
PRIVATE SLAYCROFT--
--ATTENTION TO ORDERS--
DON'T LET HIM SAY IT!
YOU DID IT, DIDN'T YOU? YOU TOOK THE PILLS.
NO.
OH, BUT YOU DID! YOU MUST HAVE.

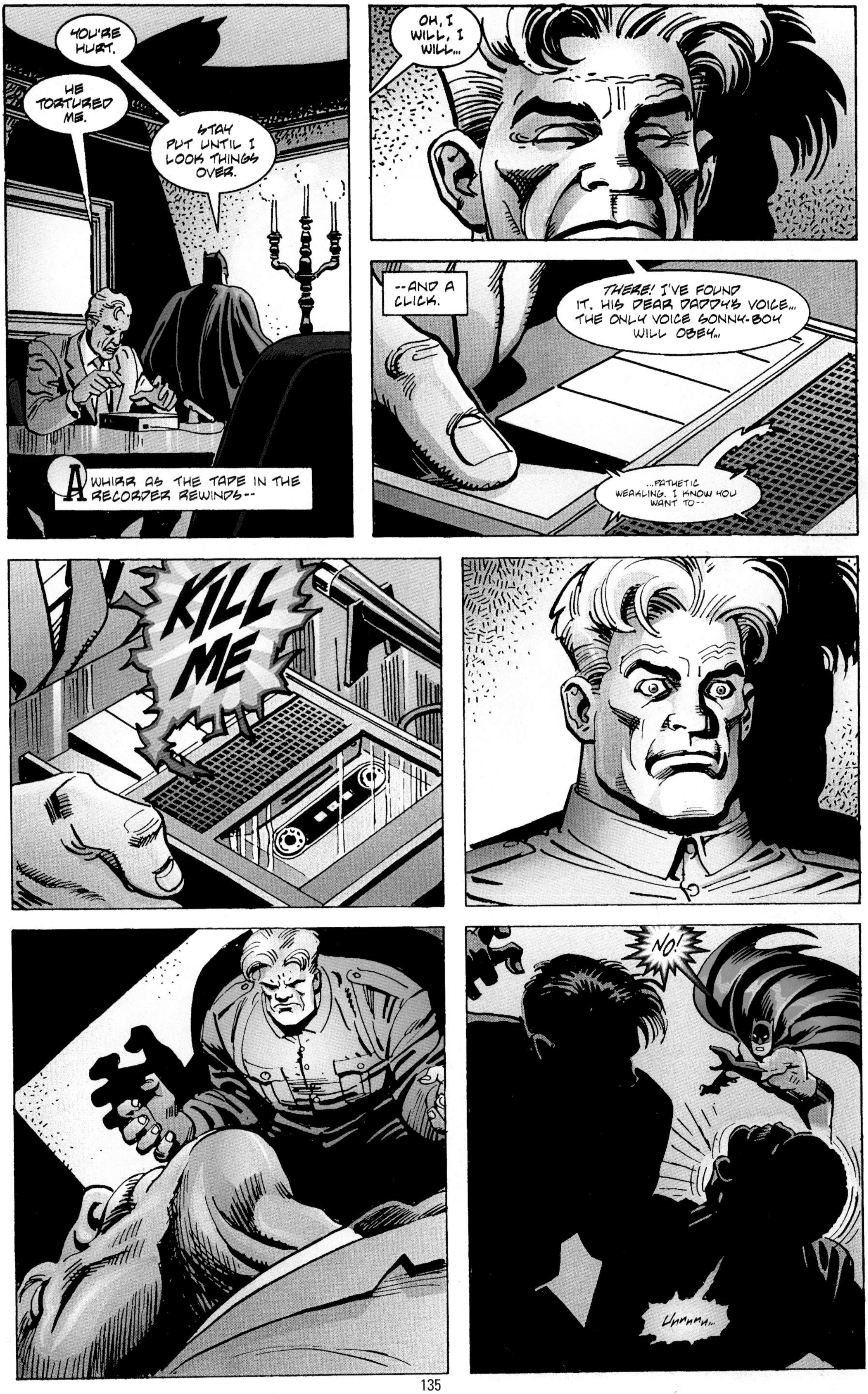

YOU'RE HURT.
HE TORTURED ME.
STAY PUT UNTIL I LOOK THINGS OVER.
A WHIRR AS THE TAPE IN THE RECORDER REWINDS--
OH, I WILL, I WILL...
--AND A CLICK.
THERE! I'VE FOUND IT. HIS DEAR DADDY'S VOICE... THE ONLY VOICE SONNY-BOY WILL OBEY...
...PATHETIC WEAKLING. I KNOW YOU WANT TO--
KILL ME
NO!
Unnnnn...

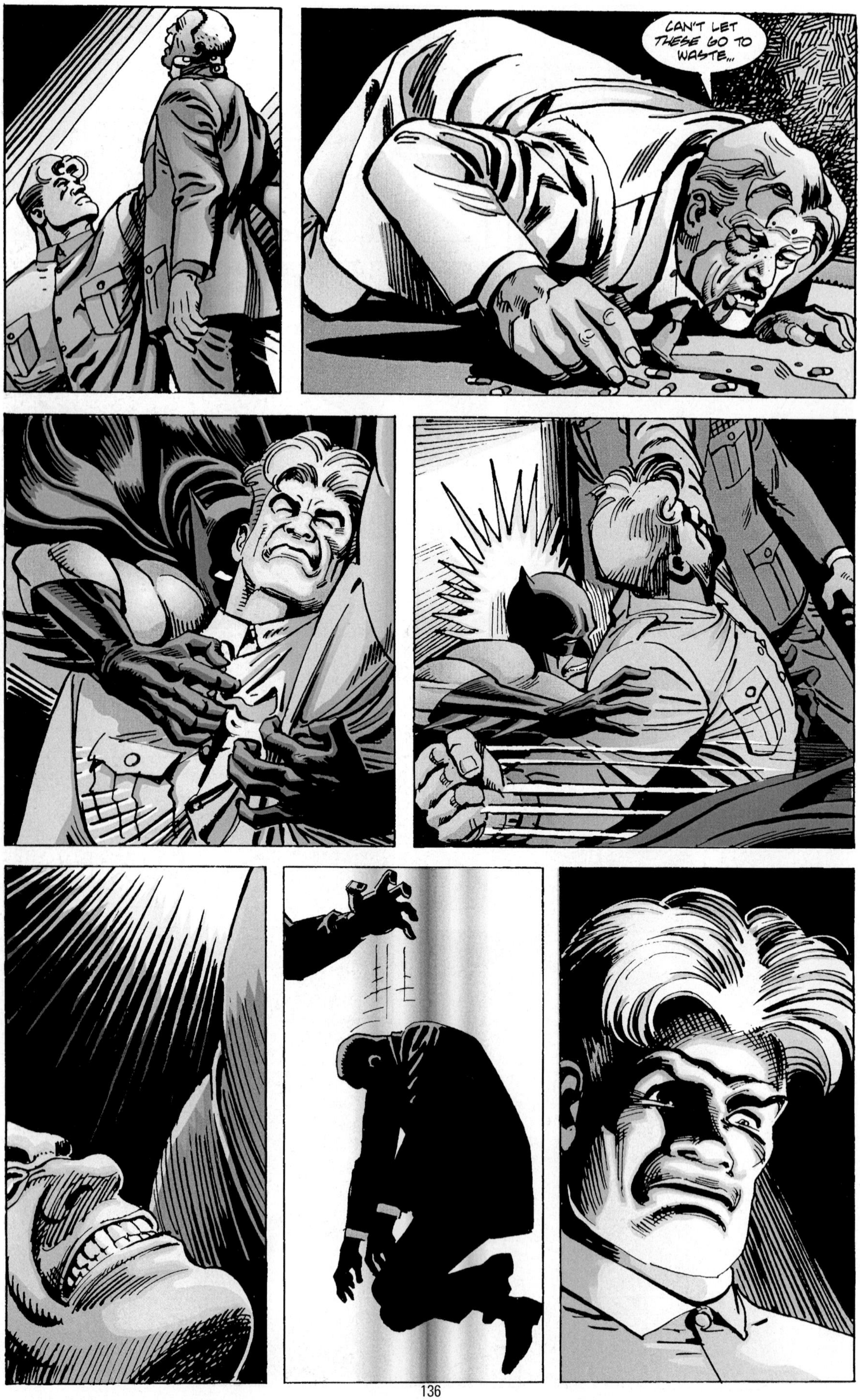
CAN'T LET THESE GO TO WASTE...

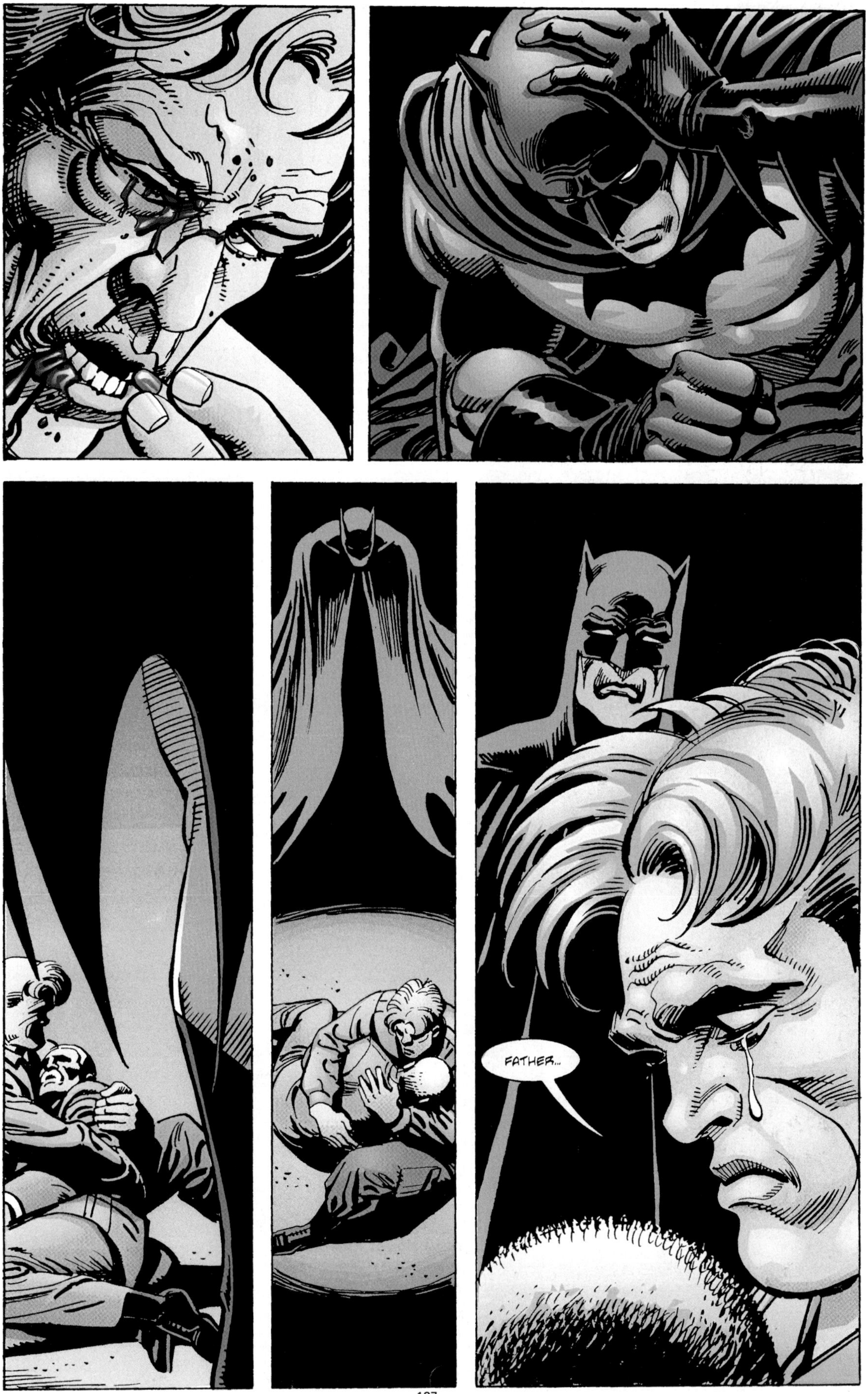
FATHER...

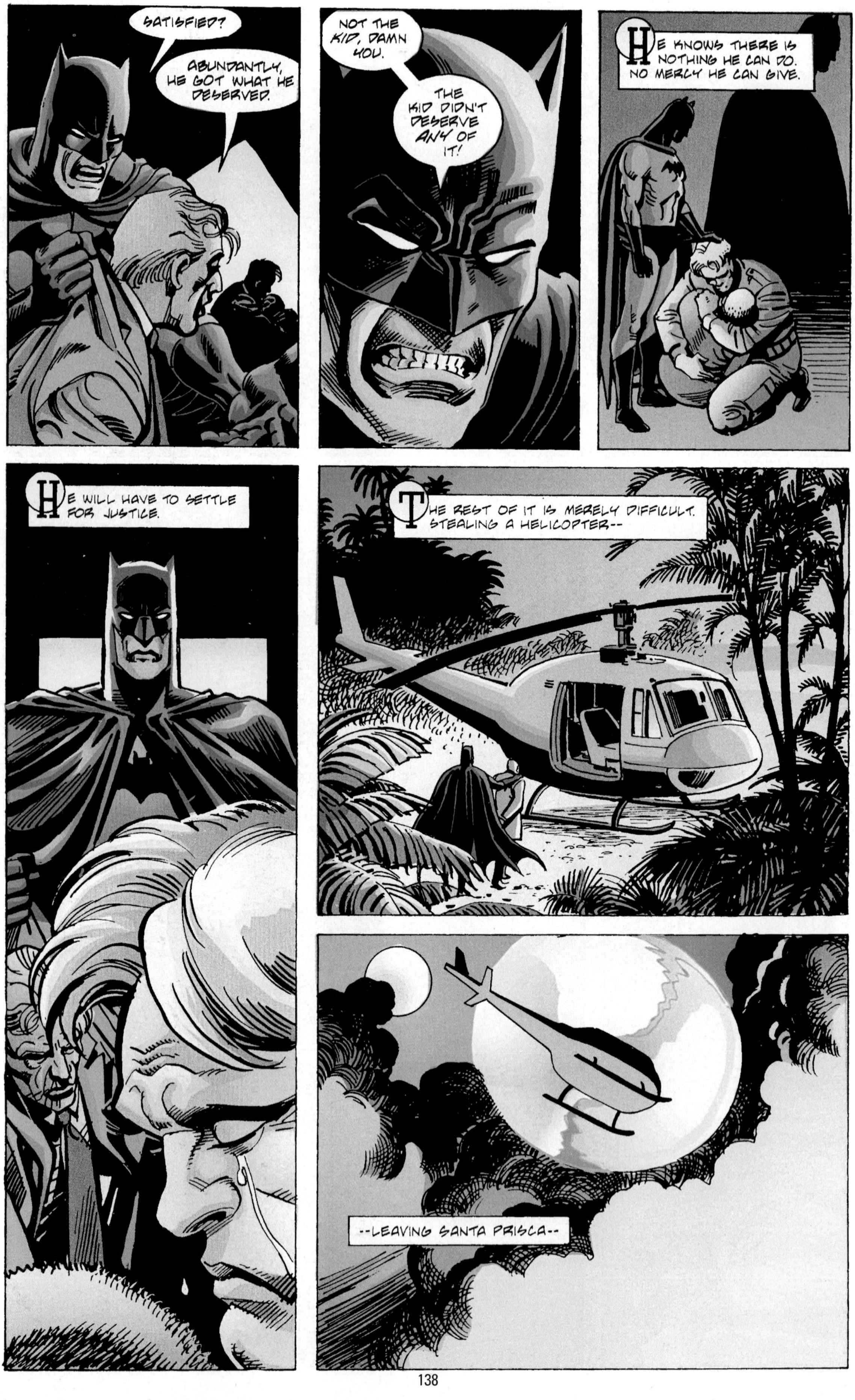
SATISFIED?
ABUNDANTLY, HE GOT WHAT HE DESERVED.
NOT THE KID, DAMN YOU.
THE KID DIDN'T DESERVE ANY OF IT!
HE KNOWS THERE IS NOTHING HE CAN DO. NO MERCY HE CAN GIVE.
HE WILL HAVE TO SETTLE FOR JUSTICE.
THE REST OF IT IS MERELY DIFFICULT. STEALING A HELICOPTER--
--LEAVING SANTA PRISCA--

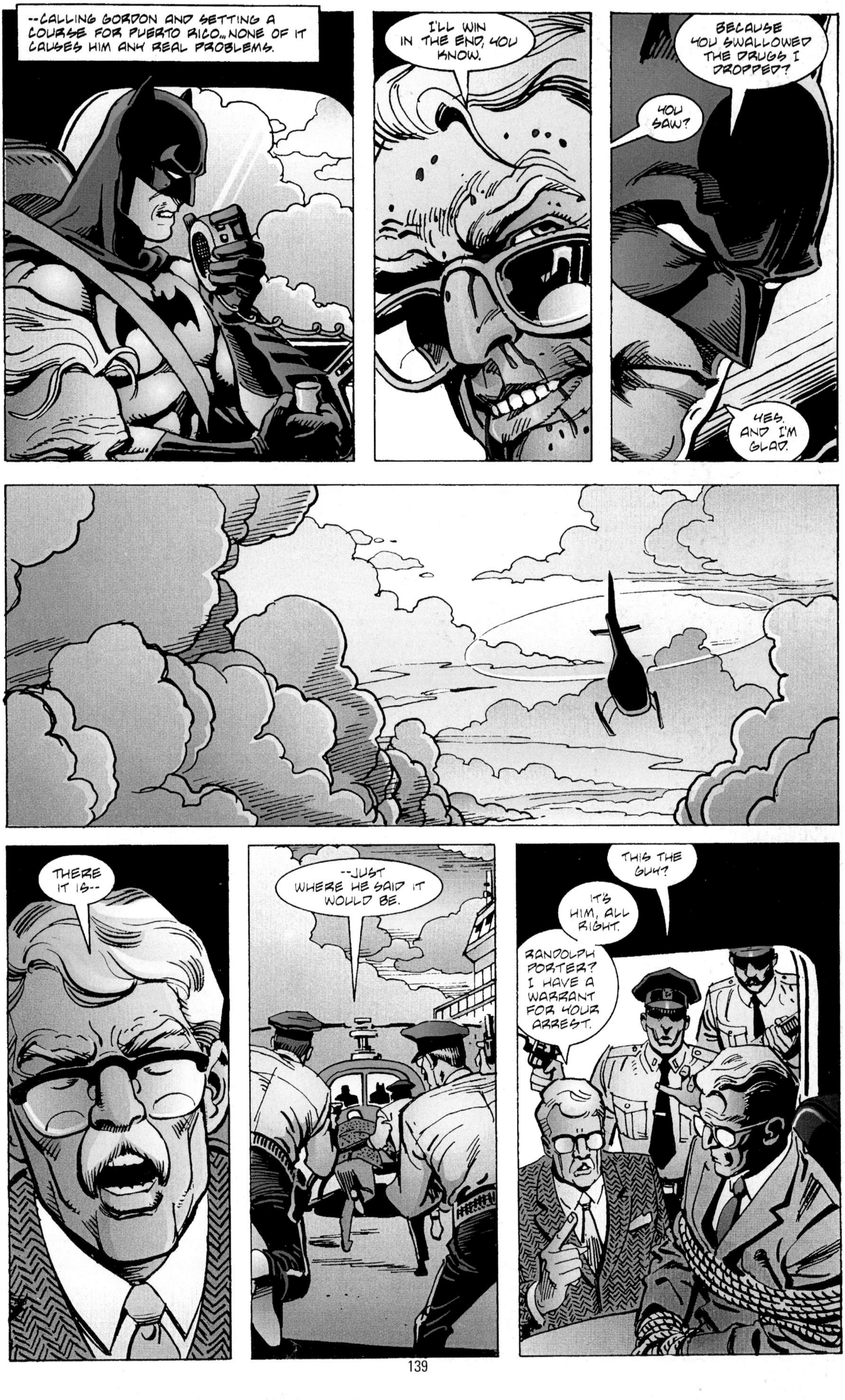
--CALLING GORDON AND SETTING A COURSE FOR PUERTO RICO... NONE OF IT CAUSES HIM ANY REAL PROBLEMS.
I'LL WIN IN THE END, YOU KNOW.
BECAUSE YOU SWALLOWED THE DRUGS I DROPPED?
YOU SAW?
YES. AND I'M GLAD.
THERE IT IS--
--JUST WHERE HE SAID IT WOULD BE.
THIS THE GUY?
IT'S HIM, ALL RIGHT.
RANDOLPH PORTER? I HAVE A WARRANT FOR YOUR ARREST.

--INCREDIBLY STRONG FOR SUCH A FRAIL-LOOKING MAN.

HE ACTUALLY BENT ONE OF THE CELL BARS. BUT HE WASN'T QUITE STRONG ENOUGH TO ESCAPE.

NO. HE WASN'T SMART ENOUGH.

THEN HE WENT INTO SOME KIND OF WITHDRAWAL. THE DOCTORS TRIED DIAZAPAM, THORZINE... NOTHING DID ANY GOOD.

THEY SAY HE SCREAMED FOR TWO DAYS.

FINALLY HIS ENTIRE SYSTEM COLLAPSED HE DIED IN INTENSIVE CARE.

ANOTHER VICTORY FOR YOU. YOU SHOULD BE HAPPY.

DID YOU HEAR ME?

HE IS REMEMBERING A GIRL NAMED SISSY... AND A BOY, TIMMY...

AND THE SHADOWS HE INHABITS ARE COLD...

...AND FILLED WITH GRIEF.

End

140

The story of Venom continues in **BATMAN: KNIGHTFALL.** When the super-drug falls into the hands of the villainous Bane, he is determined to use his Venom-enhanced strength to destroy the Batman!

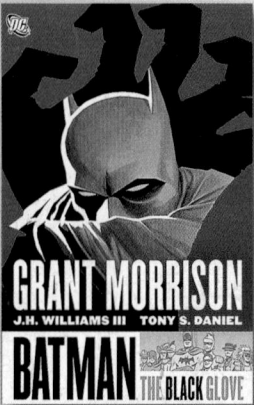  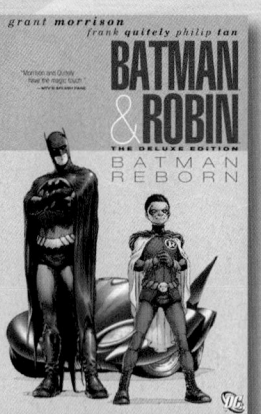 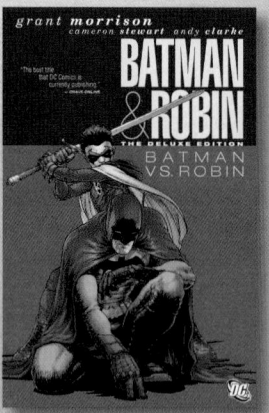

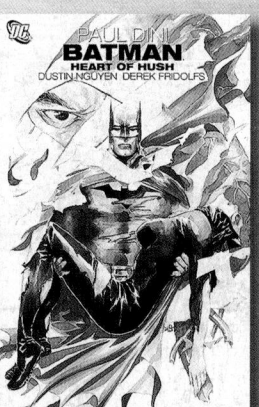